Praise for *Raising Critical Thinkers*

✳   ✳   ✳

"In a world where too many people think they know what isn't so, there are few skills more vital than critical thinking and rethinking. This is the guide parents need to teach their kids to become thoughtful consumers of information."
　　—Adam Grant, #1 *New York Times* bestselling author of *Think Again*

"Critical thinking is not merely a test of fact versus fiction. In this timely and actionable primer, Julie Bogart teaches us how imagination, self-awareness, empathy, and introspection make true critical thinking possible. These are crucial lessons for children and parents alike."
　　—Ximena Vengoechea, author of *Listen Like You Mean It*

"I am in awe. Every parent and educator needs to read this book. As a psychologist and mother, I understand the importance of raising critical thinkers, but it's not always clear what that really means day to day. *Raising Critical Thinkers* uses cutting-edge education theory and concrete practices to answer: How do we help kids separate fact from fiction? What can we do to keep kids' curiosity and 'itch' to learn alive? What fosters self-awareness and flexible perspective-taking in kids? Let Julie Bogart guide you through the wilderness of raising critical thinkers."
　　—Diana Hill, PhD, author of *ACT Daily Journal*

"With fascinating examples and age-specific activities to help kids learn to think deeply, imaginatively, and compassionately, Julie Bogart gives us *the* guide for nurturing critical thinking in the next generation."
　　—Yael Schonbrun, PhD, assistant professor of
　　psychiatry and human behavior at Brown University

"For decades, I've admired Julie Bogart's wise and humane help for parents who participate in their children's education."
　　—Peter Elbow, professor emeritus of English,
　　University of Massachusetts at Amherst

RAISING
CRITICAL
THINKERS

✳ ✳ ✳

A PARENT'S GUIDE TO GROWING
WISE KIDS IN THE DIGITAL AGE

JULIE BOGART

A TARCHERPERIGEE BOOK

tarcherperigee

An imprint of Penguin Random House LLC
penguinrandomhouse.com

A portion of the exercises have been adapted from the author's online curriculum, *The Writer's Jungle*, published in January 2000 on the website www.bravewriter.com.

TarcherPerigee with tp colophon is a registered trademark of Penguin Random House LLC.

Most TarcherPerigee books are available at special quantity discounts for bulk purchase for sales promotions, premiums, fund-raising, and educational needs. Special books or book excerpts also can be created to fit specific needs. For details, write: SpecialMarkets@penguinrandomhouse.com.

Hardcover ISBN: 9780593192283
Ebook ISBN: 9780593192290

Printed in the United States of America
2nd Printing

Book design by Elke Sigal

33614082798587

In memory of my aunt June

One life, but we're not the same. We get to carry each other.

—Bono, U2, "One"

CONTENTS

CONTENTS

FOREWORD

BY BARBARA OAKLEY

I was once asked whether a college course I was creating taught critical thinking. "It depends," I said. "What's your definition of critical thinking?"

It turned out that the university didn't *have* a definition for critical thinking. So as I perused the university catalog, looking at all the courses that supposedly taught critical thinking, I realized—critical thinking at this university means whatever anyone wants it to mean.

That university, our country's leading institutions, and most especially, *you*, need Julie Bogart's book.

Raising Critical Thinkers gives tools of self-awareness that can help you and your children catch yourselves being controlled by invisible assumptions that thwart your ability to think clearly and rationally. These invisible assumptions are why seemingly objective scientists, no matter what data and conclusions they are presented with, can find their "objectivity" tumbling forth to support their preconceived biases. It is also why judges, politicians, managers—in fact, virtually everyone—can find it so difficult to step back and look with dispassion at their decision-making.

Neuroscience is beginning to give us a sense of where those invisible assumptions come from—your brain's subconscious procedural learning system. This system detects and formulates patterns. Perhaps most important, it makes judgments. The judgments this system makes (technically, they're called the output of the "value function") sneakily intrude into what you truly believe—actually, you could *swear*—are transparently conscious, objective decisions.

Surfacing these kinds of invisible assumptions is almost supernaturally difficult. Perhaps that's why, despite their importance, most books on critical thinking barely touch on preexisting biases. Instead, they'll focus on issues such as honing your own argument—as opposed to, for example, being able to change your mind in the face of compelling reasoning. Or they'll concentrate on methods for objectively evaluating data, without discussing how the mind can fool itself into justifying how objective data can be overruled. Too often, books about teaching our children to think critically focus on how to detect bias *out there* rather than helping them develop the skills to investigate their own.

Julie approaches critical thinking in an utterly novel way. Like a master poker player, she turns her gaze not only toward the cards being dealt but also inward to the body's physical "tells" in reaction to those cards. You may not be able to directly detect the subconscious influence of the procedural system, but you can see its side effects. And these bodily reactions and thought patterns can serve as a guide for digging deeper and being more honest, both with those you are interacting with and yourself. It's this self-awareness that supports you in guiding your children as well.

Is it possible to "train" your inevitably biased procedural system to be more open and less one-sided? Julie's got you covered there, too. She recommends the heretical—reading outside your worldview. And indeed, this is precisely what neuroscience suggests. It's a little like training an artificial intelligence program to play better chess by giving that program broader data to train with. And she gives guidance about how to make room for dissenting viewpoints—if anything, this book serves as a much-needed balm for the all-too-contentious social environment we find ourselves in today. Plus, this book is loaded with activities to try with your family, including thinking critically about subjects like grammar and picture books, video games and sports.

As Julie notes, "Knowing how to develop well-formed opinions in spite of prejudice and bias is one of the goals of education (and this book)." Read on for a wonderfully insightful guide to steering yourself, and the children you love, toward a life of considered, thoughtful insight.

INTRODUCTION

He's making violent love to me, Mother!
—Mary, *It's a Wonderful Life*

I knelt next to boxes of opened letters addressed to my grandparents scattered on the carpet in the living room. My two aunts and I paged through each one to determine which to keep and which to toss. My beloved Bapa had died. His wife survived him, but she suffered from dementia.

I popped open the top of a more recent box of letters. These had been written within the last year. No stamps. I stripped the vanilla pages from their unsealed envelopes to discover love letters penned by my grandfather to his wife of sixty plus years. Eva had lost the ability to speak coherently and had forgotten her own name. My heart squeezed, imagining my grandfather writing to the woman he had loved for decades, willing her to understand, knowing she couldn't read a word. My Bapa's beautiful penmanship curled into paragraphs of memory.

He wrote, "Eva, remember when we climbed the little hilltop together, where I first made love to you?"

My jaw dropped. My Catholic grandfather—talking about his 1930s love affair with my grandmother before they were married. I stopped my two aunts from their estate duties. "June, Shevawn, listen to *this!*"

I read the paragraph aloud, and the much younger of my two aunts, Shevawn, whooped, declaring, "And they lectured me about the sanctity of my virginity before marriage! What's up with that?"

My other, more serious and older aunt, a professor of ethics and religion and a former nun, immediately capped our howling laughter. "That can't mean what you think it means!" She avoided saying the words. I did not: "You mean sex? Come on, June! Imagine Eva, Phil? Taking a roll in the hay on the hill where they first declared their love for each other? It's romantic! Incredible!" I teased her to lighten the mood.

She wasn't amused, but Shevawn laughed louder. After a moment, June leaked a small smile, considering the torrid possibility of her parents having sex before marriage, and gently told us to calm down, that we had work to do. She had allowed herself the possibility of my interpretation—a moment of amusement—but she would not be swayed from her task.

I enjoyed this impromptu sitcom moment. I knew the complexity of the ideas in conflict. In the 1930s, to "make love" to someone meant to put the moves on the woman of your dreams. It didn't mean to have sex, the way it does today. But this letter had landed us in trickier territory. My Bapa hadn't written this note in 1937. He'd written it in 1997. He referenced an experience from the 1930s, yet recorded it in the full light of the late twentieth century. Certainly, he knew the changing times and the way sexual innuendo had altered the meaning of those two words. Yet perhaps he was calling back to a previous meaning deliberately. Did he use that old-time language to jar his wife's confused mind into re-calling a sweeter period of her life? Or was he expressing nostalgia for his own memories using the idiom of that day? Or had we stumbled on a deathbed revelation—a confession—a scandal and secret he had kept until his dying day—that he and Eva, the lifelong Catholics, had been lovers before they were married?

My aunt June wanted her parents to be good Catholics for their entire lives. My younger aunt Shevawn wanted them to be rebels, revealing a long-hidden willingness to put their own values ahead of church doctrine. Each of these interpretations matched the sisters' personalities and had less to do with my grandparents than the story my aunts wanted to tell themselves about their parents. Later that weekend, I ribbed my mother that her Catholic parents may have had sex before marriage after all. She chuckled and dismissed the notion as ridiculous. Her memory of growing up Catholic with these parents shaped her beliefs—no late-in-life letter could alter what she *knew* about her parents.

You're probably wondering: *Who was right?* That's the essence of critical thought right there. We take data, experiences, language, memories, and beliefs and mix them together to form opinions. In this case, my family never agreed on the correct connotation of the "making love" idiom as written in the letter. My Bapa had passed on. Whatever the meaning, it had died with him. For me, the love letter remains a delicious enigma—one of those delightful paradoxes of textual interpretation that reminds me that critical thinking doesn't always lead to airtight conclusions.

The ability to evaluate evidence, to notice bias as it kicks into gear, to consider a variety of perspectives (even if they make you uncomfortable), and then to render a possible verdict—what you believe to be true, for now—is the heart of the critical thinking task. It's a tall order and really tough to do with your own family because your childhood beliefs are often the most familiar and undetected.

Critical thinking is more than critiquing someone else's ideas. It's the ability to question your own, too. In publishing, we have an expression: "Content is king." In academics, I like another motto: "Context is everything." What you know, how you know it, why you know it, what you don't know, why you don't know—these invisible factors shape how we understand every subject under the sun. In this book we're going to explore how your kids make meaning for themselves and how to improve the quality of those assessments. Each day, whether they're aware of it or not, kids evaluate evidence and form beliefs. They'll think again and discard some of those same beliefs years later. How they think will be responsible for their well-cultivated religious or nonreligious viewpoints. They'll arrive at political positions one year and overturn outdated ones years later for reasons they value. In truth, we all use various critical thinking tools to make all kinds of decisions. We even use critical thinking to order off a menu! We decide which items will hit the spot using personal criteria. How hungry am I? What's in season? Will this meal make me use my hands (on a first date, no thank you!)?

Naturally, some contexts for critical thinking are low stakes. You can order a meal, dislike the taste, and regret your choice without any other negative consequence. Other judgments we make have lasting implications that impact other people, not just ourselves. For example, the decision to go to war has vast consequences for all people involved and for years to come. To make a quality judgment, the thinking must be deep, rich, sober, and purposeful. That's why raising skillful critical thinkers is essential—how our children think will create the world they share.

Have you ever wondered what's going on in your children's minds after you read, study, watch a movie, teach a math process, or play a video game with them? Maybe you wonder why a sister taunts her brother, unable to imagine the distress she's causing. Perhaps your student declares a solution to a problem that seems monstrous to you. You may notice that a teenager appears "obsessed" with a video game, and you draw the worrying conclusion that that teen loves violence—but can you be sure? How do we understand the meaning kids make for themselves? How do we help them reason more effectively and compassionately?

This book is about *raising* critical thinkers—in today's global, digital environment. Today's kids are swimming in a sea of declarations. Ranting online has the appearance of confident truth. Most parents want to protect their kids from misinformation. What happens when an unsupervised child stumbles on a logical presentation of facts for a perspective that contradicts the family beliefs? You might be wondering, as I did while raising my kids: *Is it more dangerous to read the opposing view or to be protected from it?*

In my first book, *The Brave Learner*, I looked at the power of environmental and emotional context to aid learning—real-life contexts, like adding the surprise of cookies and tea to the study of poetry, providing kind collaboration to a struggling learner. In this book, I want to move the furniture around in our minds—how do we set the table to generate fresh insight rather than recycle what's been taught? Is it possible to sustain "childlike wonder" into adulthood, or does it get lost in that journey to maturity? How do we help kids discover *more* about the subjects they study, not just what standardized tests require our children to demonstrate? How do we activate our children's imaginations for subjects like history or the social sciences, and even math and science? What do we do about the endless sea of information on the internet? Can kids be critical thinkers about films, novels, and video games they love, too? In other words, how can we lead our learners to think more deeply, thoughtfully, and imaginatively about everything in their world?

If we give students the tools of inquiry, however, we have to be prepared for the results. They'll ask hard-to-hear, provocative questions. They'll jump in and use technology and social media apps without having considered their purpose or source. They'll adopt viewpoints that challenge your well-settled ones. It can be jarring to allow kids the leeway to be forthright about how they generate meaning. Hang tough, however. The electric truth is that critical thinkers become versatile readers, skilled writers, and consequential adults. They're engaged students in and out of the classroom. They innovate, they challenge the status quo, they vote and volunteer, and they make thoughtful contributions to the places where they work. They find powerful new ways to acquire the skills they need to thrive; they grow healthy families; and they become delightful, responsible adults. To be a critical thinker is to be a person with insight, empathy, humility, self-awareness, mental acuity, and intellectual aliveness. Truly, raising critical thinkers is the most exciting and important work we can do as parents and educators.

I've spent the last three decades working with all kinds of young thinkers. I home-educated my five children for seventeen years, I built a company with a team of skilled professionals that has coached thousands of students of all ages to think and write well, and I've taught incoming freshmen at Xavier University. In all those years of teaching, what shines most brightly is the incredible high students get when they experience an epiphany of insight. They're startled by their own brilliance when they generate fresh perspectives.

I've distilled my favorite lessons from those years of investment into this book—both philosophy and practice. In part 1, "What Is a Critical Thinker?," I lay the groundwork for how any of us forms a worldview. How can we teach our kids to differentiate bias from belief or facts from interpretations? Where do well-formed opinions come from, and on what basis do we hold them? How do school experiences and internet searches influence how our kids think? What role does their identity play in how they learn? In most chapters, I include activities to try with the whole family.

In part 2, "Read, Experience, Encounter: A Real Education," I explore the three key ways any of us learns. I challenge the idea that reading is enough—that a well-read person is automatically a well-educated one. We take a look at how digital life is altering our brains and our kids' ability to read closely and deeply. I provide strategies for how to recapture that depth, too. Then I take a look at the kinds of practical experiences and encounters with people that lead to breakthrough insights and a more thoughtful relationship to any subject they study or any interest they pursue.

Part 3, "The Rhetorical Imagination," is the big kahuna! Once your students understand how they build their worldviews and know how to investigate a topic deeply, they're ready to expand how many points of view they can examine at once. They will have entered the stage of development I call the "rhetorical imagination"—the capacity to think critically and imaginatively. In this section, I offer you tools to help your students interpret texts and to compare and contrast more than one viewpoint. Then I show you how to help your emerging young adults cope with the destabilization of their habits of thought. I also provide guidance to you, the parent, for how to navigate those turbulent waters, particularly when you have teens who are dead set on challenging your cherished ideals. Believe it or not, this is an essential stage of development for them. Let's embrace it and learn to do it well.

Each chapter builds on the previous one, so reading in order is advised. That said, you'll come back to this book. The practices can be used again and again, and you may notice that you need different chapters during different seasons of your child's life.

In short, this book is for you if you've asked *What's the point of all this education? There's got to be more than passing tests and getting into college.* It's especially for you if you want your children to have a big, juicy, insightful educational experience in all the subjects and beyond. You have the chance to raise good people who contribute to the well-being of one another and bring a vibrant creativity to their thinking processes. It's an exciting journey, and you get to be a part of it! Let's get started.

PART 1

What Is a Critical Thinker?

The pupil is thereby "schooled" to confuse teaching with learning, grade advancement with education, a diploma with competence, and fluency with the ability to say something new.

—Ivan Illich, *Deschooling*

Drop the belief that schooling creates thinkers. As bell hooks, revolutionary educator, expressed with cutting clarity: "Sadly, children's passion for thinking often ends when they encounter a world that seeks to educate them for conformity and obedience only. Most children are taught early on that thinking is dangerous." Ouch.

Kids are naturally curious from the moment they take their first breaths. A baby brings all the toys to her mouth—gnawing, drooling, sucking, chewing—her primary means of knowing. The toddler becomes a scientist: dropping what can be dropped, throwing what can be thrown, eating what can (whether it should or should not) be eaten. The toddler looks under, around, over, behind.

The baby and toddler are assembling worldviews that will become a

1

bedrock for how they interpret their world. They're making unconscious judgment calls every day—what they prefer, what their environment offers, what they can do for themselves, what requires support. Add another couple of years, and now the small child wants to stir, beat a drum, hammer, bike ride, splash, stomp, teeter-totter, lick, scribble, sniff, slide hands all along the dirty handrail, rip paper, smash Play-Doh, and roll down the grassy slope. As they grow, they navigate more complicated tasks, like how to find the right shaped LEGO brick in a sea of hundreds to assemble a pirate ship. They scrutinize the two-dimensional illustration and match it to the three-dimensional piece. Bigger kids' brains estimate the distance they need to jump on a skateboard to clear the bottom three steps of a staircase. They look at an unfamiliar plate of food and use data collected from previous eating experiences to decide whether it's worth the taste-test. Teens evaluate the book versus the movie to determine whether the film is faithful enough to the novel. They form passionate opinions about hot-button social issues and rank their favorite bands by criteria they design. All children figure out when to ask Mom for a cookie (while she's on the phone with the insurance company, of course).

Critical thinking is a tool kit we cultivate to help us skillfully live. Educational expert Arthur Costa explains that critical thinking is active when a student uses "strategic reasoning, insightfulness, perseverance, creativity, and craftsmanship to resolve a complex problem." I see critical thinking like this: a source of wisdom, ease in social settings, adaptability in crisis. Critical thinking puts the power in personal growth. It finds the solution to the puzzle. It's the fount of insight. It's the design in creativity. Critical thinking enables us to interpret and act. We use it when we decide to trust or to be suspicious—and to check ourselves for bias. It's the skill that connects us to the past, to larger contexts, to nature, and to narrative. There are times when we're actively aware that we're strategizing and creating. There are other times when we navigate a complex problem using an invisible sense—intuition, a hunch, loyalty to a community perspective.

Educators worth their salt want children to be critical thinkers. Yet the daily flood of inputs kids face staggers any awake brain. Children and teens are confronted with a wide array of source material—videos on YouTube, personal stories on social media apps, real-time chat while they game, TV shows and streaming movies, books they enjoy and textbooks they don't, adults they love who hold different perspectives about the same topics, accurate information and disinformation side by side in an online search. Too often, parents and instructors teach students to be critical of the stuff that's *out there* and to receive without question the information presented in the home or classroom. Yet have we considered the minds making all that meaning? Critical thinking relies on this pivot to self. Adults and children alike can learn to identify their perceptions, what causes them to trust one source of information and distrust another, and why they accept some ideas as true while they reject others as false. Researchers call this kind of self-monitoring "metacognition" or "thinking about thinking."

I prefer to call this type of brainpower "self-aware critical thinking." In the coming chapters, I explore how to teach these self-aware critical thinking skills to children and teens in an age-appropriate way. They'll learn to observe their assumptions and to question them. They'll grow in their ability to notice nuance and complexity while forging a set of personally meaningful values. These skills last a lifetime and deepen their ability to experience awe, wonder, connection, and satisfaction.

What tools help us raise these self-aware critical thinkers?

Let's find out.

CHAPTER 1

Says Who?

That's it. That's the real story. I was framed.

—Jon Scieszka, *The True Story of the 3 Little Pigs*

I dunked Noah's three-year-old head under the clean water to rinse the soap. As he popped up, he sputtered, clearing his mouth, "Tell me *The Three Little Pigs* again!" I obliged, as I had dozens of times before. Noah chimed in at the wolf's iconic refrain: "I huffed and I puffed and I blew the house in!" Noah didn't just say the words, either. He sucked in big drafts of huffy-puffy air, and he blew out his huffy-puffy, water-wet, house-blowing breath at imaginary homes of straw, twigs, and bricks. We laughed and laughed.

Months later, I stumbled upon a new book at the library that I thought my three-little-pigs-obsessed child would enjoy. It was called *The True Story of the 3 Little Pigs* by Jon Scieszka. We plunked down on the couch together, and I read it aloud. Noah's eyes widened with delight—the wolf's perspective! This pitiable wolf simply wanted to borrow a cup of sugar from his neighbors, the pigs, in order to bake his grandmother a birthday cake. I mean, what a nice guy! Poor Mr. Wolf suffered from a terrible cold. His sneezes toppled the first two houses, inadvertently killing the pigs who lived in them. The prudent wolf couldn't bear to allow all that ham to go to waste, so he ate the swine. By the time the wolf arrived at the brick house, the third little pig had reported the wolf to the police for the wolf's misdeeds. Mr. Wolf was *wrongly* convicted of his crimes and sent to prison for ten millennia. The wolf declared the injustice of his situation from his jail cell in a final plea to the reader: "That's it. That's the real story. I was framed."

Noah quickly became obsessed with the new book. It wasn't that he thought that the book, in fact, told the *true* story of the three little pigs. It was that by reading the wolf's version of the fairy tale, Noah became aware that there might even *be* another perspective. Noah's ability to be suspicious of the wolf's account was intuitive and part of what made reading the book so delightful. Until that moment, Noah had aligned automatically with the omniscient narrators in all fairy tales. There had never been a reason to question the truth-value of any story—until he heard from the wolf.

Noah had unwittingly stumbled onto the literary device known as the "unreliable narrator." An unreliable narrator is the original not-self-aware thinker. The defensive, self-interested manner in which the wolf told his story is a dead giveaway to readers that the wolf is not using his own critical thinking faculties. Instead, he showcases a self-serving defense to disguise his misdeeds, obscuring the facts and reframing them to suit his declaration of innocence. The wolf, as unreliable narrator, was Noah's first brush with examining the viewpoint of any story we read. Scieszka plays up the wolf's woe-is-me story with humor. Readers *feel* the absurdity. But how do we know that we are, in fact, reading an unreliable narrator's perspective? What makes the wolf's narcissistic point of view obvious to us, the readers?

We've arrived at the fundamental question in learning. How do we know which source of authority to trust? Which perspectives of historical events, for instance, are accurate? How do we recognize a conspiracy theorist versus a whistleblower? How do we vet our elected officials for truth-telling versus egocentric lying? Which scientific theories are reliable? Which are a sham? What mathematical process is the right one to use in a given context? Which novels ought to be canon? How do we determine which books to retire from "classic" status?

The questions cascade in a rush the minute you give yourself permission to run down that slope. What governmental policies cause people to flourish? Which cause human rights abuses? How do we evaluate the claims of religion? To what standards do we hold any claims? Whether conscious of them or not, we ask questions every time we read, listen to, or ponder any and all input. When teaching our kids, it's tempting to think we can find the truth and then teach it to them, and yet who decides what that truth is?

Each subject area can be understood as a host of stories, told by narrators, a.k.a. storytellers (educated experts, commentators, artists, scientists, firsthand witnesses, liars, believers, victims, winners). Each and every storyteller has an angle. One way to think about any subject—whether conveyed to us via book, movie, play, legend, myth, data point, poem, statistic, practice, theory, doctrine, or news report—is to ask, "Who's telling the story?" When I asked my aunts and mother to tell the story of their parents' love life, I got multiple versions of the facts. What makes any of their interpretations reliable? That's the essence of this critical thinking journey. Maybe you've experienced the sensation that someone without proper experience and authority is telling *your* story and doing it poorly. Think about the classic gender-stereotyped circumstance: a male doctor tries to tell a woman how to handle the discomforts of pregnancy and childbirth. Most women rightly respond like the character Rachel from the sitcom *Friends*: "No uterus, no opinion!" That's a bit what I mean here. The storytellers matter. Each point of view comes from a data set that is particular to that narrator. We evaluate the reliability of that narrator automatically, filtered through countless checkpoints that are frequently invisible to us.

Education is not a walk through neutral information, mastered for a test. It's the ability to identify the storytellers, to evaluate sources, to question perspectives, and to determine the usefulness of a viewpoint at a particular moment in time. In fact, interpretations of historical events, literature, scientific discoveries, and more shift generation to generation, year to year, sometimes within months. Tall order! Is critical thinking reserved, then, for subject-matter experts who poke holes in theories and assess who to trust and who to disavow? Are we supposed to just "take their word" for it? If critical thinking is only about how we evaluate *other* people's conclusions, how can we judge their viewpoints without proper experience or education? For instance, most people are not qualified to render a verdict on scientific theories about topics like greenhouse gases or the origins of the universe. I remember reading arguments for and against the big bang theory. I had my own "aha" moment as I read: *I'm not qualified to evaluate the evidence.* Yet isn't that what we do anyway? What criteria justify the opinions we adopt when we aren't skilled experts ourselves?

I'm thinking of the countless decisions parents make without expert skill: whether or not to vaccinate, which type of orthodontia is best, what sort of birth is safest, what kind of schooling is right for this child? Parents make these calls for themselves without education or training all the time, and they feel called on to do it. In fact, people of various backgrounds assertively offer critiques of all sorts of viewpoints without the relevant education, especially online. One scroll through Twitter and you can't help but notice how many tweets are unsupported assertions. Anecdotal support runs rife—we substitute personal experiences for the expertise of trained professionals all the time. Alternatively, we may amass evidence for a position we take and are mystified when other people discount those "facts" with a swipe of the delete key. The world our kids are entering is one where having a confident opinion is expected, and that opinion (regardless of qualifications) acts as a litmus test for whether they belong in a community. It turns out that we usually select the storytellers who affirm our cherished community memberships.

Name That Storyteller

Each time we consume information (data, expert opinion, studies, personal experience), we ask a pithy question: "Says who?" Every field of study—whether it's history, literature, mathematics, sociology, political theory, psychology, the arts, the trades, the sciences, statistics, religion, medicine—comes to us through a lens. Those subjects get told by the storyteller, who interprets the information. At times, the storyteller chooses to hide behind an impersonal presentation of data. For instance, the hard and social sciences are expressed as "objectively" as possible, removing personal opinion to the best of a researcher's ability. Other times, the opinion of the narrator is obvious: editorial writers, academics writing persuasive papers, or the wolf who justifies eating two little pigs. Sometimes the storyteller claims divine guidance, such as a religion's holy scriptures written by God through a human secretary. One critical thinking skill we want our kids to master is the ability to *name that storyteller.*

When students are told to examine a researcher's work, to challenge the perspective of a writer, or to compare and contrast the conflicting findings of experts, they're expected to render reasonable analysis. How do they do that? That's what this book is about, but before students can launch their insights at research, there's an even more important step they must take.

The Academic Selfie

Before anyone (our students and ourselves included) can critically think, we need to address a common blind spot: our own thinking! The most thoughtful analysis comes after flipping around the camera lens to take what I call an "academic selfie." Because we live inside our own bodies and think thoughts in our minds, we lose touch with how we make meaning and judgments. We consult a personal feeling of "rightness"— how what we choose to believe aligns with what we've learned in school, online, or on TV or radio. We compare what we think with what we've been taught in our religious communities. We think about where we live or how we were raised. Until we've done this internal work, any evaluation of someone else's thinking will be influenced by all that personal static without our realizing it.

Remember my aunts and mother as they interpreted their father's love letter? They each understood the "making love" reference differently. They justified their interpretations without asking an essential question: *What do I hope will be true?* Flipping around the lens means acknowledging that a personal bias is about to take over the reading! Recognizing bias doesn't mean that the conclusion the person draws is automatically wrong. Rather, to be a critical thinker means getting comfortable noticing our swift reactions when they come up to ensure that those automatic thoughts don't overwhelm other possible interpretations, especially in the initial research phase of study. Critical thinking includes these two skills, then: criticality (of others) and awareness (of self). Both. As we educate children, let's teach them the undervalued skill of self-awareness first.

So where do we begin? How can anyone become a *self-aware* critical thinker? High-caliber self-aware thinkers are adept at identifying the impact of their experiences, perceptions, biases, beliefs, thoughts, loyalties, and hunches on their studies. And let me tell you—that work is exhausting. Truly insightful thinking needs time to gestate. Usually we start with a slew of barely perceptible reactions as we read, like the ones in this list:

- I go blank when I have to remember numbers.
- I don't want this to be true.

- This idea makes me nervous. What would my [parent, spiritual leader, best friend, teacher] say about it?
- The main character reminds me of my mean aunt.
- Isn't this writer from the political party my dad hates?
- That fact ruins my thesis. I wonder if I can skip it and write my paper without it.
- I wish I knew more about X. I'm annoyed that the writers are ignoring X.

These thoughts are often just beneath a student's conscious awareness, so it helps to draw them out. Students can learn to live with the discomfort of contradictory evidence, a report that drills a hole in a theory, or the conflicting opinions of experts before they can comment. Have you ever had the experience of writing an angry social media post and deliberately skipping the evidence against your main point? That's your mind protecting your intellectual energy—the energy it takes to gain and grow insight (and the time it takes to rethink your thinking!). Most online conversations move too swiftly. It's energizing to rant. It's tiring to give patient consideration to a view or fact you don't want to be true.

Even adults struggle with these skills because we've been trained to see reading outside our worldview as participating in heresy. Here's a snapshot of how it may feel to patiently monitor your own reactivity. Imagine reading an editorial that contradicts a belief you hold sacred.

- You may notice a pit in your stomach:
  Why am I nervous reading this article? Am I scanning quickly to find its flaws?
- You might feel a note of triumph:
  Aha! This is the fact I can use to prove I'm right!
- You might notice that you get bored or that you feel angry.

- You might identify a shift in your tightly held understanding, which unsettles you.
- You might clear your browser history so your spouse doesn't find out you were reading from that website.
- Your mind may skitter away from what you're studying to the fear that you're too near a dissenting position. (Whatever the field, there's always orthodoxy and heresy within it.)
- You may dismiss an argument simply because you know the reputation of the news source.

It's easy to disregard information that creates emotional drag. Conversely, the adrenaline rush when someone confirms what you want to be true is heady stuff. That's the hit we want: proof that we're on the right side after all. The technical term for this validation-seeking mechanism is "confirmation bias"—the inclination to trust a report because it confirms your already-established beliefs. These body sensations, thoughts, and neurological reactions aren't easily waived off. They *are* the essence of how we form our bedrock opinions.

Naturally, children are adults in training. They're susceptible, too. Heck, they sit at our dinner tables for nearly two decades listening to us rant and pontificate. If we don't learn how to moderate our own tendency to righteously rain down the "truth," we'll short-circuit our kids' ability to think well. It takes self-control to be a thoughtful thinker. Controlling our impulses is tough for all of us.

According to psychologist Daniel Kahneman, there's a strong correlation between self-control and quality critical thinking. Kahneman, in his excellent book *Thinking Fast and Slow*, cites the famous experiment by psychologist Walter Mischel that tests the willpower of four-year-old children left alone in a room with a single Oreo cookie. The instruction? *Do not eat this cookie for fifteen minutes, and you will be rewarded with two cookies.* The children weighed the dilemma alone and were viewed through a one-way mirror. No books or toys were in the room to distract the child. If the child ate the cookie or showed signs of distress, the experiment ended.

Half of the children succeeded in waiting the full fifteen minutes. Amazing, right? What *is* astonishing is that when tracked ten to fifteen years later in their educations, the "resisters had higher measures of executive control in cognitive tasks." These "children who had shown more self-control as four-year-olds had substantially higher scores on tests of intelligence." Similar studies with computer gaming and puzzle solving demonstrated that those who score poorly on these sorts of tests "are prone to answer questions with the first idea that comes to their mind and [are] unwilling to invest the effort needed to check their intuitions." This unwillingness to "check our intuitions" is what so many of us face every day when we hear the news or read a website. It takes patience and self-control to stay open to additional information.

I found this study riveting. To be a critical thinker requires this sort of self-discipline. In a similar way, quality thinkers delay the gratification of being immediately right. They choose not to fall prey to their first hunch or impression. Kids without the patience to seek additional information will often "take the cookie" of simplest insight, instead of waiting for the payoff of two or more impressions to consider.

So let's pause and again consider *The True Story of the 3 Little Pigs* through a different lens. What if we evaluate the story not as critics, but as *self-aware* critical thinkers first? How would I engage the wolf's version of the three little pigs story?

I start by asking myself:

- What messages about wolves am I bringing with me as I read this story?

    Answer: I'm used to wolves being portrayed as bad guys in fairy tales. I remember the wolf in *Little Red*

Riding Hood and *Peter and the Wolf*. In both cases, that wolf is "big and bad."

- How might this background impact my analysis of this wolf's report?

  Answer: I'm suspicious of a wolf who appears considerate of pigs—a favorite meal choice. I doubt his assertion that he "accidentally" killed two pigs and, therefore, *had* to eat them. Yeah, *riiiight!*

- What prior experiences do I have with fairy tales?

  Answer: A fairy tale gives me a moral about good and evil. I look for the noble moral from the get-go. If I don't see one, I'm suspicious of the tale-teller. In *The True Story of the 3 Little Pigs*, there appears to be no moral—only a half-baked self-defense of immoral acts.

- What's my experience with this particular fairy tale?

  Answer: I've heard it told and seen it represented countless times where the pigs are innocent victims and the wolf is the clear villain. *Surely that must be the true version because it's the most common one.*

- Lastly, what do I know about Jon Scieszka, the author?

  Answer: I happen to know that he's hilarious.

Given this background, I went into the book expecting Scieszka to take the familiar story and flip it on its head, changing the wolf from villain to victim. And yet, because I trusted the wolf-as-villain to be the "truest" version of the fairy tale, I got the jokes! Scieszka's approach worked like a charm.

Let's pivot, now, to Noah's point of view. What caused three-year-old Noah to distrust the wolf's version of the three little pigs story so quickly? What made him see that story differently than all the other three little pig versions we had read together (that he had accepted at face value)? I can think of two factors.

First, *I* read the Scieszka picture book to Noah so it was my disposition that influenced how Noah heard it. I couldn't help but chuckle at the absurdities. I used intonation in my reading that discredited the wolf's retelling. In short, my viewpoint of any story served as the controlling lens for little Noah's interpretations and responses.

Second, Noah was so familiar with the original version of the fairy tale that he had already accepted it as the right version through sheer repetition. What if the first time Noah had ever heard the story had been from the wolf's perspective? What if he had heard the wolf's tale countless times from a variety of books and movies before he heard the version sympathetic to the pigs? Do you think Noah (or any child, for that matter) would have been able to automatically discredit the wolf's take at that point? It's an interesting question. There are clues in Scieszka's text that tell us the wolf is self-interested and making excuses. Children relate to excuse-making, which is part of why this book is an enduring favorite with kids. The book strikes a chord with them because they relate to the cover-up! But if a child is young enough and unfamiliar with the original tale or with our stereotypes about wolves, would that child be as likely to distrust the wolf? Might a child come to the conclusion that the wolf was justified in the actions he took after all? Here we arrive at the heart of the critical thinking challenge.

Noah and I suffered from what researchers call the "mere exposure effect." Kahneman explains that repetition conditions us to assign positive attributes to the item that gets repeated. Researchers conducted an experiment in American university newspapers where Turkish words (or Turkish-sounding terms) were shown inside an ad-like box each day without any context or explanation of their meanings. After some weeks, readers of the campus newspapers were asked to rate these terms, as well as others that recurred less frequently, as either "means something good" or "means something bad."

The outcome surprised Kahneman: "The results were spectacular: the words that were presented more frequently were rated much more favorably than the words that had been shown only once or twice." Repetition gives the impression of "goodness" or reliability of report. This is why during election season, signs merely bearing the names of candidates are everywhere. Familiarity, in this case, breeds trust. Kahneman goes on to explain that this naturally occurring bias has biological roots, where a stimulus that leads to a benign or positive result is cataloged in the brain as "good," which we compute as true. Cognitive ease is the result, which our brains enjoy immensely. Circling back, then, the more Noah and I heard and retold the original tale of the three little pigs and their plight, the more we believed the pigs' point of view and saw them as good! That big bad wolf didn't stand a chance with us.

Identifying these factors before we read any book is optimal. However, even if we only notice them afterward, we give ourselves the best chance to behave as self-aware critical thinkers. While this story seems an obvious parody of the original fairy tale to all of us, it's a wonderful exercise to perform with your kids who have less experience. Asking questions that provoke self-awareness is key to analyzing any text, from the founding documents of the United States to scientific studies to religious literature to novels and poetry.

All critical thought is funneled through a self, from the moment we exit the womb. Our brains are obsessive meaning-making machines, interpreting whatever comes our way with whatever limited insight is available to us at the time. Human beings are determined to wrestle information into a worldview that tells the story they love to hear. Let's help our kids identify the storytellers.

In this book, many chapters end with activities to try with your kids. (Occasionally I toss in an activity for you, too.) Most of the time, the activities are organized by age range.

- Bright-eyed: 5 to 9 years old
- Quick-witted: 10 to 12 years old
- Nimble-minded: 13 to 18 years old

✳ ACTIVITY: SAYS WHO?

The following questions focus on how your children hear a story and what sense they make of it. Hint: *do not* fire off these questions like a drill sergeant. Offer them conversationally, along the way, as you interact with your kids. Read them, say them to yourself in the shower, forget about them, and then . . . use them naturally!

Bright-Eyed (5 to 9)

Pick a story to read to your child. It can fall into one of the following categories:

- Fairy tale
- Tall tale
- Folk tale
- Aesop's fable

Read it ahead of time so you are familiar with this particular version.

Next, read it aloud with the child.

Ask several of the following questions (the ones that you find useful or helpful):

1. Who's telling the story?
2. Do you think the storyteller knows what all the characters think? Is the storyteller one of the characters or outside of the story? How can you tell?
3. Do you trust the storyteller to tell the truth? Why or why not?
4. Who do you like in the story? Who do you dislike? Is either of these characters telling the story?
5. Have you heard this story told in any other ways? Which storyteller do you prefer? Why?

You can apply these questions to video games, pretend play, television shows, and songs, too. If you know of more than one version of a story that showcases a different viewpoint, read it and ask the same set of questions. Compare the answers.

Quick-Witted (10 to 12)

This next age group is capable of a little more introspection than the bright-eyed kids. This group can play with the narrative and perspectives. Select a well-known story—it can even be a movie series like Star Wars, or a book series like Redwall.

1. Who's telling the story? How do we know?
2. Do you trust the storyteller? Why or why not?
3. Whose story is not being told? Do you trust that character? Why or why not?
4. Try telling the story from another perspective. How difficult is it? What changes did you make?
5. If you tell the story from the villain's perspective, does the moral of the story shift? To what moral? What do you think about that?

Nimble-Minded (13 to 18)

Teens are ready for deeper engagement when they read. Pick a well-known story (movie or book) for these questions. You might converse over coffee or shakes. Keep it light. This is not a quiz.

1. Who's telling the story? Is it being told in first-person experience (who is that?) or from an omniscient (all-knowing) storyteller? How can you tell?
2. Do you trust and believe the narrator? Why or why not?
3. Whose story is not being told? Can you guess why not?
4. Retell the story from a different character's perspective. What changes do you have to make? How does the character's background influence how the story is told? Do we know enough about this character to create a believable perspective?
5. Retell the story from an inanimate perspective (as a tree or flower or house in the setting). How does that shift the way the story is told?
6. Check in with your body. When you hear two different versions, is there a difference in how you feel about the story? More eager with one, more suspicious with another, more humorous with still another? Say more about that.

Now that your kids have experienced the power of a storyteller's viewpoint (whether the villain, the victim, or the innocent bystander), let's take an inventory of the language we use when we talk about those views. Is the storyteller sharing an opinion? How do we tease out the facts from a storyteller's bias? What roles do worldview and perspective play in thinking well? In the next chapter, we clarify the glossary of terms that recur throughout this book and in your quest to raise critical thinkers.

CHAPTER 2

Separating the Facts from Their Fictions

Those of us who love certainty are shocked a lot in life.

—Dr. June O'Connor, my brilliant aunt and a professor of
ethics and religion at the University of California, Riverside

How can she still believe that? I showed her the facts!"

"That's not true. She's biased."

"Everyone has a right to their opinion."

"If it's true for one person, it's true for everyone."

"I have proof!"

"God said so."

"He has an agenda."

"Objectively speaking, that's misinformation."

"I know because I was there."

"You're prejudiced!"

Ad nauseam.

You've wandered around social media, right? People toss out lines like these on the regular, hoping to shut down conversations in one fell swoop. What drives us to stop the other person from talking? Why do we expect other people to agree with us? What is this instinctual need to be right that excludes someone else's attempt to engage with a perspective that's different from ours?

Underneath our desire to have the correct point of view is a drive for sameness—the certainty of agreement rather than the discomfort of difference. And honestly, there's a pretty good reason for that drive to sameness, even if it's biting us in the rear end now. It all began with a little experiment. I now present to you a down-and-dirty history of global, public, classroom-based education (not to be taken as the definitive history, you understand). I want to peel back the possible, accidental, unintended consequences that resulted from one of the most successful human projects of all time: educating everyone.

As human society evolved, a glittering vision emerged: "Let's school all the people—from royalty with crowned jewels, to landowners, to regular folks who work for those muckety-mucks." It took time. Not everyone liked the project. Some felt public education would hinder religious training. Colonialists and slaveholders actively obstructed educating those they oppressed and exploited. Teaching girls to read and write was seen as a waste of time by many men in power. The disabled were similarly excluded from school.

In 1635, the first free public school supported by tax dollars was opened in the American colonies. More than a century later, Thomas Jefferson advocated for a widespread public school system after the Revolutionary War. It wasn't until 1837, however, that the first official board of education was opened (in Massachusetts). Around the same time, children's rights advocates fought for widespread tax-funded education in Europe to limit abusive child-labor practices. Between the mid-nineteenth and mid-twentieth centuries, modern public education expanded to the continents of South America, Asia, and Africa as well. Even so, it took significant activism to ensure that everyone (all races, sexes, abilities, and classes) had an equal right to publicly funded learning. To this day, equity in education is a fight that continues.

The best version of the public school dream went like this: reading, writing, and arithmetic would no longer be reserved for the elite (those people who could hire tutors for their heirs). Instead, by the end of the twentieth century, the global community collectively agreed that children of all backgrounds and beliefs everywhere on the planet deserved basic language and math literacy, with a side of history and science. Public schooling for the masses was built on an education model that would provide reliable workers to the booming industrial revolution, and eventually school would become the place where kids learned enough to participate in today's science and technology revolutions (among other professions).

So, governments mechanized education—creating a predictable system that would produce reliable outcomes. The results are in. Look at this astonishing world we inhabit! From standardized widgets in every field to predictable health-care practices whether you find yourself in Birmingham or Mumbai, from in-kind transportation systems on every continent to agriculture that feeds billions, from universal computer technology to space travel and global telecommunications—human beings have eclipsed any fantasy that the original modest advocates for education-for-all ever dreamed possible. In short, it works to publicly educate billions of people. We've created a shared reality, built together through the power of knowledge. Has there ever been a more successful human project in our history? I think not!

In an attempt to benefit from all this educating around the globe, sameness has been key. We consolidate research so we can advance (scale up!) together. We're skilled at creating tools that convert our differences into sameness—from transformers of electrical current to units of measure. Variations from country to country exist within a carefully created deliberate equivalence. The goal is maximum interchangeability. We've substituted mass production of goods and services for artisanal skill. Methodical distribution of all those goods is truly one of the milestone accomplishments of the twentieth century. It's remarkable, if you really think about it, that you can travel the globe and see the power of education at work wherever you go. To achieve this uniformity of outcome and purpose, global schools are remarkably similar in design. Traditional K–12 classrooms drive for consistent measurements of learning. The aspiration goes like this: if all people can be well-enough educated, the result will be mutual understanding and a shared commitment to global peace and prosperity.

But alas, disillusionment arrived swiftly. The twentieth century taught us that human expertise has limits. Einstein blew our minds by exposing that even time moves at different rates from different perspectives (shattering our faith in a fixed understanding of physics). We wondered what else might not be the reliable fact we once trusted. We learned that just because we know how to do something doesn't mean we should. Knowledge doesn't assume morality or ethics (cf. genocide, segregation, religious conflicts, nuclear weapons, air and water pollution). Our unexamined biases interfere with how we apply what we learn. Knowing what to think is not the same as knowing how to think. Martin Luther King Jr., our American civil rights hero who was assassinated for his prophetic social commentary, put it this way: "The function of education is to teach one to think intensively and to think critically. Intelligence plus character—that is the goal of true education." Part of our children's schooling, then, is recognizing the moral arc of what they learn, not just mastery of facts for tests.

Each field of study is a swiftly moving stream, and you cannot step into it in the same place twice. Certainly, there are core practices and undergirding principles that act as the bedrock of study. It only takes a little deconstruction to watch those practices and principles morph and evolve through the centuries, however. Goodness, there was a time when human beings didn't even have the digit for zero! Understanding is temporary, even if useful. Whatever you may accept as factual has likely been examined by someone else who sees the same data through another interpretive prism. We question how to use facts. We question the factuality of the facts themselves! Even when we agree on the facts, it's what we say about them that determines everything. We might agree that it's raining, but one of us will be glad and the other, pissed off!

PhD candidates write dissertations on topics that are already well understood, looking for the disregarded flaw, the hidden nuance, or the breakthrough insight that was previously overlooked. Religions have countless denominations or sects that uncover that one interpretation of a tenet the other groups missed. Political parties splinter into factions that promote different definitions of the same concepts: freedom, law, governance, common good, human rights. The study of science has demonstrated again and again that for every gain, there is a new mystery birthed worthy of a lifetime pursuit or an unintended dangerous consequence (hello, splitting the atom).

Anytime you think you're certain, you can be sure that someone somewhere uses the same words you use and means something entirely different. Even bedrock terms like "God," "country," "school," "love," "gravity," and "health" call up a wide array of associations and definitions. It's not to say that we can't land anywhere solid. Rather, insightful thinking means recognizing that every fact lives inside a story. Education ought to be more like Russian nesting dolls—recognizing that each fact is nested in others that influence its size and shape. Education is not merely identifying one set of right answers.

Intimacy over Certainty

The alternative to certainty is intimacy. Intimacy means knowing more of the subject with more of yourself. It looks like a greater and greater tenderness toward a field of study—a hunger to become close to it, to know its compelling contours and unavoidable flaws. It means reading the subject's ardent fans and listening with patience to its detractors. Intimacy leads to both a fascination with and protection of a subject's inherent value. There's inscrutability and mystery within every subject. Intimacy in learning means developing an *ongoing* relationship to that discipline, allowing it to morph and change, which requires humility. Mastery is a myth.

Don't believe me? Let me give you a benign example to drive home this point. Perhaps you believe that you read fluently. If I put a language you don't speak in front of you, or a new alphabet, or a different orthography like characters or hieroglyphs, suddenly you'll be aware of your lack of fluency in reading. Even within your own language, you might find yourself running into a brick wall of vocabulary you don't understand. I can't make sense of medical articles in academic journals because of the many unfamiliar terms. In fact, the majority of modern English speakers feel the shift from fluent to not quite when we read Shakespeare. Mastery of any subject is an illusion. Lifelong learning is expressed as a relationship, not a degree.

Yes, there are facts. But facts don't live in a vacuum. They're expressed by people in contexts. It's this contextual frame of reference that leads to the exhausting fights we've all experienced. We believe we're sharing facts, when in fact (ha!) we're sharing interpretations of facts. Leaning into the uncertainty can feel dangerous or exhilarating. Think of a ski slope. When you learn to snow ski, you take the bunny trails with a gentle gradient. As you gain skill, you increase the incline and discover new balance, leg strength, and hip-swishing action. The danger comes when you pair your current (inadequate) skills with too steep a hill.

When pursuing an education, students start with bunny hills:

- Identifying their current relationship to the topic
- Getting to know the subject matter factually

- Learning how to use the tools of the field
- Meeting the experts who have invested their lives in the work
- Discovering the broadest consensus of how the topic exists today in the world

Then, the student is ready to tackle steeper hills of critical thought:

- Dissenting opinions
- Evidence that doesn't fit neatly into the current understanding
- Ethical and moral challenges
- How it influences adjacent subjects
- Its impact on the status quo

Today, with the speed of the internet and the ability to manipulate information (graphs, statistics, images, and quotes), any of us can be led down a steep, bumpy path to conspiracy theories and misinformation. Before we guide our kids down the bunny slopes of critical thinking, let's review important vocabulary that will recur through these pages (as surely as moguls, ice, and powder) on the mountainside of thought.

Fab Vocab

The following list of ten terms is loaded with meaning and misunderstanding. Before you move on to the rest of the chapter, I invite you to freewrite for two minutes about each term (or select a few, if you don't have enough time for them all). Take a sheet of paper, turn it to landscape view, and fold it into eight boxes. Put a term at the top of each space and two on the back. Set a timer and write for two minutes each, whatever comes to mind. Scribble your own definitions and questions about the terms. What do these concepts mean in *your* mind? I use this same practice with my college students when we begin a class together. I find terms that will recur in our meetings and get their unvarnished initial impressions before we begin using them together. It helps each of us to expose the hidden assumptions we make about terminology.

Let's start here, with you (and maybe your teens!). Try it with your spouse. Talk over the terms with a sibling or best friend on the phone or via lengthy text messages. Drum up a variety of takes. The more you think about these concepts, the better!

- Fact
- Interpretation
- Evidence
- Perspective
- Opinion
- Prejudice
- Bias
- Belief
- Story
- Worldview

Next, let's take a look at my definitions. Keep your freewrites handy, too, as you read the rest of the book.

FACT

The well-known proverb, "Facts are stubborn things," is often attributed to US founding father John Adams. He did, in fact, *say* it, but he was referencing a well-known idiom that originated with Frenchman Alain-René Lesage. Even that factual attribution has additional fact layers that require interrogation. Amazing, right? So what does it mean to say a fact is stubborn? When we talk about a *fact*, we're talking about *irreducible information that can't be disputed.*

Examples:

- Water boils at 212° Fahrenheit and 100° Celsius.
- Frederick Douglass escaped slavery on September 3, 1838, by rail.
- The first atomic bomb was dropped on Hiroshima, Japan, on August 6, 1945, by the United States.
- A group of ferrets is called a business. (Bet you didn't know that!)
- At 66,000 miles in length, the human circulatory system could wrap itself around the earth more than two and a half times. (Mind blown!)
- India has 19,569 languages and dialects—twenty-two of them are official languages. (Unreal!)
- Ghana existed as a massive empire on the African continent from the seventh to the thirteenth centuries.

Facts are *actual*. They're not probabilities or interpretations. A fact can be demonstrated to be true repeatedly. Science and mathematics, in particular, truck in facts. People in these fields use data collection, tools of measurement, and verified research methods to identify facts. Facts don't tell stories. They don't offer moral or ethical guidance. Facts don't care about your religion, your political affiliation, or how many degrees you hold. That said, most of us want to *do* something with a fact. We're rarely content to state facts without making a point. We want to explain them!

INTERPRETATION

Enter *interpretation*. Philosophy, history, political science, and literature lean toward themes and interpretations of facts, which is why it can be confusing for kids to sort the facts from the interpretations we give them. Look at these two takes on the bombing of Hiroshima:

> *Dropping the atomic bomb on Hiroshima, Japan, on August 6, 1945, was an unjustified act of war by the United States.*

> *Dropping the atomic bomb on Hiroshima, Japan, on August 6, 1945, was a necessary act of war by the United States.*

The information is factual (that is the sort of bomb that was used, it is when the bomb was dropped, and that is the city it devastated). The first comment asserts that dropping the bomb was "an unjustified act." That's an interpretation of the facts—it's the story that the storyteller is telling (chapter 1). The second comment interprets the same facts differently. It uses the phrase "a necessary act" to describe the bombing. If your kids encounter either of these takes in a textbook, these word choices create vastly different impressions in a child's mind. The presence of either commentary doesn't alter the truthfulness of the facts, though. You can have your fact cake and interpret it, too. But it's important to separate facts from interpretations when you read and study. (See the end of this chapter for an activity to help your students do just that.)

One of the inherent dangers of textbooks is that they reek of unacknowledged authority. When a student summarizes a chapter or answers comprehension questions, the student learns to treat the (sometimes subtle, sometimes less so) *interpretation* of the facts in the textbook as equally factual. This is why students need to be trained to differentiate between interpretation and facts. More takes (multiple viewpoints of the same data) can offset this tendency to conflate facts with their interpretations as well.

EVIDENCE

Courtroom dramas aside, *evidence* is key to the study of history, political science, all the sciences, law, and even literature. Evidence is the source material that allows students to make claims about facts to support those interpretations. What counts as evidence? Sources and data from research are two of the most common types. Primary sources encompass a wide range of artifacts and reports: objects, paintings, dig sites, documents (letters, treaties, records, diary entries, manuscripts, speeches, newspapers), film, and firsthand eyewitness accounts. Secondary sources are those that comment on original sources—like a newspaper article that cites a research study, a textbook that describes an era in history, or a commentary on a work of literature. Sources can be ranked by their reliability, their consistency across multiple versions, the credibility of the author/creator/witness, and so on. Evidence is also drawn from research data. Research can be presented in its raw form (without interpretation). When it is explained by the researcher, the researcher is interpreting the data. This is what happens in a courtroom—an expert interprets the data that acts as evidence in a trial. Evidence, then, is what we call a fact after we explain how that fact supports a claim or an assertion.

PERSPECTIVE

When we talk about taking a *perspective*, we mean that once we've compiled the facts, evidence, and interpretations currently available to us, we now see the topic from a particular frame of reference. From where I sit, this is how this issue appears to me, for now. Given who I am, what I know, how much I've read or studied, I have this to say about it. One of the compelling ideas I enjoyed considering when I looked into perspective was advanced by Glenn Parry in his book *Original Thinking*. He suggests that the idea that my personal point of view (perspective) matters got its start in the arts over half a century ago. Parry explains that a seismic shift occurred during the Renaissance. "Perspective, as any art student knows, is the technique of drawing a landscape from the single point of the eye in sight lines that recede away from its vantage point. Things closer to the viewer are larger and therefore assume greater importance, while things farther away are diminished." In this painting style, the individual's perception was placed at the center of the design.

Parry convincingly points out that an important shift in how humans think occurred as a result of this artistic revolution. "After perspective, the human eye and consciousness came to be thought of as separate from all else; humans became the detached observers of what came to be seen as a disenchanted and desouled world. Before perspective, human beings were an integral part of the world, not set apart from it." Human beings moved into the analyst's role—poking, prodding, exploring, examining, and understanding the world, rather than merely participating with it. The tool called perspective in painting shifted what we consider important, too.

Perspective enabled us to see ourselves as "detached observers." Over time, we've granted ourselves authority to take perspectives with confidence—many times without considering how the world looks to others. In his groundbreaking book *The Overview Effect*, Frank White addresses the way perspectives can be developed and shattered as the vantage point shifts. Until space travel, the only point of view any of us had of our planet home was an experience of Earth as flat and the solid ground on which we stood. Even while scientists had persuaded us of the earth's round shape, our experience of living on the planet did not give us that information directly. When astronauts escaped the atmosphere and viewed the earth as a whole from space, photographing our blue marble home, they confirmed what scientists had deduced. Suddenly, the astronauts' perspective (how they saw and understood the earth) shifted. Michael Collins, an astronaut on the Apollo 11 mission, described this shift: "The thing that really surprised me was that it [Earth] projected an air of fragility. And why, I don't know. I don't know to this day. I had a feeling it's tiny, it's shiny, it's beautiful, it's home, and it's fragile." This enormous planet suddenly appeared vulnerable from a different vantage point. Perspectives, then, are snapshots in time. They rely on limited information and make what is close to you appear larger than what is in the distance or not yet in your immediate field of vision. Perspective is about seeing—what you see, how you see it, why you see it the way you do, and what you don't see yet.

OPINION, PREJUDICE, AND BIAS

An *opinion* is not the same as being biased. (More on bias in a moment.) A well-crafted opinion is formed after you've considered a variety of perspectives (not merely your own), examined research, and then reached a conclusion (for now). An opinion is a claim you make after interpreting the data—a judgment based on facts. Many people express prejudices and biases, calling these opinions. They're not.

Prejudice is not based on data. It's based on faulty assumptions that often draw on stereotypes. For instance: "Boys like to play in the mud and girls don't." To develop a sound opinion requires studying the behaviors of a large sample of kids in lots of settings with mud and drawing a conclusion based on the data collection and subsequent interpretation of the facts.

A *bias* is when you use your own experience as the reference point for the view you adopt. For instance, if you asked me about mud and children, I'd immediately tell you about my five kids. Both genders delighted in muddying themselves, much to my chagrin, and so I'd be inclined to assume everyone's kids loved mud as much as mine, regardless of gender—my bias. We all have a bias (unavoidable if you live in a body, which we all do). Knowing you're biased is half the journey to self-aware critical thinking. We can shed our prejudices and separate from our biases as we're made aware of them. Then we can choose to consider the information in front of us. Knowing how to develop well-formed opinions in spite of prejudice and bias is one of the goals of education (and this book).

The next time someone says to you, "That's just my opinion," find out if it is, in fact, an opinion, a prejudice, or a bias by asking them for evidence. If they respond with a stereotype or personal experience, that's not an opinion. Get it? I see you! You're headed straight to your keyboard and a social media comment section right now, aren't you?

BELIEF

A *belief* is different from an opinion, prejudice, or bias. A belief is a conviction that is shaped by religion, identity, and culture. A belief doesn't rely on evidence, but springs from a cluster of ideas you choose for yourself. A great example of beliefs in conflict happened in India preceding the Indian Revolution in 1857. The skirmish began with the introduction of a new cartridge for the Enfield rifle. Indian *sepoys* (soldiers) of both Muslim and Hindu backgrounds were trained to use their teeth to rip open the casings holding the gun powder and then to dump the powder into their rifles. Rumors spread that the casings were oiled with pork and beef fat. As a result, Muslims refused to load their guns because of their belief that eating pork was *haram* (forbidden). Hindus refused on similar grounds, believing cows to be sacred; therefore, they could not ingest beef fat. The British, who did not accept these beliefs and instead had beliefs of their own—namely, that a soldier must not refuse orders from a senior officer—court-martialed the sepoys for their disobedience. The soldiers were imprisoned and sentenced to hard labor. This clash of beliefs is cited by many as the spark that lit the Indian Revolt, even while many other factors were also at play.

Our beliefs are felt as personal in a way that an opinion may not be. Our beliefs are more fragile, too. They rest on a constellation of interconnections between faith, reason, culture, personal conviction, and community identity. Popular beliefs include how we see religious texts, what codes we follow when we eat, how we form our morals, and what we expect to be true about our allies and perceived opponents. Many of our hottest debates stem from a difference of beliefs. Beliefs are tenacious and often come first. Facts are rounded up to support a belief, not the other way around. It often takes a compelling experience or encounter to overturn a belief. (More on that in part 2.) Our beliefs can be resistant to facts that contradict them.

STORY

Story in the context of critical thinking does not refer to novels and picture books. Human beings put facts and experiences, reason and logic together to generate stories that affirm someone's place in the world. The story is the *fiction or narrative* we create to bring together all those intersecting pieces of data, opinion, beliefs, and perspective to explain reality as we see it. In traditional cultures, narratives are the most powerful tools for capturing truths that sustain those communities. Modern culture often mistakes its obsession with science and data as being objective, forgetting that experts put research into stories all the time. Even in history and the sciences, how we understand information is informed by the larger "stories" that our culture endorses. Many modern nonfiction books (those by Malcolm Gladwell, Jim Collins, Brené Brown, and Isabel Wilkerson, for example) are built on this exact premise—including this book.

A familiar example of how story works in our culture can be seen in weight-loss programs. Each method identifies studies that showcase how following a particular type of diet results in losing weight. That said, the programs go well beyond the calculus of calories consumed versus calories burned. A story of health, beauty, and fitness are often part of the explanation of benefits when adopting the proven diet. Identifying the "plot" of the interpretation reveals the aims of the storytellers. We'll continue to see the role storytelling plays in critical thinking throughout this book.

WORLDVIEW

The last term in our critical thinking glossary is *worldview*. A worldview is exactly what the compound noun says: it's how you *view* your *world*.

Worldviews are more comprehensive than perspectives. A perspective is a snapshot in time. A worldview encompasses the totality of what you know and don't know. It often acts as an unconscious filter when you read new information. Worldviews are more difficult to identify because they feel like skin—the invisible layer of protection that allows your mind to bump into other people's minds while remaining separate. Your worldview defines how you make bottom-line sense of every interaction, every bit of data, every hiccup in what you expect to be true.

One of my favorite illustrations of worldview clashes occurred with the 1998 release of the animated Disney movie *Mulan*. The film features a female lead who impersonates a man to fight in the military so her elderly infirm father does not have to risk his life as a soldier. The Disney version includes songs about Mulan's search to be known and understood as her own person, not confined to patriarchal stereotypes. Americans thrilled to the story, seeing their worldview of independence and individuality celebrated. When the film was exported to China, however, the Chinese audiences were puzzled. Mulan is *their* story. The moral of the story as they tell it is that good people in traditional society put the welfare of their families and communities ahead of personal ambitions. Given that this tale originated in China, it's telling that the Disney version flopped so badly there. Yet it's not a mystery why: the story was reimagined to play to an American worldview.

Academic Disposition

All of these terms seem clear enough until you find yourself in a debate with someone you love who sees the same issues differently. Suddenly you wonder if they are simply showing bias or are articulating an opinion or whether they're spewing actual facts that you don't want to hear. Perhaps you've chugged along comfortably in your beliefs until . . . bam! What you always trusted to be true is dashed by direct, incontrovertible evidence. Maybe you made the "mistake" of reading the other side, and it made sudden sense to you, and now you can't figure out where to put this new information. Destabilization of viewpoint is especially painful when it costs you your community or marriage or family members. It's no wonder that when we teach our kids, we're protective of our own points of view. Everyone wants to recruit new members to "Team Right Ideas," and we're the biggest champions of our own perspectives!

Education, however, depends on the ability to be *dispassionately curious*. Shouldn't we be passionate about our opinions and beliefs? Yes— for ourselves. But we also have a responsibility to teach our children and ourselves to be curious without defensiveness. The good news is that academic work can be a safe place to explore and think. The academic disposition protects the student, if the student adopts it. The task of a learner is not to render verdicts every time the student runs into a new perspective. In other words, reading viewpoints the learner doesn't hold is not a challenge to anyone's integrity. Reading is not voting. The only task is to *pass the eyes along the page or screen*. That's it.

The academic disposition can be expressed this way:

- Be a witness to the writer.
- Know that the writer's perspective exists; know how it exists for the writer.
- Allow the viewpoint a place alongside your current views.
- Make tea. Sit patiently. Read. Be curious. Incubate.
- Grow your understanding first, and later, your critique.

When we make room for dissenting viewpoints, we open understanding. It's as though we're repainting our Renaissance landscapes with more vantage points rather than a single one. Learn first and then generate insight. Flip back to these pages anytime you run across these terms in the coming chapters and need a refresher.

✳ ACTIVITY: THE FACT STRAINER

This activity is a great one to try yourself first. Then invite a teenager to join you, if you have one at home. As you become comfortable with this practice, you can use that understanding to guide your conversations with younger children as well. To strain facts from the narratives we tell about them, we start by identifying what's *irreducible*. Let's practice with a news item. Look for names, dates, verifiable activities or actions, locations, and objects involved in the event.

1. Pick a current news item.
2. Find multiple news sources for the story. Print several (three or four) articles if you are able.
3. Highlight all the facts in one of the articles.
4. Go to the next article and highlight the facts as they are stated in that article. Do the same for all the news sources.
5. Double-check to see if there are any facts omitted from any of the stories. Make a note of which facts are omitted from which stories (if indeed any are). Remember: facts are irreducible.
6. Notice where the facts are placed in each article (at the top, middle, bottom, strewn throughout).
7. List the facts on a clean sheet of paper. Read them in the order they appeared in the article without interpreting them. Do this for each article.
8. Does the sequence of the facts say anything about the priorities in the articles?
9. Are any of the facts you identified actually interpretations rather than facts (now that you've read multiple stories about the same topic)? For instance, if you're reading

about a shooting, are the motives of the shooter spoken of as fact or suggested as possible? If reading about a wildfire, is the cause described as a fact or a theory?

Identifying facts first helps to neutralize the influence of the writer's interpretation. Reading the same story multiple times makes it easier to strain the facts from interpretation.

Pro tip: Reading a story with a bias you don't hold sometimes makes the facts easier to strain. You can see the interpretation more easily because you are more aware of the bias.

Let's take our critical thinking vocabulary into the next chapter and think about the ways traditional schooling treats facts, bias, interpretation, and more.

CHAPTER 3

Curiouser and Curiouser:
A Problem-Posing Education

I think what I learned from Trix was more the ability to ask
questions and less the need to feel like I had the answers.
—Mo Willems, children's author and illustrator

It's difficult to sit with questions—the door knock without an answer. Yet the most powerful learning of all comes through incessant questioning. And you know who excels at that level of interrogation, right? You got it: your three-year-old! Oh, and your five-year-old. In fact, anyone under age ten. By ten, we teach that questioning nature right out of our kids. By sixth grade, the majority of children have lost their "childlike wonder" and are either cooperative test-takers or relegated to the "not very good student" category of education. By sixteen, most kids have come over to the dark side of smug, self-righteous know-it-all-ness with confident, single-identity answers. We wonder: *How on earth did this happen?*

The strident, opinionated teen is not merely a developmental mile-stone, unavoidable and annoying. Our education system has worked extra hard at removing childlike wonder and replacing it with confident answer-giving for a decade. "Frequently, by the time children reach 3rd grade, the sense of wonder with which they entered kindergarten—wonder out of which authentic thinking and thus thinking for oneself develops—has begun to diminish. *By 6th grade it has practically disap-peared.* Children's thinking focuses on what the teacher expects. A major contributing factor to this loss of wonder is the failure to properly nurture the true voices of children" (emphasis mine). True voices of children? You mean those loud, incessant, follow-me-into-the-bathroom-with-all-their-questions voices? Yes. Those voices!

On its worst day, traditional education is designed to promote mastery of methods and right answers. It's not a forum for persistent (read: irritating, intrusive, repetitive) curiosity. It's not a place to get lost down a rabbit trail of interconnections that matter to the child. In fact, too often, teachers determine which problems students should care to solve. A child's natural inquisitiveness is expected to thrive outside school hours, *thankyouverymuch.*

Asking questions—the deconstructing, provocative, and curiouser and curiouser kind—is, however, the key to the most vibrant education, leading to breakthrough insights and, well, a side effect: happiness. In-novation, creative thought, fluency—these become the currency (and joy!) of a well-educated person. How did we (as a group of schooled humans) lose our incessant want-to-know and trade it in for the know-it-all temperament instead?

Don't Bank on It–the Academic Task

Most teachers use exams and writing assignments as proofs of learning. Recitation (test-taking, oral reporting, explanatory writing) focuses on what education reformer Paulo Freire calls the "banking concept" of schooling. The all-knowing teacher makes *deposits* of information that the teacher deems appropriate into the student's ostensibly empty mind. The student then narrates that information through writing or tests or oral presentations. The pupil is then evaluated on the basis of the teacher's agenda, never mind what may have been the meaning and intent of the child. It's not to say that narrating information can't be valuable in a student's life. Rather, what Freire is asking us to consider is what's lost when recitation becomes the chief method of instruction.

This style of education assumes that there is correct information (deemed necessary by a textbook, teacher, or school board) to be mastered. History teachers concur: "Students are generally used to working with a textbook and viewing history as a collection of right answers." Freire describes this sort of learning this way: "Education is suffering from narration sickness." He explains, "The teacher talks about reality as if it were motionless, static, compartmentalized, and predictable."

And we wonder why school feels tedious. Freire reminds us that our kids come to class filled to the brim with experiences and beliefs already active in their lives, guiding how they engage with whatever material is being taught. They have bodies they want to involve, not just minds. They have cultures, families, and traditions that impact the meanings they make for themselves.

Too often, a child's lack of interest is subordinated to this "narration sickness"—the relentless proving that a teacher's lessons are the right ones, expressed in the right ways, for right now. Remember reciting the times tables? *Four times four is sixteen.* We learn the "sonority" of the words (the cadence of recitation), but too frequently without grasping the meaning. Marcy Cook, mathematics specialist and educator, concurs: "If students are only to memorize facts and rules told to them by the teacher, they are being treated as empty receptacles to be filled with knowledge rather than as decision-making, thinking individuals who will succeed with new, different problematic situations."

I experienced this exact crisis in math, where memorization and recitation failed me once I got to higher levels, like Algebra 2. The truth was, I was fed rules and rhymes without understanding. Remember this adage about dividing fractions: "Yours is not to reason why. Just invert and multiply"? What a mind-scramble! I wanted to know why. That's how my mind works. Without the meaning, holding on to the process alone was impossible. Decades later, when I went to teach fractions to my oldest son, I had to hide in a garage and practice alone with the math book in an attempt to reteach myself. None of it had stuck.

Multiple-Choice Madness

This "narration sickness" Freire talks about is easily seen in one of the most prized testing methods in school: the multiple-choice test (complete with Scantron—where no additional words can be added). One of my friends shared with me that her son had a particularly tough time with multiple-choice tests. One time, he gave an answer so perplexing, it prompted the principal to call my friend to discuss it.

The student's "mistake" illustrates my point perfectly. Here's the test question my friend's son "got wrong," although objectively speaking, he was not only correct but the question itself has *two* right answers. See if you can discern what's going on here:

Which unit of measure would you use to measure this?

(a) feet
(b) centimeters
(c) kilometers
(d) quarts

My friend's son chose (b) for "centimeters." The "correct" answer was (a) for "feet." It was assumed the students knew that the illustration represented a living tree in the woods. This student saw the illustration on the page and assumed the test was asking what unit of measure ought to be used to measure the *drawing* of the tree. So logical! In this way, "centimeters" is a better answer than "feet" and perfectly correct.

Yet let's pause and take this one step further. What if my friend's son had understood that the illustration was meant to represent a living, breathing tree off the page? *Both* feet and centimeters are correct answers in that case, technically. Both are units of length. Someone may prefer using feet to measure a tall tree, but there could be a reason for measuring in centimeters. It's not *wrong* to measure a tree in centimeters. In fact, from an illustration, would we know if the drawing represented a tall tree in a forest or a small bonsai sitting on a tabletop? If one student lived in the woods and another student's family kept bonsai, the drawing might catalyze completely different mental images in each student's mind, causing different answers (both correct). Even so, both feet and centimeters describe an item's length, so they both work as "right answers." In this case, the student was being asked to guess which answer was the *most likely one* in the mind of the test-creator. That's a mind-reading skill many kids never develop well enough to be considered great students. It takes careful effort to craft effective multiple-choice tests that lead to the kind of critical thinking that empowers students rather than confuses them.

The multiple-choice test "right answer" thinking is what often derails thoughtfulness—evidence of caring about the question, not just surmising the answer a test-maker had in mind. It's unreasonable, in my opinion, to assume that a child should get inside the mind of a test-maker and add the following thought: *The test is looking for me to provide the most common unit of measure for a tall living tree.* In fact, if that is the thought process, haven't we just admitted that education is about jettisoning your own perceptions and learning to become more and more proficient at guessing the thoughts of experts and authorities instead?

By emphasizing single answers under timed pressure, the student is prevented from thoughtfully considering the question and all its possible variables. Instead, the student is expected to identify the right answer the test-maker had in mind as swiftly as possible. Worse, that answer may be the least imaginative, most stereotypical one because it must be identified quickly, without reflection, before the bell rings.

I wonder if this kind of testing is what leads to the high stakes of modern discourse where each participant feels the need to get everyone to agree swiftly, particularly online. We assume that one right answer, delivered by whomever we choose as an authority, can be found and applied—quickly—and everyone will agree! This practice is so frequent in our education that once we leave school, we forget that we're allowed to consider myriad possibilities when confronted with complex issues. Instead, we feel pressure to pick a side and stay there as proof we were right. We've been trained to ignore the impact of personal interpretations and past experiences. Too often, the multiple-choice test is about time efficiency, snap judgments, invisible authorities, and declarative answers. It's a staggering question to consider: why does modern education value speed over thoughtfulness?

Now you try. Consider this multiple-choice question:

Pick the adjective that describes this image:

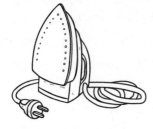

(a) hot
(b) cold
(c) iron
(d) blue

Most savvy test-takers would exclude the word "iron" (a noun) and ignore "blue" because the drawing is a line illustration without any apparent color. Did you select "hot" or "cold"? Most people will pick "hot" rather than "cold" because irons are routinely associated with heat. But if you're a nuanced thinker, you might notice something peculiar about this iron. *It's not plugged into an electrical outlet.* Therefore, can it actually *be* hot? If you patiently consider the illustration in totality, you might pick "cold" as your answer—because it describes the truth of the iron's current state. So logical. Yet, that choice is likely wrong. Most tests want the test-taker to associate heat with irons, which is the most common word association. Without any chance to explain why "cold" makes more sense in this case, the score you get for making this "error" will define you as "not smart" rather than the more careful, nimble-minded thinker you actually are.

Artist and educator Betty Edwards, who inspired this thought puzzle in her book *Drawing on the Artist Within*, makes it painfully clear where this sort of testing goes: "Such rigidity is maddening, and I believe its eventual effect on student test takers with undamaged brains is to make them try *not* to see what is in front of their eyes, but instead to arrive at abstract verbal concepts which may in fact contradict their visual perceptions." In other words, students are rewarded with better scores when they train themselves to *not see*, meaning they reshape their direct perceptions to match stereotypes and well-accepted relationships: *irons are hot.*

What a loss! Edwards does explain that much of education works to exclude visual variables. Naturally, abstract mathematical processes, for instance, are much easier to assess by exam. Edwards explains that "Two plus two is four, no matter how the appearance of the numbers changes." That said: the numerical representations are still symbols of quantities, not the items themselves. For children, the abstract concept of adding symbols may undermine their ability to grasp math (back to Freire's sonority of the multiplication tables over true understanding). If, however, we take that abstract number and assign it to two pairs of items—like two feathers added to two other feathers—we will have four *feathers*, not just the abstract numeral 4. If we hold the feathers in our hands, we experience their softness. If we try to stack them or lay them to each other, we may notice they are not identical in size, yet any two feathers added to any other two feathers is surely four feathers. What if we then add two cast-iron frying pans to two other cast-iron frying pans? We'd have four frying pans, certainly. These pans are heavy, difficult to stack, and have a much different "feel" than the feathers, and yet they all still add up to four.

The weights and dimensions of these two groupings of "four" are vastly different, and our awareness of those features has an impact on the how we think about the combinations, inescapably. For instance, while the count is four in both two plus two operations, if we were to measure them by weight, we'd get completely different numbers. Our bodies and intuition sense that difference, and it could be important to name it to our kids. Combining for a count is not the same as combining two items by weight. Once we talk about *why* we might add two feathers to two others or two frying pans to two others, we'll unavoidably consider whether it's a good idea to arrive at four of them! If we combine two feathers with two frying pans, we are now even more flummoxed—what is the goal of all this combining?

Naturally, advanced mathematics cannot always be worked out using items we hold in our hands. The key to critical thinking, however, is making that connection between the abstract and the practical as often as we can, as early as we can, particularly at the start of a new academic journey. In this way, we lay the foundation for greater complexity and skill. We're letting our students know that there's always more to consider, even when we use a reliable process or practice. Ethical decision-making counts on the persistent drive to see the implications of any mathematical operation, any interpretation of science or history, any application of insight. A question you might be asking, now, is: *If worksheets and tests are not the way forward, then what is?*

Problem-Posing Education

Fortunately, Freire suggests a different method of schooling—the "problem-posing" education. Children are not taught *what* to think by instructors. Instead, the children are trusted partners in solving meaningful problems with the collaborating power of the adult. Educator bell hooks explains that "as teachers, our role is to take our students on the adventure of critical thinking. Learning and talking together, we break with the notion that our experience of gaining knowledge is private, individualistic, and competitive."

Marcy Cook draws the same conclusion: "The art of questioning becomes the key to the thinking classroom. Educators should be questioning not to guide student thinking in line with theirs but to provoke thinking and to discover what students know and understand." Critical thinking grows in an emotionally stable, supportive environment, where real problems are explored by teacher and student together.

In a subject like math, the critical thinking skills we most want to cultivate are "asking good questions, providing good problems, challenging and even frustrating students by provoking thought. . . ." I got to see how this approach worked in a public school math class. My oldest son studied Algebra 2 at the local high school while he was still home-schooled in the other subjects. When I met with his teacher at the parent-teacher conference, I learned that she started each day with a math problem on the whiteboard. She would ask the students to suggest an approach for how to solve it. She told me that it took some work to get students to take the risk—to make a guess about how to solve the problem. Her goal was to grow mathematical minds, not merely great test-takers. Yet, the students had been so conditioned to wait for the teacher to tell them what to do and how to do it that it took some coaxing at the beginning of the school year to draw them out. By the end of the year, they were eager to participate. Today's education experts agree that this method of instruction, especially if it is the habitual approach combined with explicit instruction of mathematical processes, leads to the best outcomes for students. They learn to think like problem-solvers rather than only answer-givers. Savvy teachers and parents can ask questions like these:

- Are there other ways to approach this problem? Can you show me?
- What real-world situation might require using this mathematical operation?
- Why do you think this process works?

These kinds of questions help students remember that there's a "why" to learning. They can then make links between action and reflection. I remember when I learned to multiply zeros and ones, I got mixed up and learned the "trick" backward. I thought $0 \times 3 = 3$ and $1 \times 3 = 1$. Clearly, I didn't know what multiplication was meant to achieve. I relied solely on process instruction and mis-memorized the answers. Receiving a failing grade didn't help me across that bridge. No one asked me what I thought I was doing. Instead, I was left to re-memorize more meaningless number sequences. Cook explains: "We do not want the intellectual life of a classroom turned into a training ground for test preparation." Traditional math instruction has misled many of us into believing a pair of myths: that math is governed by step-by-step methods to find right answers, and that textbooks and teachers are the authorities that know those answers.

We can provoke our students' curiosity by offering them meaningful problems to solve. I've long declared the value of what I call "big juicy conversations"—that is, conversations that ramble, that create the basis for a free exchange of ideas. As bell hooks confirms for us: "Conversations are not one-dimensional; they always confront us with different ways of seeing and knowing." To raise a critical thinker means giving our kids opportunities to discover what they know intimately and their barriers to understanding. Both.

Itch to Fit

The good news is that we can tip the scales of education toward questions. In *The Brave Learner*, I recommended creating a "Great Wall of Questions" where parents jot down every question their kids ask for a week on sticky notes and then stick them to a wall. At the end of the week, I suggest that they peel off the notes and discuss the questions at dinner. By valuing questions and not answering them immediately, we inspire our children and teens to sit with curiosity rather than push for declarations of right answers. The next step is to grow the quality of those questions.

How do we do that? Recent brain fMRI scans confirm what is known as the "gap theory of curiosity," advanced by George Loewenstein of Carnegie Mellon University in the 1990s. Researchers discovered that our curiosity follows an inverted U-shaped curve. "We're most curious when we know a little about a subject (our curiosity has been piqued) but not too much (we're still uncertain of the answer)." Loewenstein explains that when we feel a gap between what we know already and what we want to know, there are "emotional consequences: it feels like a mental itch, a mosquito bite on the brain. We seek out new knowledge because that's how we scratch the itch."

John Dewey, the father of modern education, addresses the role of curiosity in his school model—what he calls the "problem-solving" education. British educator Dr. Michael Luntley suggests that for Dewey, problems are those that are felt as an "itch." A disturbance in the child's natural expectations leads to this "itchiness." The search then becomes: how does this new information "fit" into what I currently know? Luntley names Dewey's construct the "itch to fit" practice. A teacher's chief task, then, is to create the disruption in expectations that triggers an "itch"— or, a need to know. Learn to "trigger the itch," and you'll see curiosity bloom. The experience is similar to locating the right LEGO piece for a build. After repeated attempts to *fit* the right piece in the right spot, the right LEGO snaps into place. Itch? Scratched. As Luntley explains: "Learning is timely, not timeless." What is learned is relevant now, for this moment's question.

✳ ACTIVITY: ITCH TO FIT GRAMMAR

Try the following activities with your kids to get a sense of how a problem-posing and problem-solving education capitalizes on an "itch to fit" strategy.

Let's start with everyone's least favorite subject (except for you "word nerds"): grammar. Grammar has a terrible reputation. It's the most opaque, least enjoyable trudge through a collection of lifeless terms and definitions of any school subject. Grammar gets taught as a list of abstract words that are assigned to other words. It's most often taught through workbooks. The trouble is, native speakers don't rely on a firm understanding of grammar to create meaningful sentences. They speak by ear—whatever sounds right. The "it sounds right" mechanism is nearly flawless for developing fluency in your heart language.

Grammar can be experienced as an exciting encounter with the structure of language. It's also possible to discover its inherent power to enliven writing. Both of these goals are possible if we approach grammar as *critical thinkers*. The following activities are designed to show you how to take a traditionally dull subject and use the "itch to fit" pattern to generate both interest and understanding. These same principles can be applied to other school subjects as well.

Ready? Trust me: these are fun!

Bright-Eyed (5 to 9): Whimsical Words

Have you ever noticed how easily small children play with language? *"Muddle, puddle, scruddle, plum!"* The way they slip into mimicking patterns? "The sheeps sleeped on the hill." They make staggeringly good guesses while they learn and test their language skills. When they miss, adults are delighted and rarely worried that children won't eventually catch on to the fluent pattern of speech adults use.

Introducing terms like "adverb" and "preposition" to kids under eight feels like overkill because, frankly, it is. Children are particularly fond of rhyme schemes. They memorize songs, board books, and simple poetry easily.

Word Play

Pick any end-rhyme scheme (like "ay" or "end"). Recite with your children as many rhyming words (even nonsense terms) in a row as you can for that one ending. Count them and see if you can break your record using a different ending rhyme.

- How many of the terms are made up for fun, and how many are words we use in English?
- Try them in sentences, even the nonsense words. What do they mean? How do you know?
- Are some of the words describing things?
- Are some of them items you have in the house?
- Are some of the words actions you can take?

Now cluster them according to the way they work in sentences. Put items together, put descriptive terms together, put action words together. Group them by syllable count. Group them by your favorites and least favorites. Put them on sticky notes and stick them on items in your house to see them each day. Take a lot of time with this activity. It's got endless riches in it. Don't worry too much if a child says that an adjective is one of the words that you "do." Right now, official classification is less important than identifying what the words imply. You could spend a week playing with rhyming lists over lunch each day. Next, play with rhyme in poetry.

Nursery Rhyme

1. Pick a nursery rhyme (one stanza) your child knows well. Read it together, enjoying the rhyming words. For instance, you might pick "Twinkle, Twinkle, Little Star."

> *Twinkle, twinkle, little star,*
> *How I wonder what you are.*
> *Up above the world so high,*
> *Like a diamond in the sky.*
> *Twinkle, twinkle, little star,*
> *How I wonder what you are.*

2. Identify the rhyme scheme: /ar/ and /igh/ in this case.
3. Brainstorm other words that rhyme with these endings. (Nonsense words are encouraged, too!)
4. Next, type out the whole nursery rhyme with extra space around each word. Type the additional rhyming words you brainstormed together. Use a large font and triple space.

5. Cut each word into its own square using a pair of scissors. Alternatively, handwrite each word on a single note card.

6. Shuffle the words and strew them faceup on a cleared table or on the floor. Begin by making sentences that are playful, not necessarily sensible. Reassemble the rhyme multiple times. Try swapping other rhyming words into the poem. How do these terms alter the meaning? Working together, change the story of the poem by rewriting lines to include your brainstormed rhyming terms. (You can do that by handwriting the new lines on a sheet of paper, or you can assemble sentences using your word cards if you have enough words.)

> Twinkle, twinkle, little star,
> *I can see you from my car.*
> Up above the world so high,
> *In a rocket I would fly.*
> Twinkle, twinkle, little star,
> *Catch your starshine in a jar.*

You'll do the heavy lifting here in terms of rewriting a nursery rhyme, but the idea is to expand what can be known— the rhythm, the rhyme, and how the meanings shift based on the assembly of the lines; yet the satisfying pattern remains.

Quick-Witted (10 to 12): Grasping Grammar

In our native languages, we consult our ears to make sure our sentences sound right. In a language we don't speak, we must have a working knowledge of the parts of speech in order to assemble sentences that make sense. To teach grammar, then, requires an approach that helps kids make the dynamic connection between the label (part of speech) and the word's function (role) in any sentence. To simply call one word a "noun" and another a "verb" doesn't make that connection for the child. The native speaker already knows the word we call a noun is in the right place. The label doesn't improve the speaker's chances of using it correctly, so the grammar term doesn't feel relevant. It's like memorizing times tables without understanding the actual shortcut to addition behind multiplication.

So where do you begin? By doing a little violence to the original sentence structure, of course!

Instructions

You'll need a whiteboard and a sheet of paper.

On the whiteboard, write:

The black dog barked loudly at the garbage truck.

On the sheet of paper oriented in landscape view, create two columns. Label the columns "Essential" and "Nonessential." In the steps that follow, you and your kids will generate clusters of similar terms. Keep these terms together under either the Essential or Nonessential headings.

The following steps ask your child to remove and add back terms in the sentence to determine the role they play in making the sentence meaningful.

1. Remove all occurrences of "the" by having your child erase "the" from each place you find it.
    Black dog barked loudly at garbage truck.

    Have your child read it aloud.

    Ask: Does it sound right? (It doesn't.)

Ask: Are there any words that could be put in the sentence to make it sound right?

See if they can figure out that there are two: "a" and "the."

Put them in the first column under Essential.

Now, re-add both instances of "the" back to the sentence on the whiteboard.

2. Erase "black" this time. Read the sentence. Does it sound right?
The dog barked loudly at the garbage truck.

It works! Put the word "black" in the second column under Nonessential.

Add "black" back to the original sentence.

3. Next, erase "barked."
The black dog loudly at the garbage truck.

How does that sound? Feels incomplete, doesn't it? What kind of word is missing?

Is it possible to put any other words where "barked" used to be?

Try a word that's not a verb with your kids. Toss out the word "mouth" and see if it works instead of "barked."

The black dog mouth loudly at the garbage truck.

How did they react? Can they hear that it doesn't sound right? You've provoked an "itch to fit" scenario. Their minds are busy searching for a term that will make that sentence work. Their minds want to know: *What did that dog do?* That's what's missing—what the dog did.

Ask: Can any other similar words replace "barked" for the sentence to make sense? They may think of one or more of these terms:

- Whined
- Yipped
- Growled
- Woofed
- Howled

Each of these verbs can replace "barked," and the sentence still makes sense. The meaning shifts a bit, though, and that's worth noticing. Discuss.

Other questions to ask: Do each of these words work with "loudly"? Is one better than another? Put these words together in column one under Essential.

Add "barked" back to the sentence on the whiteboard.

4. Now remove "loudly."
    The black dog barked at the garbage truck.

    The sentence still works, right? Can you swap in other words that would work instead of "loudly"? Naturally, quite a number of similarly styled "ly" words work in this space: "quietly," "happily," "nervously," "sheepishly." Put several of them into a cluster in column two, Nonessential.

5. Move "loudly" around in the sentence. Does it work in other spots?
   Loudly, the black dog barked. Good.

   The black dog barked at the garbage truck loudly. Yes!

   The black loudly dog barked. Nope!

   Ask questions:

   Why does "loudly" work in some places and not others?

   What word does it go with (modify, change, alter, improve)?

6. Next, remove "dog" and "truck."
   Are they essential to the sentence? Read the sentence without those words first.

   The black barked loudly at the garbage.

   Note: the term "garbage" became an item, rather than a description when the word "truck" got removed!

   Can "dog" and "truck" be replaced by any of the following words?

- Cat
- Turtle
- Pretty
- Very
- Sister
- Bike
- Walked

Notice which terms in the above list "work" even if the meaning isn't precise. You can use the word "cat" or "sister," and the sentence makes a kind of nonsense but sounds right. You can't replace "dog" or "truck" with "pretty," "very," or "walked." Those words throw the sentence out of whack. You might ask what "cat," "turtle," "sister," and "bike" have in common with "dog" and "truck." (They are entities or things.) Then ask what is different about "pretty," "very," and "walked."

What else can be discovered about the words in the sentence? The word "garbage" is describing "truck" in this sentence so it's nonessential. In other sentences, it is essential because "garbage" is the item (noun). Try playing with other nouns to see if they can become words that describe (adjectives).

7. Identify the parts of speech for your word clusters in each column.

This is not a quiz, but a chance to give a name to the types of words that emerged in this exploration.

Essential		Nonessential	
a, the	article		
barked whined yipped growled woofed howled	verbs	black garbage	adjective
dog truck cat turtle sister bike	nouns	loudly nervously quietly happily sheepishly	adverb

Next, you can move on to using sentences from books your kids are reading and create a lexicon of terms that can be cataloged under each part of speech within the Essential and Nonessential columns. Over time, your grammarians can determine which words shape-shift—shuttling between the two categories.

Grammar is a particularly satisfying subject for practicing critical thinking skills because nearly everyone finds grammar terms stuffy and difficult to remember, yet all of us have confidence in our fluency in English. Most of us were not taught grammar in a way that makes it relevant to our daily speaking. Learning to examine what feels "right" and why is the bedrock of self-awareness. Sometimes we are startled into an insight—for instance, the new awareness that "garbage" can be both a noun and an adjective!

Nimble-Minded (13 to 18): "Jabberwocky"

One time, my kids and I read "Jabberwocky" by Lewis Carroll and became intrigued with each of the invented terms. The study of this poem became one of the most powerful grammar lessons we ever experienced. We assigned definitions and parts of speech to the nonsense terms. You can work through the entire poem this way. As an example, take a look at the two opening lines:

> *'Twas brillig, and the slithy toves*
> *Did gyre and gimble in the wabe:*

In the first stanza of the famous poem, we're confronted with brand-new vocabulary invented by Carroll: "brillig," "slithy toves," "gyre," "gimble," "wabe." These words sound like English but have no identifiable, objective definitions. I saw a grammar lesson hiding in plain sight!

When my kids and I examined this passage, we asked questions about the words. What do you think "brillig" means? Why? Lots of ideas tumbled from their mouths: "bright" and "gloomy" were both offered. The word conveys an ambiguous sound to our English-speaking ears. We could justify either possible meaning. We landed quickly on adjectives because we were used to "'Twas" leading to a descriptive term like "sunny" or "cloudy." But then an interesting shift occurred. Couldn't "brillig" also be a season or a month of the year or a time of day—like "spring," or "January," or "afternoon"? And wouldn't those words be nouns rather than adjectives? Blimey, it was true! Both nouns and adjectives worked in that sentence.

As we made our way through the poem, we made up possible meanings for each nonsense word, letting the sounds and familiar sentence structures guide us. We also had to keep in mind the previous choices we had made and how those definitions might influence our next definition for a consistent story line. We tested our ideas to see all the possibilities, not to get the meaning right.

We created a glossary of terms with our own definitions (each child had their own printout of the same poem, and by the end, their own version of what it meant based on their unique definitions of the invented language). One of the delightful by-products of this process was the realization that the same term could be understood as more than one part of speech depending on how you defined it. That turns out to be true in English, but we often forget it in our fluency of speech.

Now you try!

1. Triple space and print a copy of the "Jabberwocky" poem for your child. Work through the poem stanza by stanza, one at a time.

2. A grammar reference book or website will be handy for this project, too. Keep it on the table or nearby to consult as you analyze the poem.

3. Give your child highlighter pens. Instruct them to highlight any word they don't know. They may highlight an English term, too. That's okay! They're going to apply the same skills to words in English that they apply to Carroll's invented language.

4. Next, talk about the possible meanings of the words they've selected to define. Perhaps they want to define "brillig" and "slithy." Your children may not yet know the grammatical terms to assign to any of the nonsense words, but they can tell you why they think "gyre" and

"gimble" sound like "dance" and "leap," or "flounce" and "bumble," or "crawl" and "climb." Substitute the invented-language word pair, and discover how those meanings impact the poem.

> *'Twas morning, and the happy toves*
> *Did flounce and bumble in the wabe*

5. Once you have a stanza's worth of terms, ask: Is this term a verb or an adverb? How do you know which is which?

6. Next you might ask: What's a "wabe"? Another host of possibilities unfolds. Do the "gyre" and "gimble" definitions influence how you see a "wabe" and its personality? Is a "wabe" a person, place, thing, or idea? Nouns can be any of these. Can your child identify what kind of noun "wabe" is meant to be from the context? The phrase "in the wabe" provides a clue. What other nouns can follow "in the"? It could be an item or location—"in the basket" or "in the forest" are two that come to mind.

7. Ask: How do the sounds of the invented words impact the definitions you give them? Do they remind you of other English words? Which ones?

8. As you explore each term, use your grammar reference to help you. Compare the invented term to a known English word and then identify the part of speech. By the end of this exercise, your children will have operated as grammarians!

9. Once all the words are defined and sorted, consider writing a stanza or two as a sequel using some of the invented language as the student has defined it.

It's wild to realize that Carroll created a meaningful poem rife with language we don't understand, yet somehow we *do* believe we've understood it. We make meaning of any words we read. We think we understand them, too, by assigning even familiar words automatic definitions without asking questions. The deep dive into *"Jabberwocky"* is a great starting point to discover that our subjectivity plays a role in how we read anything. Our impressions form our interpretations.

In the next chapter, we take these powers of examination further. What else can be known about anything we read or study or witness? Our kids are fantastic leaders in keenly observing the world around them. All we need to do is point them in the right direction through well-conceived questions and give them the tools to express what they find!

CHAPTER 4

Keen Observation: Through the Looking Glass

We mostly see what we have learned to expect to see.
—Betty Edwards, *Color*

Alice Liddell tumbled through a looking glass and found herself in an enigmatic land of talking caterpillars, a mad hatter, and a rabbit who tells time. Dorothy Gale twisted her way to a mysterious colorful world with good witches, a road of yellow bricks, and flying monkeys. Tristan Strong punched a hole in the sky and entered a universe with a burning sea, haunted bone ships, and an iron monster. Each time you leave your comfort zone, you expand to include a new way of knowing and being in the world. The disorientation can be as profound as Alice's, Dorothy's, and Tristan's, yet the mark it leaves is indelible. You never see the world in the same way again. The ability to take in new perspectives is not only fueled by good questions, but it also requires seeing differently—changing your field of vision.

When I was twenty-one years old, in 1983, I visited Berlin. After World War II, Germany was split in two: the Allied powers controlled the western half of the country, labeled West Germany, and the Soviet Union controlled the eastern half, called East Germany. Berlin, Germany's capital, is located in what was then East Germany—one hundred miles from the border with West Germany. Just like the rest of the country, Berlin itself was split into two halves, one controlled by the Allied powers and the other by the Soviet Union. The west side of Berlin had become an island of thriving capitalist democracy surrounded by communist East Germany. To get to it, visitors had to travel by plane or train from West Germany.

In my mind, the countries in the Soviet Bloc (all the communist states under Soviet control) were dingy, gray places. American politicians, the Olympics, newspapers, the nightly news on TV, dinnertime conversations with my Republican dad, church sermons, speeches by then president Ronald Reagan, and lectures in college created a powerful impression. My friend Craig and I booked train tickets to West Berlin that traveled overnight. Blackout windows prevented us from seeing anything of East Germany as we rolled through. We arrived at 6:00 a.m. to a rosy sunrise. West Berlin impressed us with its active city center bustling with people so early in the morning. Craig and I decided to visit the communist side of Berlin that day, which meant a nerve-racking customs trip through Checkpoint Charlie (the infamous gate between west and east).

We flashed our passports and were guided from sunny West Berlin through a rectangular canvas makeshift tunnel. We emerged one hundred yards later in East Berlin, and to my shock—the sun still shone. Unexpected! We walked past buildings with windows glinting. We crossed a charming bridge over the Spree River where the light was so glittering I had to shade my eyes. I took the lens cap off my camera to capture the gorgeous view, and it slipped from my hand to be lost forever in the gently moving, sparkling water below. My senses were dazzled. I had never imagined communist countries in sunlight, and I hadn't known that about myself until I was baffled by the bright light of a summer morning in East Berlin. I came to.

How had I cultivated a mental image of East Berlin so not in keeping with reality—as though the weather would reflect an American inter-pretation of the harsh conditions of communism? My irrational reaction to the sunshine pointed to something deeper. In my mind, eastern Europe was barely worth visiting. I had conflated the city (its people, culture, weather, and geography) with the oppressive political system, as though they were one. I had built an unconscious negative construct that could be traced back to the "evil empire" rhetoric.

Thirty years later, my mother and I took a river cruise through now free eastern Europe. We visited countries that had at one time been communist—places to and from which few could travel in the 1980s. When we visited Bratislava, Slovakia, we enjoyed the company of a young Slovakian woman named Sophia who hosted several of us for coffee in her tiny cinder block apartment on the tenth floor of her building. These Brutalist structures, called Paneláks, are world famous as examples of basic communist housing. The residents paint the com-plexes in bright colors to offset the functional, boxlike shapes of the buildings. Our hostess had grown up in her lime-green apartment building, but not under communism. Her parents (who were my age) had. So I asked her what I had wondered since my visit to East Berlin: "Did your parents like communism? Are they glad they are free of it now?"

Her response staggered me. First Sophia explained that she loved her own freedom to travel, to speak her mind, to have access to the in-ternet and American television. She reported that her parents, however, were finding the new way of life difficult at their ages—hard to find decent jobs, retirement insecure. During the communist years, they had enough work, holidays and family traditions, and a home they loved. Sophia concluded: "They were happy."

I hadn't expected to hear that anyone living in a Panelák could have been happy. My mind wouldn't differentiate the nostalgia of family life from the oppressive political conditions of Czechoslovakia. I wondered: *Do human beings have a need to affirm the hand they've been dealt despite the well-documented abuses of their own government? Just how difficult is it to think critically about your own culture, country, or life?* I wanted to dismiss Sophia (which surprised me). I wanted her parents to admit the superiority of our system and the failure of theirs. I wanted . . . What did I want . . . ? What had I expected her to say and why? That was the nagging question that stayed with me.

Silent Films

One way our point of view is formed is through what I call "silent films"—the wordless (unconsciously fashioned) images that scroll through our minds. My mind had conjured silent films of life under communism that played in the background of my thinking. When the word "communism" was spoken, it was like pressing the play button, and suddenly unbidden images, labels, and feelings flooded my nervous system. I automatically rejected the idea that "happiness" or "sunlight" could go with the word "communism."

What we *know* comes from this imaginative space inside. Because images are often impressions or glimpses, it's easy to undervalue their role in the creation of our thoughts. The images we involuntarily build to house our beliefs evoke physical sensations in the body and a host of emotions. The language used to describe communism under Soviet control influenced my imagination. An "evil empire" does not exist in a sunlit landscape. Noted scholar Alice Brand cites research that validates what was happening to me:

Psychologist Lev Vygotsky . . . contended that linguistic thought develops as social speech moves inward. Speech syntax becomes increasingly abbreviated. Articles and adjectives disappear, pronouns drop off, and predicates shrink to verbs—until what remains in our mind is only the single naming word. Fully internalized, that single word carries the most information and comes closest to pure meaning. . . . Pure meaning is endowed with images and connotation. Pure meaning is saturated with affect.

In other words, pure meaning drives our strong emotions. The silent films we make for ourselves are not three-hour movies with complex moral dilemmas. They spring from a monosyllabic voice we create from our impressions. We do it automatically. "The construct of memory is central to cognition. . . . But perceiving an entire visual field or retrieving all of memory is humanly impossible. We choose." In other words: we choose the image that clarifies an impression built from language. Our minds prefer a visual shorthand to the more layered and complicated thoughts we might have if we were more patient in our thinking.

What would happen, however, if we spent time becoming aware of those involuntary impressions that control our reactions before we listen to the news, attend a lecture, see a film, or travel to a foreign country? This is the true stuff of education, and it's the hidden, personally created curriculum that exerts influence every time you read a book to your kids, or teach them about history, or watch a film together. These undetected impressions are the background operating system that control how your children understand politics and social issues, religion and history, what constitutes a good life, and how to learn math. Yet how often do kids get the chance to shake out their impressions like sheets and hang them on a line to observe and consider?

Deeper thinking depends on the ability to expand the field of vision, to notice our emotional reactivity, and to assess the judgments we've made on that basis. Let's practice now. I want to start with you, my reader. Take a journey with me through your mind's eye to notice how your body relaxes or tenses based on suggested experiences and the images you conjure in your imagination. While there are other activities for your kids, this exercise is for you. It offers you a way to dive into the vulnerable waters of how your mind and imagination create instantaneous reactions.

 ## ACTIVITY: SILENT FILMS

Sit quietly, and read the following directions. Close your eyes (if you can) to imagine each scene before moving to the next suggested scenario.

Hiking Trail

1. Imagine walking on a trail in a state park that is familiar to you in the warm afternoon sunshine. What do you see? Give yourself time to be detailed: sky, trees, path, lake or creek or ocean, birds, insects. . . . Now, tune in to your body. What sensations do you have? Relaxed or tense? Warm or chilled? Notice the surface of your skin, your jaw, your neck. Imagine your feet hitting the trail—what sensation or sound? What else? Name the overarching experience: peaceful or worrying? Safe or dangerous? Enjoyable or disquieting?

2. Next, imagine walking on the same trail at night without a flashlight. Check your body now. What can't you see? What sensations do you have at nighttime? How does darkness impact your confidence in walking? Are you

wondering about a pothole? Stumbling over a tree root that is raised above the trail? Coming upon an opossum or skunk too late? A snake on the ground, a bat overhead? Walking into a cactus? Amazed at the sea of stars above you? Are you comforted or disquieted by the darkness? Note whatever comes up.

3. Now picture walking the same trail at night with a flashlight. How does the light beam change your body response? How is it different from walking in full daylight?

4. Next, imagine bringing an experienced hiker with you as you hike without a flashlight in the dark. Are you more or less comfortable?

City Alley

1. Let's switch locations. Imagine walking in a new-to-you alley between tall buildings downtown in a big city. Picture that walk in the daylight. What do you see? Give details: the name of the area if you know it, descriptions of the buildings, the kind of pavement. What's happening in your body now? How do you feel compared to the walk during the day on the hiking trail? Name the overarching experience: peaceful or worrying? Safe or dangerous? Enjoyable or disquieting?

2. Picture walking through the same alley at midnight, alone. What changes for you? Anything? What worries or comforts you? What happens if you add a streetlamp to the scene? Does that change how you feel? In what ways?

3. Next, imagine walking through the alley at night with a local. How does that companionship impact your body

sensations? Pause and think about the ways your
breathing shifted or your imagination conjured images.

Does your body experience slight shifts in its reaction to
each location, each time of day, and with or without lighting or
companions? In this simple thought experiment, you were able
to guide your body to have unbidden reactions to scenes you
created in your imagination, in your mind. Stop. Now actually
go for these walks in both places at these times of day and night,
with and without flashlights/streetlamps and companions. Did
that instruction jolt you? Imagine how much more you'd learn if
you actually *did* take those walks!

The places you walked in your mind just now are real to you. Your
attitude about why you would feel safe or unsafe in each scenario is built
from facts you know; fears of what could be; and beliefs you've accumu-
lated through experience, news reports, and stories told in your family
and community—just like my unbidden impressions of eastern Europe.
Your bodily reactions are truest to what you really believe—whether
they're built from verifiable fact or from what you think *ought* to be true.
For instance, you may *know* that the hiking trail is safe, yet the introduction of nightfall shifts how you feel about it (because night has so
often been associated with danger). You may *want* to feel safe in a
downtown alley, but your body finds it difficult to overcome the programming of the nightly news that treats that location as dangerous.
Conversely, if you live downtown, you may find the hiking trail more
treacherous and the alley to feel perfectly safe because it's your home.

Think, for a moment, about Dorothy from Kansas landing in Oz.
Remember how the munchkins all titter when Dorothy is surprised that
Glinda is a *good* witch? Dorothy ran smack into her preconceptions:
witches are bad; they wear black; they're mean. Her programming told

her so. The image in her mind didn't match the glittery, pink-clad beauty arriving in a bubble with a wand and performing good deeds.

Our mental and emotional gymnastics—the sorting of how we take in information—must be identified in order for us to become self-aware critical thinkers. One place we start is by calling up the unbidden images and then asking them questions to expose hidden bias or incomplete information. As you gain facility with this kind of self-inquiry, you'll be better able to guide children in your care as well. Learning to pose questions to ourselves (the problem-posing education we discussed in the last chapter) is one of the ways we both call forth insight and expose our current incomplete thinking. What's exciting is that children are naturally curious and far more willing to upend their preconceptions— and when they're really young, they don't yet have preconceptions to upend! That's one reason we are endlessly delighted by babies and toddlers. They bring a fresh perspective to what we see as old hat and routine.

Like good detectives, kids must put their magnifying glasses right up to the item under scrutiny—what I call "keen observation." To keenly observe means to pay careful attention to our perceptions (while reserving judgments). When our children are small (bright-eyed and bushy-tailed), we help them dial up their sensory experiences first. We give them toys, tools, and tastes that help them tune in to sight, sound, touch, smell, and flavor. We provide names for what they experience, like "bright," "loud," "soft," "fragrant," and "sour." As children grow older, they learn to interpret those perceptions with greater and greater skill and personally created meaning. "Bright" might indicate that the lights are assaulting the eyes, or it might mean that the dark space is now well lit. The child makes a judgment.

Kids learn to associate a "fragrant" scent with perfume and a "sour" taste with lemons. As children become teens, their sensory perceptions lead them to even more personal interpretations. They may correlate the fragrant perfume with a person—and that fragrance may be experienced as a threat if the person who wears it has been cruel. The sourness of a lemon, however, may be experienced as comforting, reminding a teen of visits to Grandma's home in Florida where lemon trees grew in her backyard. Observation, combined with personal experience, leads to interpretation.

ACTIVITY: KEEN OBSERVATIONS

The following three keen observation activities are a joy! See them as processes with no right answers. Ah, that feels better, right? We're not here to bludgeon ourselves for warped worldviews. We're here to discover more richness and beauty. We start with our magnificent five senses. Let's enjoyably (productively!) "waste time" in observation, becoming intimate with a subject for study. The ground floor of critical thinking, then, is learning to notice, name, identify, and interpret.

Use N squared, I squared (N^2I^2) to remind you of these four keen observation skills.

Notice: Be alert to a personal impression or reaction.

Name: What's the impression being created?

Identify: Explore the source of the impression.

Interpret: Give preliminary meaning to your impressions.

As you work through these activities, remind yourself that these are personally created meanings drawn from what each child notices, names, identifies, and interprets. In other words, if you believe the perfume is sweetly fragrant and your child identifies it as having a horrid, pungent odor, that's completely acceptable.

Bright-Eyed (5 to 9): Sensory Treasure Hunt

How we understand our detailed sensory perceptions is the basis of interpreting the world around us. "The brain is the ultimate reductionist. It reduces the world to its elementary parts: photons of light, molecules of smell, sound waves, vibrations of touch—which send electrochemical signals to individual brain cells that store information about lines, movements, colors, smells and other sensory inputs." We gather that information through our senses and then we make it make, well, sense (ha!). These sensory experiences create the silent films that live in our minds and guide our reactions. Sensory input is rich source material for personal writing and thinking, too. Let's get started!

Touch

Send your child to find five to ten items in the house with a variety of textures, weights, odors or fragrances, and colors. Bring the items to the kitchen table. Take notes for your child while the child makes observations (using the questions that follow).

Notice

....

- Which item do you like to hold or touch?
- Which item makes you handle it with care?
- Which one feels strange in your hand?
- Do any of the items offer a temperature change (makes your hand cooler or warmer)? Which ones do and which don't?
- Put the items in order of their weights (lift two at a time—if possible—and compare weights, and then

sequence them). Which sequence did you choose (lightest to heaviest or heaviest to lightest)? Why? Try them in the other sequence. How does that look to you? Are some of the heavier items smaller in size than lighter items? Are any of the items similar in weight? Is there a big difference between the heaviest and lightest objects? Jot down the sequences. Snap a photo!

- Now sequence them according to size. Did you start with the smallest or the largest? Snap a picture. Are you measuring by height or width when you compare sizes? Try it the other way. How does that change the lineup? How different are these lineups than the ones based on weight? Compare photos.

Name

....

- Name the textures of each item: rough, smooth, prickly, fuzzy . . .
- What scents do you detect for each item? Odor or fragrance? Sweet or pungent?
- What colors? Count them.
- What color does it show in the light? In the shade? From above or below?
- How many yellows or greens can you detect in a monochrome item?
- Compare the colors to a box of Crayola crayons and see if you can find other color names for your items.
- How many more colors did you find after this careful observation?

- Put the items in groups that make sense to you (colors, textures, shapes, scents).
- Count how many items there are in each group.
- Sequence them according to which ones you like holding the most.
- Sequence them according to which ones you like looking at the most.
- What do the items have in common? What makes them different from each other?
- Identify the ones that look the most similar and most dissimilar.

Interpret

- What drew you to these items when you looked around the house? Were there any items you considered and chose not to bring to the table? Why?
- What causes a heavy item to be heavy? Why is another item light? Can you tell?
- Think about the colors again. Why do you think we see "one" color when we look at an item quickly and more colors when we observe closely?
- What's the difference between a fragrance and an odor?
- What else would you like to say about these items and your experience exploring them?

Add your child's questions to these, and invite your child to ask *you* these questions, too. Compare your answers. The goal is to recognize how probing with questions leads to greater awareness of the detailed way an item can be known.

Quick-Witted (10 to 12): Grab Bag

Betty Edwards, author of *Drawing on the Right Side of the Brain*, explains that the reason so many of us feel we can't draw is because we haven't been taught to see. When we take our pencils to the page, we *think* we know what we're seeing and attempt to draw *that* image. For example, because in our daily lives we look people in the eye rather than at their forehead, our minds imagine the eyes taking up more space on the face than they do. When a child goes to draw a face, the eyes are frequently drawn too large and high up on the head. When we stand back to evaluate our drawing, it doesn't look right, but we find it difficult to know how to fix the mistake.

What happens if we use an objective tool, like a ruler, to discover what went wrong? We'd see that the eyes are fully halfway down the head from the top of the hair to the bottom of the chin. The forehead is much larger than expected, and the eyes are much smaller proportionately. To draw accurately requires a kind of "forgetting" of our assumptions and a willingness to have accurate data overturn what we think we know. We have to trick our minds—our eyes—into seeing the relationships and proportions (not the ones we think we see). In Edwards's book, she instructs students to turn the image that they're drawing upside down so that the artist's assumptions are confounded.

In a similar way, critical thinking depends on the fresh eyes of the mind. We let go of what we assume is accurate information. We open ourselves to a new thought or perspective on the off chance that there's information we've misrepresented to ourselves. We get to that place of openness by deliberately subverting our expectations. Because our eyes account for the greatest source of data that we take as factual, this first activity removes the power of sight.

Instructions

Gather a selection of items from your home, such as these:

- Perfume bottle
- Pinecone
- Kazoo
- Starfruit
- Puppet
- Bottle brush
- Seashell
- Feather
- Pipe
- Velvet pillow
- River stone

. . . and so on. Feel free to pick any item that has multiple dimensions to it.

- Next, put each item inside a single paper bag (the bag should be opaque—not see-through).
- Put the bags in "stations" on your kitchen table or on a coffee table.
- Place a blindfold (could be a sleeping mask or a bandana tied around the eyes) on your child.
- Your child will work with one bag at a time, but feel free to do all the bags. (It's a fun activity.)
- Ask the following set of questions and then jot down your child's responses on a clipboard as they

investigate the item. Let them know ahead of time that even if they *know* what the item is, they are to avoid naming it until they are done "noticing" it.

Questions

Read these questions aloud to your child in a conversational tone. It's perfectly natural to chat back and forth.

Notice

- Open the bag and put your hand on the item. What's the first sensory observation you can make?
- Move it around in your hands. Can you give an impression of how it impacts you right away? Pleasure to hold, off-putting, uncomfortable, cozy, prickly, warm, cold?
- How heavy or light? How large or small? How many parts? What sort of edges (smooth, hard, angular, curvy)?
- Bring the item out of the bag to sniff it. Does it give you pleasure to smell it? Or is it offending? Or perhaps it's neutral?
- Can it be shaken to produce a sound? What noise? Pleasing or not?
- Let the child know if the item can be tasted. If so: What flavor?

Name

- What is the texture? How would you describe it?
- What is the shape?
- How many sides or dimensions?

- What geometric shape is it most like?
- Name the scent and taste (if edible). Any comparisons to other scents and tastes that occur to you?

Identify

- Can you identify what gives it its texture, weight, and shape?
- Can you name the parts? What are they?
- Can you imagine the item's use (edible, a tool, a decoration, a part of nature . . .)?
- Can you guess what item it is?

Interpret

- Take off the blindfold. Examine the item with your eyes.
- Looking over your previous answers, what did you miss when you weren't allowed to use sight as an observation tool? What new aspects of the item can you observe now (for instance, color)?
- Do your observations match the purpose of the item (for instance, if you said that the smell was offensive but it turned out to be perfume, is that a mismatch of its goal)?
- Can you elaborate on the item's purpose: How does its weight, shape, texture, fragrance, color, or taste help the item achieve its purpose? What thwarts it?
- Are you surprised by any of your observations? Which ones, and why?

Remember, there are no right answers. All observations are equally meaningful, even if not equally elaborate or articulate.

Detailed investigation without a set of preconceived right answers is the foundation of quality, enjoyable critical examination.

Nimble-Minded (13 to 18):
Keen Observation of Images

For the teenagers in your family, let's look at images associated with social issues. These observations will be aimed at abstract topics rather than concrete objects. Remember, mental images influence interpretation. Think back to my journey in eastern Europe. I wasn't even aware of the silent film playing in the background. It wasn't until I had the opportunity to compare reality against that silent film that I saw what I had created in my own mind. This exercise invites teens to answer questions about the images in their minds related to one of the social issues listed here (or the teen can pick one of their own).

Hint: it can be useful to go through this process a few times, over a period of weeks. The first time, select a topic that provokes a strong reaction. The second time, pick a topic that doesn't evoke a strong belief or opinion. Compare and contrast the experiences.

- College athletes: Should they be paid to play?
- Photo editing and filtering tools: Is it ethical to alter the faces and bodies of models in advertising?
- Homeschool regulations: Should parents be allowed to teach their children without government oversight?
- Violent video games: Do they play a role in increased aggressive behavior in those who play them?
- Gender-based toys: Should toys be marketed to cater to a specific gender?

- Animal rights: Is it ethical to use animals in medical or cosmetic testing?
- Social media: Does social media suppress free speech?
- Cell phones: Are laws restricting cell phone use while driving appropriate?
- Music and films: Is it ethical to download music and films for free?
- Fencing at the US-Mexico border: Is fencing an effective immigration strategy?

Put the selected topic at the top of a blank sheet of paper. Ask the questions and type or handwrite the oral answers on your teen's behalf. (Some students like to work alone, which is fine, too.) Urge your student to take all the time needed. Recommend that your teens close their eyes and move the camera lens of their imagination around to see into the corners, to see behind the foreground, to consider all the bits of information their vision gives them. Not all of the following questions are relevant to the suggested topics. Skip any that aren't a match.

Questions

- When you stop to think of your topic, what scenes flash before your mind? Describe them in as much detail as possible. Then go on to the following questions to add detail.
- Do you see people? What skin tones? Can you identify gender? Consider the wide array of people, not only the ones you are used to seeing. Under-resourced, middle-class, or wealthy? Which sort of clothing are they wearing? Are they adults or kids? Are they from a religious group—which one? What foods do they

enjoy? If you were to get them a hot drink, what would it be?

- Where do they live? House? Apartment? Condominium? Yurt? Tent? Rural, urban, or suburban setting? What are the people doing? Are they sitting, standing, cooking, cleaning, watching television, working on a hobby, working at home, eating a meal, studying, praying? What is the ratio of children to adults? Who's in charge? Who likes being there? Who doesn't? How do you know?
- What are they doing? What's the primary activity? Where is it conducted? In a lab? At a photoshoot? On a game controller? In a boardroom? At a home?
- Can you detect the emotional state of the people? Consider some of these possibilities: content, worried, fearful, angry, fierce, indifferent, excited, purposeful, curious, convinced . . .
- Where are these scenes? In your city? In another state or country? In your living room? Indoors or outdoors?
- What's the weather like? What season of the year? What colors or absence of color? Warm or cold? More than one season?
- What do you see in the room, yard, campus, lab? Are there new scenes crowding into the original one as you think more about your topic? What are they, and what do you make of them?
- If your topic were on a billboard, what would be on it?
- If your topic were a photo without words, what would you put in the picture?
- If your topic were a meme on social media, what image and message would it use?

- If your topic relies on equipment, what kind is it? What is the ideal equipment for this topic? Safe or unsafe?
- If your topic were an ad, would it be pro or against? What images or story would show that perspective? Is there a brand that promotes your viewpoint now with their own ads? Picture it in your head now. Which is it?

Share the following with your student:

The images you summoned in your mind influence how you read articles and books about your topic. They impact how you listen to news reports and what you feel when you meet people who make up these groups. Your silent films shape your own vocabulary in how you talk about the topic. You've named, noted, and identified those impressions. Now it's time to interpret.

- What did you discover that surprised you about the images you see in your mind's eye?
- Did any of the questions trigger a change in how you see your topic? For instance, if you were to think about home education, perhaps you only ever imagined it in a house, but the question about apartments made you consider that yes, some families may actually home-educate in apartments. You might have read the question about where the people from your topic live only to realize for the first time that at the border wall, there are people living in tents.
- How does the overall picture you created influence how you think about the topic? For instance, my mistaken notion that the sun didn't shine in

communist countries made me think the people who lived in those places were always unhappy.

- When you think about your topic now, after this inventory, name your overall impression/disposition toward the topic—positive or negative? Any shift from before you began? New information you didn't consider?

As you review the activities with your children, you can share this summary that goes with the activities.

The purpose of keenly observing is to put you, the observer, in touch with the story you tell yourself about any item or topic. The storyteller, in this case, is you! Your own viewpoint may have been invisible to you since it is the way your mind directs your attention or creates the impressions you carry with you all the time. By slowing down and looking in the nooks and crannies of an item or a topic, you uncover how those assumptions shape how you feel about the topic or item. The next steps in your critical thinking journey will deepen your understanding of how you form your impressions.

Once you've tried these activities with your kids (and feel free to do them more than once!), move on to the next chapter. What's the point of all this observing? Where does it lead?

CHAPTER 5

Critical Thinking Starts with Caring

In brief, the ideal critical thinker is disposed to care.

—Robert Ennis

Before we get too far, it helps to think about the goal of all this edu-ma-catin'! "Getting through" and "getting done"—are these adequate measures of having learned? Or is there a more personal measurement we ought to use? Raising critical thinkers must be purposeful, or why bother? As I thought about the point of education, I stumbled on a comment Nobel Prize recipient Toni Morrison made in the documentary about her life, *Toni Morrison: The Pieces I Am*, that nailed it for me. During the US civil rights movement of the 1960s, when so many of Morrison's friends were taking to the streets demonstrating, Morrison found herself raising two sons as a single mother. She worked as a senior editor for Random House, a publishing company in New York

City. Her sense of responsibility precluded travel and risking arrest, yet she wanted to show solidarity with the protestors.

So she asked herself a clarifying question: "What can I do where I am?"

What can I do where I am?

What *can* I do where I am?

What can *I* do where I am?

What can I *do* where I am?

What can I do *where* I am?

Each word is loaded with potency. Morrison realized that she could use her talents and position as an editor to make a difference. She solicited book contracts for the biographies of civil rights activists Angela Davis and Muhammad Ali. She advanced the social change that mattered to her—putting her education and her unique position to work. "What can I do where I am?" indeed.

Caring to Matter

In the context of formal education, I hear that question this way: How can I, the person I am, in the place I am, use the tools, research, and insights of my field for the betterment of humankind—here, now? In the context of kidlets, I hear it this way: "How on Earth does this subject relate to who my child is and can be for themselves and others?" That's a powerful why for schooling, don't you agree? Let me get big and dramatic. In my opinion, we learn so that we can participate in the transformation of the world, even if that contribution means using a chemistry degree to improve the quality of shampoo. All of our contributions add up to better living (or at least, shouldn't they?). Isn't that what Morrison meant by the provocative question she posed to herself?

Each age is charged with this great mission: to develop the latest, best understanding of a field of study and then to develop the most liberating, effective, humanizing manifestations of it on behalf of others (the great I-Thou project). Learning is not primarily for the purpose of amassing money or power but for gaining wisdom and putting that knowledge to use for the bettering of life for all people. I'm gobsmacked that I get to live in this era. I can fly to the other side of the world in twenty-four hours. I can talk by video phone for an unlimited number of minutes to my son in Bangkok for the price of internet service. I can click "search" on an iPad and find statistics I want to know in seconds flat. My household chores are completed by machines. Truly, these technological marvels are the result of billions of educated human beings around the globe pooling their talents to improve life for everyone, everywhere.

The academic task is about service—each of us contributing to the centuries-old great conversation in our field of study, using our voices to expand the symphony of ideas, for the flourishing of all people (my people, your people), everywhere. "What can I do where I am?" *is* the clarifying goal for a robust, meaningful education. Too often, schooling feels more like this: "I have to pass the math test so I can take another math test."

Math, as an example, matters because it enables people to care more precisely. What if a child saw math as valuable—as the best tool to measure what matters? For instance: cups of flour for a bread-baking recipe, the ratio of compost to soil for the vegetable garden, the temperature of a chicken pox–induced fever, the angles for how to miter a corner of a quilt, the percentage of life left in the video game? What if we saw math as a critical thinking tool? Math makes it possible to understand all the data that's shouted at us online, in books, and during press conferences. What if fluency in numbers gives us a better sense of scale when we study history, rendering particular dates and the span of centuries meaningful?

One of my sons became fascinated with math because of the massive distances (read: really big numbers) between planets and stars. When my children were in elementary school, we invited several neighboring families to join us to re-create the solar system. We stood distanced apart based on a scaled model reduced by a factor of a billion(!). The kids lined up in measurable distances from the sun at the end of the street, adding planets at the correct distances, until we got to the outer planets (including Pluto, recently demoted from planet status). We discovered that our Pluto representative would have to be over three miles away from the rest of us. Our kids gasped in shock at the vastness of our solar system.

Math doesn't have to be an abstract subject for worksheets. It's a critical thinking mechanism that makes it possible to care with precision. If a student appreciates the *value* of math, that student will be more likely to react with an accurate proportion of outrage or appreciation to whatever the numbers convey. Without caring, education is just another "purchase." Math skill becomes a key card to a better club of degree-holders. We can ask the same question about reading or history or learning another language: *Why does it matter?* Mastering information is not as important, then, as asking how the subject causes us to care: caring more about the subject itself, each other, and how that subject matters to all of us.

Critical thinking starts with caring.

Caring to Think Well

To think well means to care enough to improve your thinking. Amazingly, your kids are already sold on one of the most powerful tools to improve how they think: games. All kinds—board, video, dice, card. Author Bernard Suits gives my all-time favorite definition of gaming: "Playing a game is the voluntary attempt to overcome unnecessary obstacles." There are two keys terms in this definition I want to highlight: "voluntary" and "overcome." Game play is unique in your children's lives because they choose it and feel motivated to overcome the unnecessary challenges it provides them. These are optimal conditions for *caring to think well.* Your kids care about playing correctly, playing to win, and improving their game play. Games lead to a bevy of great thinking skills: flexibility of mind, persistence, questioning, striving for accuracy, imagining and innovating, and thinking with clarity and precision. Plus, games are fun. Sometimes we forget how important pleasure is to the ability to think well. A mind at ease (seeking both pleasure and meaningful risk) is relaxed and alert.

Games provide the high-challenge, low-threat conditions that are optimal for learning, too. Brain researchers Renate and Geoffrey Caine identify one of the key factors of the relaxed alert state: what they call "thematic attractors." These are focal points "around which we organize our thoughts and ideas." Activities that are thematic attractors (like playing sports, enjoying comic books, or participating in a 4-H competition) give kids the experience of personal power and direction. "They provide a personalized focal point and framework around which patterns can form, so that attractors 'seed' the felt meaning, much as an oyster builds a pearl around a fragment of grit." The personal meaning a gamer makes for themselves through game play fuels their eagerness to problem-solve and attack bigger challenges. They learn to "think creatively, tolerate ambiguity, and delay gratification, all of which are essential for the genuine expansion of knowledge."

My oldest son, Noah, now an adult, is passionate about games. He owns hundreds of them. He's the lead designer for an open-source online game. He's got a basement full of board, card, and role-playing games. Each time he plays a new game, he deliberately loses, trying each possible iteration of game-play to discover the game's limits and opportunities. Once he's seen all the ways a player can fail at a game, he becomes a formidable opponent. Over his thirty some years, he's played thousands of games in all varieties: online, console, tabletop, card, role-playing, and dice games.

When Noah opens a board game, he *explores* all the components, popping out the pieces, putting cards inside plastic protective covers, reading instructions, fingering the tokens, unfolding the game board. The exploration stage is important. It allows the mind to set the table for the coming experience.

Next, he *experiments* by imagining an opponent, testing the way the game is supposed to work, and envisioning possible outcomes. He consults the instructions again and again.

He then *explains* the game to the best of his ability to new players. The explanation phase consolidates all that he understands about the game to that point.

Regardless of how well we, the new players, grasp his instructions, we begin—he, the novice expert, and the rest of us, eager learners. As the game progresses, questions come fast and furious:

- What if I play this card now?
- What if she wants to stop me? How would she do that?
- Am I allowed to ask for *X*?
- What happens if I run out of tokens?
- How much is that move worth?
- What would it cost me if I made this move?

We each explore the game, experiment with a variety of moves, and explain to one another how it ought to work or what we think the outcome will be. Questions relate to specific actions taken in the context of the game. We uncover strategies that work and those that fail spectacularly (often to the merriment of the players who narrowly escape!). Players drive for the same aim: winning the game. With some games, an individual player wins. In other games, a team wins. Today, some games pit all the players against the game itself; the goal of the game is for *everybody* to win! Because kids care to win, the critical thinking skillbuilding looks effortless.

It's rare that a parent worries about board game play. These games bring back happy memories from childhood. They are out on the table where adults can supervise and eavesdrop. Bring up video games, however, and a gusher of anxiety is released. Even though video games offer similar benefits to board games, the fact that all that learning happens between a mind and a machine without oversight worries adults. To be fair, the research is confusing and many times alarmist. Recent longitudinal studies, however, are promising in this regard. One thorough collection of current data draws these tentative conclusions:

> The discussion about video games has focused on fears about a large part of players becoming addicted. Given their wide-spread popularity, many policymakers are concerned about negative effects of play time on well-being. Our results challenge that view. The relation between play time and well-being was positive in two large samples. Therefore, our study speaks against an immediate need to regulate video games as a preventive measure to limit video game addiction. If anything, our results suggest that play can be an activity that relates positively to people's mental health—and regulating games could withhold those benefits from players.

Additional studies show, ironically, that it may be the kids who don't game at all who are more at risk for unregulated emotions and lower reported levels of well-being. "Non-gaming has been found to put boys, in particular, at greater risk for problems" while "gaming positively contributed to creative, social, and emotional benefits" in gamers. There are now studies that show equally positive results even when gamers played violent video games like *Grand Theft Auto*, *Resident Evil*, *Mortal Kombat*, and *Prince of Persia*. While there are blue light considerations for the eyes, neck strain from long sessions looking at a screen, and worries about the Wild, Wild West of online life itself (from YouTube ads to social media apps), the actual game play itself is proving to be valuable for children's mental well-being, emotional regulation, and sense of autonomy.

Kids who play seven to ten hours per week feel less lonely and experience deep absorption, enjoyment, and healthy concentration. This research confirms what the Caines have been telling us for decades: "Positive stress helps players achieve 'flow' and the experience of being in the 'zone,' as players are pushed by the game's tasks and challenges where there is likelihood of experiencing success." The benefits to gaming go well beyond entertainment and emotional health. Gaming matters to kids. When they care, they apply themselves and experience a surge of competence and self-regard. When they care, they persist through setbacks, innovate solutions, think with precision, and overcome obstacles.

Years back, my family took a trip to Italy. My husband, Jon, and I opened a large, unwieldy map to find our way to an obscure museum. Orienting ourselves was a first, labored step. After a frustrating minute or two, our three boys stepped forward, peeked over Jon's shoulder, and declared: "We go this way." As a trio, they pointed in the same direction and set off confidently. Jon and I were flummoxed—and didn't quite believe they could read a map that quickly. Lo and behold, the boys led us the whole way without a misstep. When I asked later how they knew which way to go so quickly, Jacob spoke on their behalf: "Mom, we play online games on maps every day. Maps are easy to read." Truly, gaming is not adjacent to life. It's a passcode to it. When kids care, they have the best chance to think well. Naturally, in the spirit of this entire book, be sure to conduct your own research into video games. Your mileage may vary, and the research continually updates. The rest of this chapter helps you vet that research, too.

One of the critiques of video gaming is that children will play to excess. Similar to how we help our kids regulate their eating habits or their bathing routines, we can guide children to use digital devices at the times we deem appropriate. One digital media expert and educator I interviewed made the following observation that I found incredibly helpful. Ash Brandin explains that one of the reasons children enjoy gaming so much is that the gaming world comes with a fixed set of rules that never change. They rely on these clearly delineated protocols every time they play. They would find it appalling to use the B key to jump one day and then the next day discover that the B key no longer causes a jump. The rules provide the framework for both enjoyment and skill-building. When regulating game play with your children, set expectations in a similar way. Ash told me: "Kids can't self-regulate almost anything when young—it's our job as adults to help them regulate and to find out how to have a healthy relationship with all kinds of stimuli." You might talk about those boundaries as the framework for the best life you can live together at home or school, just like there are rules that help them succeed in *SimCity* or *Animal Crossing*. The key is not to see these limits as punitive or to offer them in fear. Enjoy their gaming, note the amazing brain activity it inspires, and then actively include other activities in your children's lives that are similar "thematic attractors." Thinking well will be one of the delightful benefits.

No matter how you slice it, games themselves (of all sorts) are powerful as critical thinking skill-builders for several reasons:

1. The rules of a game act as a reassuring framework for play. Players know what to expect and how to behave inside the confines of that system. They learn respect for boundaries.
2. Each action taken alters the course of the game. No two game plays are alike. Opportunities to innovate and create are served up regularly.
3. Strategies vary depending on the strength or weakness of a player's position at any point in the game. Everyone hopes to be in the strong position eventually, so they keep playing.
4. Most games make use of basic mathematics—counting, combining, multiplying, dividing, spatial awareness, bidding, resource management, logic, strategizing, even map reading.

5. Games encourage autonomy: taking responsibility for one's actions and experiencing the consequences immediately when those actions succeed or fail. In fact, research shows that students *enjoy* the experience of exercising control (autonomy) when faced with gaming challenges.

Caring About Accuracy

Today's world offers kids a smorgasbord of choices for study, play, information, and entertainment. As quickly as wonderfulness expands, so does chicanery—phony statistics, propaganda, bias, greed, conspiracy theories, racism, misogyny, and those who exploit technology for selfish gain or perversion. Our kids are being asked to hop on this fast-moving treadmill of information to make instantaneous judgments about facts, opinions, ethics, personal safety, and the validity of research—sometimes in seconds! Our teens want to know: "Is this social media platform a reliable source of data? When is it and when isn't it?" Or worse, they may not even know yet that they should want to know.

One mother wrote to me, sharing that her daughter, Yazmin, wanted to learn to vape (smoke e-cigarettes). Yazmin explained that she knew vaping was safe because of a video she watched on social media. Her distressed mother wondered how to equip her daughter to verify what her phone told her. A good question. Where do we get reliable information? How do we judge a source's credibility? Yet behind that question (How do we know which sources to trust?) is an even more important disposition: caring to know. If our kids are passive recipients of information and data, trusting it because a celebrity on a media platform makes a bold claim, they may conclude: it must be so! Conversely, they may choose to distrust information you give them because they don't want you to be right.

Today's glut of misinformation is largely due to the absence of *caring to be accurate.* The antidote? Learning how to verify information—both data and sources. Joel Best, a sociologist well known for his work in the field of statistical analysis, cuts to the heart of this challenge. He explains that for many of us, there's an aura around numbers. When we read them, we become spellbound: *This statistic must be true. An important number is attached to this idea.* Too often, because of our school experience, we're easily impressed when numbers get added to any story because quantities and measurements carry authority. If that celebrated son-of-a-gun stated it or cited it, it must be an important fact. In a similar way, conspiracy theorists use numbers to bolster their credibility. They cite data that they believe has been suppressed or overlooked by mainstream sources. How do we differentiate between the two? Once you've taught your kids to care enough to vet information, we have to give them the critical thinking tools to do it! Let's look at two important steps students can take to verify the reliability of any data they encounter.

IDENTIFYING MEASUREMENTS AND BENCHMARKS

Not every statistic is true. According to Best, in the internet age, a "bad stat is harder to kill than a vampire." When those stats are shocking or are added to impressive-looking websites or get displayed on a four-color graph, we're susceptible to believing them. To evaluate statistics, Best explains that there are two requirements. First, you have to understand how the data is measured. Second, you need to know its benchmarks, which are the fundamental measures in the field.

For example, sports often measure ball speeds to compare the athletic skill of one player to another. A professional female tennis player can serve a tennis ball at about 108 miles per hour fairly regularly. The fastest tennis serve ever recorded was by a male player—John Isner—measured at 157.2 miles per hour. Without knowing these benchmarks, I accidentally credited the 2021 world's number-one female tennis player, Naomi Osaka, with a serve of 193 miles per hour. I got challenged by a tennis fan—"That can't be right!" As it turned out, the stat I had read had been recorded in kilometers per hour (taken during the Australian Open). I simply missed the KPH after the digits. Without establishing the metric of measurement or knowing the benchmark for typical speeds of serves, I didn't even question what I thought I had read. I was too busy passing along misinformation. That's how it happens. Armed with the right benchmarks, a discerning reader can spot exaggerated claims or flat-out lies.

Teach your kids to ask these two questions:

- How's the data measured?
- What are its benchmarks?

Caring About Credibility

Naturally, while statistics lend an air of credibility to an argument, it's smart to figure out who's providing the information before relying on it. How do we evaluate claims made in the media or in a textbook or online? How can we know if a source is reliable or not? Thinkers who care vet their sources. They are especially careful to vet them before passing along information they read (unlike me, who passed along the wrong information about Osaka's amaze-balls serve!). Not only that, just because a source says it's reputable doesn't mean it is. Conversely, just because a source has a bias doesn't mean it can't deliver facts, either.

There's a practice researchers at Stanford have recommended for evaluating the reliability of websites. They call it "reading laterally." Rather than allowing yourself to be pulled down the rabbit hole of a single page by giving all your attention to the case the writer makes, begin by gathering information about the writer or organization first. Reading laterally means opening several browser windows to verify the source before allowing the website to cast its spell of credibility on you. The people Stanford researchers found most effective at ferreting out facts from misinformation are, as their name implies, fact-checkers. They use a practice they call "taking bearings." It reminds me of "taking benchmarks" in statistics.

The Stanford researchers explained the practice in their paper "Lateral Reading: Reading Less and Learning More When Evaluating Digital Information":

> Exploring an unfamiliar forest, experienced hikers know how easy it is to lose their way. Only foolhardy hikers trust their instincts and go traipsing off. Instead they rotate their compass's bezel to determine bearings—the angle, measured in degrees, between North and their desired destination. Obviously, taking bearings on the web is not as precise as measuring an angle in degrees. It begins, however, with a similar premise: When navigating unfamiliar terrain, first gain a sense of direction.

TAKING BEARINGS

In the same way we wanted to compare statistics to reliable, common data in a field, taking bearings means getting a clear idea of who is providing the interpretation to the research you consume. In a study conducted by the Stanford research team, they discovered that their impressively talented and straight-A students were more easily drawn in by the aesthetics of a website, for instance—the logo, the .org URL, an abstract, PhDs listed—than the fact-checkers were. Students found it difficult to differentiate between a website for a historic medical organization with decades of peer-reviewed articles available and a much newer website that mimicked the official organization's name, created an official-looking logo, and purported to have its own academic credentials. The second site appeared to give reliable data, but upon deeper investigation, each item was skewed to promote a particular political agenda designed to influence public policy. The similarity between the two sites was a deliberate design choice on the part of the political site to approximate the credibility of the historic organization for the sake of misleading the public.

In the study, the fact-checkers were flawless in their ability to determine which website had the more impartial information and superior credentials. How did they do it? Rather than comparing the look of the two sites and then reading the articles, the fact-checkers took their bearings. They left each website almost immediately to research the organization. They got a sense of the organization's history by corroborating it with other respected sites. In fact, this is one way Wikipedia is valuable as a shortcut. It allows anyone to get a quick overview of established organizations and offers additional sources to check in the footnotes, even though the entry itself can't be relied on as authoritative in academic writing. The fact-checkers also vetted the listed experts on the "about" pages by googling their names and reading about them in additional contexts. Fairly quickly, the fact-checkers were able to determine which site was more trustworthy.

READING LATERALLY

A habit you can cultivate with your kids, then, is to *read laterally*. Anytime they reference a book or a website, ask them:

- What else do you know about the organization?
- Who are their experts?
- What standing does that writer have in their field?

One of the challenges of online conversation is that people assume that if they can link to a website, then the report or data must have been vetted by someone for its factual standing. But that is often not the case. Anyone can host a website and say whatever they want!

So what constitutes a reliable and credible source? Usually we want the writing to meet the following criteria:

- Be current (for research) or current to the era (if a primary source is used as historical evidence)
- Include accurate information that is verifiable
- Provide good detail on the topic
- Come from an expert in the field
- Strive for a balanced view of the subject (including caveats or addressing counterclaims)

The most reliable sources are not overtly biased. This means the evidence comes from experts we trust—researchers, statisticians, doctors, professors, government agencies, subject-area specialists, practitioners in the field with a long tenure. It's also helpful if the information has been properly investigated by colleagues in the field (what we call "peer-reviewed"). Bloggers, columnists, and writers might report that research and offer their own opinions, but they aren't necessarily considered subject-area experts. One of my students cited a senator's view on climate change as "expert opinion" in his essay. I pointed out that while the senator was a well-known politician, he was neither a subject-matter expert on climate change nor a scientist. The senator's view was a conclusion he had drawn for himself, but it did not carry the credibility of someone who had dedicated their career to researching the climate. This is why understanding whose statistics and opinions you cite matters. When deciding if the information in an article or on a website is credible, we can help our kids look for certain *clues* or "red flags." Here are a few to keep in mind:

Tone and language: Notice when an author "rants" rather than writes. You'll notice inflammatory language meant to cause a strong emotional reaction. For instance, on the People for Ethical Treatment of Animals website, one headline reads: "PETA Rips Lid off Chinchilla Mill That Supplies Labs and Pet Stores." Notice the words "rips" and "mill." Both of these are intended to provoke a reaction of outrage and concern.

Assumptions and generalizations: The writer provides lots of opinion without citing sources or crediting the research in those assumptions. Your teens may confuse a video that talks about why vaping is safe as legitimate just because it was a video, even though there were no references to clinical studies.

Crowdsourced information: Another danger online is that a lot of information is crowdsourced. It's easy to fall down a rabbit hole of collected experiences on discussion boards or in social media communities. Remember, a webpage like Wikipedia is good for an overview of a topic and for finding credible sources to examine, but it's not reliable as a source of expert testimony.

Opinion pieces: An opinion piece can be seen as a red flag if the student relies heavily on one source with one viewpoint. Ironically, when schools rely on one set of textbooks, they are creating a similar effect. It's easy to tilt toward positions you already hold to get reinforcement. That said, opinion pieces by journalists or researchers are often a great source of arguments for and against a topic. An opinion piece can help to clarify what's at stake in the discussion of the topic. That's one of its best uses. Be sure to include more than one perspective to hear strong cases made for and against. One of the dangers of opinion pieces or news media that openly choose a political slant is that the merits of the opposing case are belittled and dismissed. Deliberately seeking to read strong cases from more than one perspective is a way to effectively use opinion in a student's studies. I've also found that opinion pieces lead to rich conversations more often than factual data from, say, a government website that catalogs research and statistics. Using the data collection from a government site, however, is a way to take a benchmark and apply it to the data in that opinion article.

Once you've taken a look at the red flags, you can dig a little deeper into the source itself. In Brave Writer, we use a handy acronym in our online writing classes to help students remember what to look for when evaluating a source: CACAO. While cacao is the ingredient in our favorite chocolate treats, it's also a good device to help you look at sources with a critical eye. Writing that doesn't raise red flags but demonstrates CACAO—currency, accuracy, coverage, authority, objectivity—means you're using your critical thinking skills at a high level in your reading and research.

Currency

Was the information updated or published recently? A credible article will include the information about publishing dates. If the article or source is more than five to ten years old, it's important to look to see if the information has been updated since the time of publication. Population-driven information is updated every ten years with the census, for instance.

Accuracy

Is the information provided factual and well documented (multiple sources from a variety of disciplines, when possible)? Are the sources of information provided, either through links in the article or in a list of sources at the end? Can a reader verify this information by finding other sources that affirm what's stated in the article? If a statistic or report goes against the conventional understanding of a field, it matters to find corroboration. In circles that are intent on challenging the broader consensus of a particular field (science, history, medicine, sociology), ask the question: What drives the challenge? Some red flag considerations would be to consider whether the writer is using the less commonly held data to do the following:

- Explain a negative personal experience
- Prove a theological position
- Support a political goal
- Protect corporate profits
- Launch a personal brand

Challenges to the status quo require a bigger burden of proof, and that information and research ought to come from a cross section of sources.

Coverage

Does the article provide enough detail on the topic? Is everything in the article cited correctly, or is information on cited sources missing? The reader should be able to follow source information to verify it. For instance, if the writer relies on government research, does the link take you to a government site? If the writer discusses a study, can the reader find the study?

Authority

Are the author's credentials and contact information stated? If no author is listed, does this information come from an organization with a well-established reputation? Educational institutions and government agencies have more credibility than advocacy groups or commercial sites that want to sell you something.

Objectivity

When presenting information, particularly online, objectivity is elusive. Every website designer knows that color, layout, font choices, and prioritization of information create an impact on the reader. Even the attempt to create the impression of objectivity is a tacit acknowledgment that design can influence how we read and what we believe. Additionally, writers decide what information to include and what information to omit. Our aim is to seek sources that limit that subjectivity as best they can.

When we look at information, we can ask: What is the goal of this article, website, blog, or book? Is it primarily to provide accurate data? Does it wish to persuade? Does it provide a fair and balanced view on the subject—meaning it acknowledges considerations from more than one point of view? Does the writing have a purpose other than providing information?

Learning the art of evaluating a source takes time. Lots of kids may not master this skill until college! I dare say, we adults need to return to these skills ourselves. Online life makes all of us a little lazy, but it also provides tools and resources for practicing these research skills regularly. Adopt the attitude of "practice makes progress."

An Example: Birth

Let's take a look at birth, a topic everyone has experienced, even if you can't remember being born. Birth can be understood biologically—from how to achieve pregnancy all the way to how the baby grows in the uterus and then descends the birth canal during labor until the baby is pushed out into the world with first breaths. There are dangers associated with birth. Over the centuries, countless mothers and babies have died due to infection or traumatic deliveries. Medical interventions and caesarean sections over the last century in particular have led to a remarkable reduction in stillbirths and maternal morbidity. Birth is both a natural process and one fraught with some danger to mother and baby. These are facts.

But birth is more than these facts. Birth is also a cultural story. Some storytellers explain that birth is painful, must be medicated, and requires the help of medical professionals to ensure safety. Birth is also a story told for laughs on sitcoms showing women screaming for drugs. Other storytellers emphasize that birth is a natural process that needs support from experienced companions rather than medical intervention. Midwives and doulas recognize time-honored practices that ensure an unmedicated delivery. Whether a pregnant person decides to give birth in a hospital or at home will have a lot to do with which storytellers are seen as more trustworthy. How would someone decide to choose a home birth over a hospital birth?

To examine birth, we'd establish benchmarks first. How many people are born each year in the United States? Which websites provide credible statistics? Next, we'd determine how many births happen in a hospital compared with how many happen at home. A related question: What constitutes a home birth? Do births in cars or births in living rooms by accident count, too? Next, we'd identify who can give birth successfully at home. Who is better off in a hospital? What conditions lead to a healthy birth? What conditions don't?

A choice to give birth at home means doing a lot more research and taking responsibility for the sparse information available. Data for home birth is more limited. This is where *caring to know* becomes critical. We'd have to draw from additional types of sources, such as firsthand experiences and professionals outside the medical mainstream, like midwives. A person who considers a home birth must be more educated about the birth process, the risks, and how to prepare for emergencies than those who give birth in a hospital. Data is not the only way people form opinions or choose to take on risk. In the end, it's what we say about birth that shapes how we understand all that factual information.

To care means to do the work to gain a wider understanding of any topic in order to make informed judgments that include nuances, not just a thumbs-up or thumbs-down reaction. Our values are not only shaped by hard data, but by the stories that appeal to us, too. An education ought to provide a pathway to examining all of it so our students (who become employees and business owners, professionals and academics, researchers and politicians) can make high-quality, ethically sound decisions for themselves and in their future careers and families.

✳ ACTIVITY: CARING WELL

Kids of all ages can learn the habits of caring to think well and to vet information. Here are a trio of activities that support that development.

Bright-Eyed (5 to 9): Good Habits

For little kids, cultivate the habit of caring early.

1. Read author and illustrator names when you read picture books aloud to your children.
2. Get your "bearings." What other kinds of books does this author or illustrator write? Who are the publishers? Point out where the publisher is listed. Notice publication dates. Can you put the author's books in order of when they were written, if you have more than one?
3. Take a "benchmark." Notice how many pages a book is. Compare one book to another. Get a feel for the number of pages in the books this author writes. Are there any outliers? Are there shorter or longer books that don't fit the pattern? Can you guess why? (Hint: possibly a different genre of book.)

Quick-Witted (10 to 12): Give Credit

Giving credit to a source is like sending a thank-you note after receiving a gift. Passing off someone else's work as your own does not enhance a writer's credibility. It undermines it. Yet in this world of blogging and tweeting, it's easy to forget to cite a source. Try these ideas to get in that good habit.

1. Keep a collection of quotes about a particular subject. Put the author, book title, and page number after each passage this week.
2. Type quotes from several sources (an article, a novel, a poem, a historical record or document). Then on a separate

page, type the names of the authors. On a third page, type the source location (article, novel, poem, historical record or document). Clip the quotes, names, and locations into individual strips. Put them in three groups on a table and then play a matching game. Which goes with which? Allow your students to do some googling, if they need to, to identify which quote belongs to whom.

3. Practice citing themselves as if they had written a novel or a nonfiction book! How would a beat reporter cite your student in an article? How would your student like to be cited? In what kind of pretend source were they cited (interview from a documentary, in a news article, with a quote from a novel or nonfiction piece the student "wrote")? Look up a citation method for how to write that citation. Try another one!

Nimble-Minded (13 to 18): Gather Research

Teens can be tasked with finding more research online. For every source, can they find two more? Can they vet the sources and identify the benchmarks for each one? The goal is to identify reputable sources even if they oppose each other!

1. Identify a controversial topic. Type the topic plus the word "controversy" into an online search engine. Once you identify a controversy within the topic, go to step 2.
2. Find three or four articles about the topic. The articles should represent more than one perspective.
3. Read laterally about each one. Vet the credibility of the writers and/or organization.
4. Identify one benchmark to compare to statistics in each article.

5. Make a bullet list that summarizes the following:
   (a) Reliability of each source
   (b) Validity of a major statistic
   (c) Goal of each article
6. Did the articles support their claims? Why or why not?

Consider it a big achievement to teach a child or teen to care. Caring is the foundation of academic growth and provides the ethical framework for developing well-considered values and beliefs. That said, it can be difficult to maintain an even-keeled disposition when doing research. Our identities and communities influence how our kids read, think, evaluate, and reason. In the next chapter, we look at ways to honor those meaningful aspects of who they are, all while helping our students learn to think critically about any number of topics they may study.

CHAPTER 6

Identity: The Force to Reckon With

And all the worlds you are . . . gather into one world called You.
—Jacqueline Woodson, *Brown Girl Dreaming*

B y now it's obvious that where we live, who we are, and how we understand our world have a big impact on how we think. Our backgrounds and experiences provide the invisible, silent films that play easily in our mind's eye when we take in new information. We hardly notice that our responses are tweaked, torqued, and twisted to fit what we want to be true, what we expect to be true, what we've been conditioned to see as natural. The controlling lens for those silent films comes from our identities. When we talk about self-aware critical thinking, then, we're talking about first identifying the key features that make us who we are.

As we grow up, we learn at the knee—how to be, what outlook to have, who to trust, and who to avoid. Marcus Mescher, Catholic theologian and a professor at my alma mater, Xavier University, addresses how we form these habits of thinking in his wonderful book *The Ethics of Encounter*:

> Imitation is part of the learned pattern of dispositions and actions that take place in the *habitus*, a term used by sociologist Pierre Bourdieu to describe the structures that structure what we hold in common (i.e., what becomes "common sense"). The *habitus* regulates and reproduces unwritten rules. It does not explicitly instruct how to perceive the world or think about the self and others, but it is home to the embodied learning we take for granted: this is how I greet other people—or ignore them—because this is how I see others around me behaving, for example.

Our habits of being and thought come from the identities we absorb unconsciously in our families and communities. "Children imitate parents, adults emulate those they admire, and beliefs and values get passed down."

In other words, we're a bundle of needs and a collection of quirks, learned from our favorite people! That mixture of stuff lives in our bodies and leads to instantaneous, unbidden reactions. We filter what we read and learn through those direct experiences and the point of view we create because of them. Julie (the California girl; UCLA alum; home-birthing, homeschooling mother of five; former speaker of Arabic; divorcée; and white woman of Irish Catholic descent) is an amalgamation of all these influences. Each of us is a composite—a composted person. Noted journalist Ezra Klein expresses it well in his book *Why We're Polarized*: "We will never know how fully we've been shaped by our contexts. Who we are, where we grew up, whom we've learned to trust and fear, love and hate, respect and dismiss—it's deeper than conscious thought. The slate of mental processes built around the millisecond it takes an identity to activate isn't something we can simply slough off." That's why it matters to name the features of what make us who we are so that we can become more conscious of when they're activated when we teach, learn, lead, and parent. Similarly, our students and children do well to keep their identities in mind as they learn.

Our identities have a lot to do with how we imagine we'll be treated in a variety of contexts, which we adjust and adapt as we decide which features to highlight and which to hide, which make us proud and which cause us shame. Sociologist Jessica Calarco points out that fellow "Sociologist C. Wright Mills . . . described using a 'sociological imagination' [to see] how individual human lives are shaped both by 'history and biography.'" She explains: "This means recognizing that people's experiences, decisions, and outcomes are shaped by the larger social contexts in which they live and also their status within those social contexts. . . ." Peggy McIntosh, fellow at Wellesley College, a trailblazer for antiracist work, and a woman who shares my birthday (I liked her better instantly!), wrote an essay called "Unpacking the Invisible Knapsack of Privilege" to highlight ways in which white identity is featured and celebrated in many contexts where nonwhite identity has been actively suppressed. "I have come to see white privilege as an invisible package of unearned assets which I can count on cashing in each day, but about which I was 'meant' to remain oblivious. White privilege is like an invisible weightless knapsack of special provisions, maps, passports, codebooks, visas, clothes, tools and blank checks."

When we talk about privilege, that's what we mean. It's the ease of identity versus the struggle to be seen and valued as you are. Each of us is on that continuum in different ways. Economics, gender, race, religion, location, profession, education—these factors add up to providing us with prospects or barriers to participation. Our expectations of fairness, opportunity, and eventual success and happiness are deeply connected to how we understand ourselves in relationship to others. This self-understanding, in turn, influences how we interact with the issues of the day and with the ideas on offer from social critics, religious leaders, school teachers, and political pundits. The same me (and the same you) shifts and adapts, always creating a story for how we see the world and how we make sense of it. Then, we pass on these stories and expectations to our kids, who in turn form their identities. Parents and educators teach children in their charge narratives about their ancestors, their communities, their nation-state, their religion (or its absence), and their families of origin. Our children do not think in a vacuum. To be a self-aware critical thinker means to take stock of all those identity pieces.

Early in a child's life, identity is the unconscious assumption that the way the world looks to each of us is universal. Each of our identities is felt as natural or true. We bring these perceptions of self with us as we learn. A healthy education expands how a child sees their identity as one among many in the multifaceted world they inhabit. Our identities impact the questions we ask, the assessments we make, our emotional disposition as we read, the credit we give to a source or why we might discount it instead. Identity is the chief factor that must be taken into account to become that flexible, problem-solving, empathetic, strategic thinker! But maybe you're asking: Mary, Mary, quite contrary, how does your identity grow?

Lenses and Filters

Raising children is a dance with lots of tricky steps. It starts reasonably well when your kids adore you and think you're hilarious. There's a moment, though, when they stop laughing because of you, and they start laughing at you. There's a time when your children run into the brick wall of ideas they can't explain away and consider your worldview brittle and backward. Suddenly, your reasonable logic is seen as out-of-date irrelevance. If you pause, you'll remember that moment in your own life—the day you questioned the reasonableness of a belief your parents held as "truth." It may have led to a shouting match! Not to worry.

Challenging assumptions is a developmental milestone and solid evidence of a growing mind.

As I've done research and thought about critical thinking, I've identified four key influences that shape how each of us sees the world. These are the lenses and filters that create a worldview. We each weight these factors differently, which helps make up the rich variety of people who inhabit our big, bold, beautiful globe.

LENSES

These are the prisms through which we look out at the world:

- As an *individual* (inside my skin, on my behalf)
- In a *community* (shared with my "people," shaped by our collective values)

FILTERS

Filters adjust the lenses:

- Via *perception* (the way my body, emotions, and mind make meaning)
- Using *reason* (how my community interprets facts and figures into a story of logic I accept)

LENSES	1 Individual	3 Community
FILTERS	2 Perception	4 Reason

We process information as it comes to us through two primary lenses (the top of the grid): as individuals and as members of a prized community. Then we find a way to express and explain (justify) how we interpret the world using a blend of the two filters at the bottom of the grid: perception and reason. The grid moves from left to right and top to bottom in abstraction and complexity.

Individual + Perception

Let's start with the left column. As an individual, most of your daily choices will be guided by your perceptions of what you need and want. If left to yourself, you will follow those internal nudges to trust or to mistrust, to meet a need or to deny it. If you perceive danger, you'll be cautious. If you need sleep, you'll take a nap. If you're hungry, you'll crave foods that you know taste good and satisfy you. Perceptions are personal—unique to you—and subject to change. They are responsive to the latest, most available input.

Community + Reason

Looking at the right column, as a member of a community, you learn the parameters of membership. Your community will give a reasonable account (a logic story) to explain its beliefs. For instance, you may be a part of a religious or diet community that has something to say about the foods members can and can't eat. Without their teachings, you wouldn't know which foods should be avoided—in one community, for religious reasons; in the other, for health reasons. Communities come in a number of varieties. They range from family of origin to being a student in a school, from following a fitness program to joining a political protest movement, from becoming a foster parent to working in the Corps of Engineers. Even our media choices can be considered communities that help shape our worldview.

Individuals adjust their perceptions to fit with a community's belief package. We use reason to help bridge that gap. Our communities provide a logic story to justify why an individual should modify their personal practices to suit the community's values. One way to understand faith study groups or online membership communities is that they provide a place for members to rehearse the logic story of their beliefs to help individuals stay the course in spite of their natural perceptions or preferences. In other words, if you're a member of a diabetes diet community, you'll learn to lay off sugar, for instance, despite the pleasure of eating a cookie!

Individual + Community

Looking at the top row, let's examine the relationship between an individual and a community. The right to free speech is considered an unalienable right of the individual. Yet our judiciary has affirmed restrictions as to time, place, and manner of use. Individuals are not allowed to yell "There's a bomb" in an airport when there isn't one. Free speech is restricted if it incites chaos or danger for others. The individual right is modified by community needs. A benign example of individual rights versus community values is the homeowner's association. These organizations enforce community standards, like a prohibition against line-drying laundry. Even if you want to hang your own laundry in your own backyard, you can't. The priority is on community values over individual choice. It might be possible to get an exception, as an individual, if you can demonstrate that your laundry line will be hidden from view or your electricity is out. That said, the community has the power to grant or withhold those permissions. The nexus of most court cases happens right here—between individual rights and community values. Which gets priority and to what extent in each case?

Perception + Reason

The bottom row of the grid describes the filters we use to bolster our views (whether protecting an individual right or advocating for a community value). Our perceptions govern us at an individual level. Our perceptions are created through emotions, direct and indirect experiences, anecdotes that stay with us, triumphs, and trauma. We build an internal framework of what makes the world feel right side up or what feels like a threat. Perceptions can be accurate or inaccurate. Communities use reason to create a coherent logic story to explain personal perceptions in light of community values. These stories, too, can be accurate or inaccurate.

For instance, we consult our personal experiences to determine whether or not we feel we're getting a fair deal. A woman might believe that she was overlooked for a job promotion because she was pregnant. If the woman is active in a feminist organization, her community may confirm her suspicions by providing statistics about pregnant women in the workplace. If the woman is a member of a conservative religious community, however, she might be guided to reconsider her perception. She may be told to consider that her boss chose to prioritize her calling as a mother by not promoting her. It's possible that both interpretations are wrong! It could be that the woman didn't get the job advancement due to poor performance. That's why it's so critical to take in more than one viewpoint when we are tempted to form interpretations.

Our first interactions with the world come via individual perceptions. As children, we become accustomed to meeting our personal needs or getting adults to meet them for us. The first community that helps kids interpret their perceptions is their family. Each of us develops a "family habits and beliefs" fluency—the *habitus*. Our dinnertime conversations, weekly routines, the television shows we watch, the radio shows we listen to, the family's religious identity (or lack thereof), how we vote—all of this is taught explicitly and modeled implicitly. For instance, parents tell a logic story of why their kids need to bathe every day, using facts about invisible germs to coerce a child to wash, in spite of the child's perception: "I don't like how the water feels on my skin." The family community uses the logic story of hygiene to override the child's personal perception. See how it works? Children absorb the content of the parental beliefs and practices by osmosis, uncritically, as true, even though initially the "unconverted" toddler may still throw a tantrum of resistance before eventually adopting the family belief system. By the time those same kids are teenagers, they begin to challenge the family's logic stories and assert their new community's identity: the logic story of other teens! And naturally, they may also be bumping up against other communities, learning other interpretive lenses to apply to their personal perceptions.

Communities often tell their most powerful logic stories when they want to *overturn* individual perception: requirements around food and sex, how to think about death, what constitutes a legitimate marriage, who should own guns, how we should treat the environment, how to view people different from us, what to do with moral failings, when war is justified, understanding our origins, what keeps us accountable, how we should be governed, who's trustworthy and who isn't. Communities excel at filtering the overwhelming experience of being human—subject to our own perceptions—by giving our experiences order and meaning.

Conspiracy theories are a powerful example of the logic story in action. If you take the list of purported "facts" of a theory and strip them of their narrative context (without motive and personality, intention and strategy), oftentimes the theory falls apart. The "why" is the powerful thread that holds the unproven claims together. For instance, the conspiracy theory that the moon landing happened in a basement in Hollywood is meaningless without a motive of some kind. The staying power of a conspiracy theory is the story it tells—regardless of the facts (carefully vetted or not).

In the United States, the original framers of the Constitution sought to provide a flexible-enough framework for the plurality of individual rights and community values. They believed that the country was big enough and fair enough for a variety of communities to exist alongside one another without requiring everyone to adopt the same logic story or belief system. As political theorist John Rawls explains in *Justice as*

Fairness, a democratic society views individuals as free and equal. These individuals choose to enter into a social and political arrangement that provides for the smooth functioning of society, even while protecting the unique beliefs and doctrines of various communities. Rawls summarizes: "The most fundamental idea in this conception of justice is the idea of society as a fair system of social cooperation over time, one generation to the next." This balancing act between free individuals and community identities is pretty high-level stuff. Naturally, the question becomes: What do we do when an individual right and community logic story come into conflict? Which one is prioritized? Lots of court cases litigate that question. Their task? Providing for maximum freedom to each individual and protection of community values without impinging on the similar rights granted to others.

A great example of how this works is seen in our use of zoning laws. In 1926, a case called *The Village of Euclid v. Amber Realty Co.* came before the Supreme Court. Euclid sought to prohibit businesses from setting up shop in suburban neighborhoods. The court ruled in Euclid's favor and established the right of communities to enact zoning laws "for the purpose of promoting the health, safety, morals, or general welfare of the community." According to legal expert David Christiansen:

> The central concern in Euclid was whether the creation of residential districts that excluded all industrial uses was valid. The Court held that the community's health and safety would be promoted by separating the dwellings, diminishing traffic flow of vehicles, and reducing the influx of strange persons into the residential neighborhoods. Therefore, under the Euclid reasoning, although an intangible, the quality of life is an interest that a community can attempt to control through zoning regulations.

How's that for a classic description of individual rights and community values going toe-to-toe in the courts? In the ensuing decades, zoning laws have been used to regulate the location of so-called adult stores, like Hustler. In the states of Ohio, Kentucky, and Indiana, Larry Flynt (Hustler CEO) repeatedly sued municipalities over what he perceived as violations of his right to put his stores in the most lucrative locations. The zoning laws were cited as justification for regulating where Hustler could conduct business. The clash between promoting individual rights to engage in commerce versus protecting community and family values has been resolved more than once by moving "adult stores" beyond city limits, away from neighborhoods.

Community values and individual rights negotiate how to live together all the time. It's an ongoing challenge. Paying attention to which of these two impulses is guiding our thinking is part of being a self-aware critical thinker and goes to the heart of the identity question. Which do we foreground, our personal rights or our community values? You can take a quick inventory of your cherished beliefs and you'll see which ones derive from what you value for yourself and which promote your community's logic story—or some combination of the two.

Teach Your Children Well

Whew. Is your head throbbing? That's a lot to take in quickly. What's all this got to do with raising critical thinkers, you ask? The worldview of each child exerts a tremendous influence on how they learn, what they learn, and what they believe about themselves. Parents and educators also bring a well-formed worldview to the teaching task. Unmasking that belief structure is essential. Incidentally, "objectivity in teaching" is a logic story academics tell—that there's a way to engage with a topic that removes bias. The fact is, however, even what gets included or excluded in a lesson impacts that so-called objectivity. To be objective is a noble goal left over from the Enlightenment, but we've learned in the centuries since that it can never be perfectly achieved.

Try these questions to get to the heart of worldview and build the skills of self-awareness. Sometimes we focus too much on how a child feels when a whole lot more is going on inside.

- Where did you get that idea?
- Why do you think that is?
- Who told you that?
- Do you think that's true?
- How do you know that's true?
- What are other possible explanations?
- What do you think X person might say about that?
- Is this what you believe, or is it what you think you should believe?
- Who do you think benefits from that viewpoint, and who might be harmed by it, if anyone?

Aspects of Identity

I looked for research done into the role of identity in critical thinking and stumbled upon the excellent work of Dr. Gholdy Muhammad, literacy and language expert and author of the best-selling book *Cultivating Genius*. Muhammad promotes the study of identity as a key component for becoming a well-educated person. Identity, according to Muhammad, has three key features: "who we are, who others say we are (both positive and negative features), and whom we desire to be." These three aspects of identity are important to consider about ourselves, but also about anyone whose work we study. As we saw in the worldview grid, identity is more than naming your race, religion, and politics. It's discovering that the who-you-are-ness of who you are is essential to the academic task.

Let's dig a little deeper into the three aspects of identity that Muhammad itemizes. "Who you are" is the sense of self that is inherent—it's the "what you know to be true" about you: where you're from, what likes and dislikes make you yourself, how you make sense of your life, what particular personality quirks and personal needs are present. Your individual perceptions influence how you see yourself. "Who others say you are" points to the community to which you belong and the communities beyond your own that define you. Our first community identity is our own family. As we've seen, our families belong to other groups such as faith communities or racial and ethnic groups or neighborhoods or political parties.

"Who others say you are" exerts a surprising influence on how you see yourself. We're not only defined by communities that approve of us, but also by those who disapprove. Sometimes those voices are the loudest in our heads. Parents, relatives, coaches, faith leaders, teachers, and friends suggest from earliest childhood who a child ought to aspire to be, or conversely, they may imply limits to what can be achieved. One of the students I taught told me her mother didn't want her to go to college because she "shouldn't try to reach beyond her 'raisin's"—how she was raised. A limit like that can derail a student's ambitions.

Textbooks, news media, billboards, films, novels, and popular culture also tell us who we are. We internalize those portraits and then make judgments about who we will become on that basis. Some of us don't realize until our thirties and forties that our ladders of success were leaning against the wrong wall—the wall someone else chose for us!

Not only that, for individuals who experience the effects of discrimination at the hands of the dominant culture, they grapple with multiple portraits of their identities from members inside and outside their communities. They may experience solidarity and value from within their own group, they may be given coping strategies for those times they are in the minority, they may feel pressure by their families to represent their community well, and they may endure the weight of unfair expectations or prejudices by the larger culture. Identity is complex.

The third category—"whom you desire to be"—is another fascinating way to think about yourself. As important as origin is, this hunger to become an idealized version of self in order to be *seen* in a specific way exerts an enormous influence on who you become. The classic A student may be more interested in class rank than mastery of subject matter, for instance. A child may never grasp why math is essential to his education if his singular goal is to be a YouTube gaming star.

"Our students, and arguably adults, are always looking for themselves in spaces and places," Muhammad writes. Because of that drive, critical thinking needs to take into account the impact of both our identity's presence and absence in the subject matter being taught. We can aspire to a future if we can imagine ourselves in it. I'm reminded of Newbery Medal–winning author Kwame Alexander expressing his hunger to see himself represented in novels as a child. He shared that his school library did not have books featuring people of color as main characters or authors. However, growing up in his family home, with parents who were writers and publishers, he enjoyed walls of books written by Black authors, populated by Black main characters. As a Black author today, he expressed how critical it was for him to see that it was possible both to be featured in a story as a main character and to discover that Black writers could become published authors, writing about their unique experiences. According to Kwame, "My parents were my first teachers, and my first librarians." A rich education is a representative one.

Books and classrooms that feature the same group, same experiences, same perspective again and again lead to a feeling of exclusion and alienation for those who don't identify with that group. Conversely, if a child is a member of a group that is repeatedly displayed as normative, children can get the mistaken sense that their worldview is the exclusively right one.

Personhood

So let's start with the individual child. We pay deep respect to the personhood of each learner—recognizing how important it is to be *seen* and *known*. It can be difficult to name what's invisible to you. It isn't until you leave the house and enter someone else's home that you may realize there are other ways to exist in the world that make sense, too. When I was six years old, I visited the home of my Chinese American neighbors. They asked me to remove my shoes before entering the house. I can still see that home in my mind's eye—the plastic-covered couches, the white carpeting, the uncluttered space. It made such an impression. Keeping a clean house was a high priority for this family. When I lived in Morocco and visited Japan in my twenties, I discovered two more places that treated shoe-wearing indoors as unhygienic. It was a moment, twenty years in the making, when I finally asked the question: "Was my family the anomaly here? Do most people on the planet see it as recklessly unsanitary to wear shoes indoors?" The plates tilted—my experience no longer the dominant story.

Identity, then, is the taken-for-granted perspective we carry with us naturally day after day. To grow a mind, meeting a wide range of people from a variety of backgrounds is essential. It's often only through contrast with other stories and experiences that we grow our capacity to think critically about our *own* stories, the essential first step in self-aware thinking. Let's do that now. Let's help our children name their own stories as a step toward self-aware thinking. (By the way: you can do this identity work, too.) In the ensuing chapters, we look at what to do with the experiences of others.

The Composted Self

The self is a compost of many contributing nutrients, large and small, that slowly merge to form the soil in which an identity forms. The body contains these selves who evolve and change, who react and reform, who combust to create new perspectives. Think of a fertile garden that grows insight. Insight needs fertilizer. Our children, as they read and absorb information, do best when the soil is rich—drawing from a variety of sources. Our perspectives suffer when we are limited to a narrow diet (like only learning history through a textbook, or only learning math as an act of paper and pencil, or only learning to write using formats).

We're going to look at the three key components of that compost (reading, experiences, and encounters with other people—in part 2). Before we do, it helps to take a soil sample, as it were. Because they are children, we'll start with concrete observations that they can easily make. No conclusions need to be drawn, just keenly observing (as discussed in chapter 4) their own rich soil of identity.

✳ ACTIVITY: "I AM FROM" POEM

This poem can be written for all levels (bright-eyed, quick-witted, and nimble-minded: 5 to 18 years old). You'll provide a lot more support to your youngest kids. For your teens, invite them to draw outside the lines—they can go beyond literal answers. The "I Am From" poem is a pleasure to write. The structure is simple. Each new line starts with the phrase "I am from. . . ." Naturally, geographical location is part of what it means to be "from" somewhere. But we are also from a kind of cooking, a religious or nonreligious tradition, from sounds and sights, from memories and holidays, from pain and joy.

My son Liam wrote a powerful "I am from . . ." poem that I'd like to share here with you as an example:

Liam Bogart (15 years of age)

I am from the burning of Christmas trees
I am from the journaling of swirling listless leaves
I am from homemade paper cranes, haikus, and calendars
I am from Easter, pipe smoking, and golden eggs

I am from candles, lopsided beeswax

I am from nonexistent Santa myths

I am from vegan cinnamon rolls

I am from Blessing, Mr. Darcy and the blessings of Mr. Darcy

I am from Frodo Baggins

I am from *Redwall*

I am from *Harry Potter*, passed around in Italy

I am from the *Odyssey*, read aloud to silent children

I am from *History of the World* and a sleeping mom

I am from *The Name of the Wind* in Chicago

I am from myopic Jake and Noah the Duke

I am from silver-tongued Caitrin and Johannah the only 6 of 5

I am from obscenities yelled over *Starcraft* lost

I am from subconsciously learned grammar, Chomsky,
and Julie

I am from brave thinking and brave writing

I am from nonexistent science and Ing Wan's math

I am from homeschool, unschool, high school and college

Instructions

Everyone can participate, even parents and teachers! Share the writing risk—be collaborators in learning.

Use a whiteboard or clipboard to record these initial answers.

Ask the following questions to stir up concepts to include, initially recording the answers on a whiteboard or clipboard:

- Identify your background (ethnic, religious, cultural, nationality . . . whatever defines you for you).
- Name where you live (and have lived). Describe those places with a few words: nouns or adjectives.
- Name places you've visited.

- Name your favorite foods.
- Select four adjectives to describe yourself.
- Select a few adjectives to describe your family.
- What family holidays and traditions are important to you? Think about particular traditions, too. Like in our family, we burn the Christmas tree in July and we smoke corn cob pipes on Easter.
- Name the communities that you are a part of.
- What habits are your own? What habits have you learned from your community?
- What stories, songs, or legends and myths do you love?
- List two or three memorable experiences in your life (could be a happy memory, like winning a tournament, or an unhappy one, like going in for surgery). Could be how you found a book on a tram in Chicago and read it there (like *The Name of the Wind* by Patrick Rothfuss, in Liam's poem).
- What textures, scents, tastes, and sounds do you associate with your childhood so far? Might be vanilla-scented candles or dust, could be Lysol or chili in a Crock-Pot . . .

Consider these categories, too:

- Who I say I am
- Who others say I am
- Who I aspire to be

Take these lists and add "I am from" to the start of each phrase or word. Type the list and triple space. Then print. Snip the sentences into strips and rearrange them into the most

- pleasing sequence. Staple each one to a page in the order you approve, rearrange on the computer, and print the final copy. Feel free to embellish or change words as you read and reread.
- It helps to read the sentences aloud—to hear the words and sequence as you revise. Some kids prefer to handwrite the final version and illustrate it with sketches.

Identity is the foundation for all of what your students do as critical thinkers. Keep the "I Am From . . ." poems handy as a useful portrait to return to.

As Ezra Klein says, "[I]dentity doesn't just shape how we treat each other. It shapes how we understand the world." As we've seen in part 1, identity is more than a couple of boxes to tick on a census form. Our children's storytellers, their individual perceptions, their community's values, how much they care about what they're learning, and how they understand who they are determine the lens for how they interpret anything they learn.

PART 2

. . . .

Read, Experience, Encounter:
A Real Education

The best way to be kind to bears is not to be very close to them.
—Margaret Atwood, *MaddAddam*

Ready for a striptease? Academic subjects are typically bundled in bulky, ill-fitting clothes, like a dense, tedious textbook or a lecture so dull, college students schedule their naps during it. The heart of any field of study, however, is exciting and provocative. Now that we've figured out who *your kids are*, let's see if we can undress the academic task and look beneath all those layers.

Beware the Bear

When my children were small, they became enamored with animals, particularly bears. We read books about bears. The two-dimensional pages, no more than 8½ × 11 inches in size, contained the two-thousand-pound animal and often depicted those bears with hats, dresses, and smiles. We knew the bears as a porridge-loving family whose home was invaded by a blond human. We knew the bears as a family called Berenstain whose squabbles were as familiar as our own. We knew Paddington bear, wearing a mackintosh and hat, who traveled with a suitcase and umbrella around the world.

Realistic bears populated our nonfiction titles. We read about polar and brown bears, black bears and giant pandas. We were happily safe from the bears in our books. They lived on two-dimensional paper, and we could leave those bears on a bookshelf at any time. As a result, we romanticized bears as lovable and enjoyed them as stuffed animals so small that my children were comforted by cuddling teddy bears as they slept.

To give my kids a greater experience of "bear," I took them to the zoo. There, real bears paced back and forth inside their animal enclosures. These living bears were huge to our eyes; they smelled like musty fur and droppings; their claws curved sharp and dangerous; and the bears yawned or grumbled audibly with a deep, throaty resonance. Suddenly, all that we thought we knew about bears deepened. We were still at a safe distance (behind the barrier), but we had a new appreciation for the scary scale and majesty of the bear. At home, we watched films about bears so we could see their behavior in the wild, too, not just in a zoo context. Both of these experiences deepened our relationship with "bear."

My mother, however, has known bears in far more precarious and personal ways. She's gone backpacking every summer in the mountains of California for forty years. She learned to take precautions to protect her food, tent, and herself from bear encounters. Even with all that painstaking care, she's run into a few bears in the wild, directly. Imagine waking up to pee in the middle of the night, leaving your flimsy tent behind to find a private spot in the woods, dropping your drawers, only to look up and see eight feet of brown bear on hind legs only fifty yards away. That brush with the bear? No time for careful thought. The ferocity, the odor, the unpredictability, the danger were all-consuming.

This bear encounter completely overwhelmed and simultaneously overturned anything my mother thought she understood about bears from field guides and zoos. Naturally, reading about bears conveys more detailed and specific factual information about "What is a bear?" and, "How shall I protect my campsite from bears?" than seeing one in the mountains, by moonlight, while trying to pee in peace. That said, running into a real bear in the wild delivered a kind of message no book could—what it feels like to be in the bear's natural habitat, to be the interloper, to be vulnerable to the unpredictable movements and instincts of a real bear.

My mother survived all her bear encounters (and there were many) and put them in a book to share with my children at bedtime. Once again, we gratefully enjoyed the two-dimensional bear on the page, under our control, allowing us to laugh in the face of danger—and then leave the bears in the book at any time.

How We Learn

The handiest, safest way to learn is through *reading*. We can read about any topic, consuming the information quickly with detail. If we want to read about violins, we can learn how they are made, what kinds of music are written for them, who has played violins, and more. Yet reading about the violin falls short of *knowing* the violin. No one would say that to read extensively about a violin is a sufficient way to understand a violin (no matter how beautifully the writer describes its sound). We could even learn to read music written for violin, but short of hearing it played, we still wouldn't know a violin as it's meant to be enjoyed.

The next best way to deepen learning is to add direct *experience*. Perhaps you listen to a violin solo on YouTube or watch a violinist on a television special. You might go to a symphony one night and then to a local bar to hear a fiddler play bluegrass the next—two kinds of violin music. Could you visit a luthier and watch how a violin is made?

Sure. These experiences put us in more proximal contact with violins. However, even if I had a vast knowledge of orchestral music, *playing* a violin is a whole other level. Hand me a violin, and instantly I'll feel at a loss as to how to make even the scratchiest of sounds. There's an art, a feel, a skill to playing that you can't get through reading and experiencing violin music.

That leads us to the next way of knowing: encounter. A direct *encounter* with "violin" means grappling with the instrument directly. It means developing skills, not merely appreciating its beautiful music. Encounter gives way to respect—an appreciation for the skill it takes to play that overrides flippant criticisms from the peanut gallery. In fact, you're likely to enjoy listening to violins even more after trying to play one. Encounter is transformational. A true encounter (whether with a topic, or a person, or a musical instrument, or a bear in the wild) overturns preconceptions, often inspires empathy and respect, and deepens the mystery of what is being known in an up-close and personal way.

The more we engage with a topic for study, the more nuance and intimacy we discover. Each time we read about a topic, then add experiences to that understanding, and finally encounter it directly, we put more and more of ourselves at risk—which may lead to being pleasantly surprised and reassured by what we find, or startled into new insight, or challenged to grow, or moved to appropriate levels of distress. Each layer leads to a more skillful relationship to the topic because we come to know it with more of ourselves.

Naturally, we can't all become expert violinists or meet every animal in the wild in order to have a comprehensive education. However, becoming a skilled thinker does mean using these three vehicles whenever possible. A surprising side benefit of this approach is humility. Many online conversations would be far more productive if people recognized the limits to their understanding by thinking through these three levels of engagement with any topic. How can we speak with authority if we've only read about the topic and have never heard its music?

As we raise kids to be critical thinkers, it's great modeling to admit the limits of our own understanding. If all we've ever known about a topic is what we've read, then we aren't experts—no matter how persuaded we feel. We may have extensive information, but that's it. How much can you really know about another country without having lived there? How skillfully can you evaluate a theory in a scientific field, for instance, if you haven't been trained in the tools that allow experts to draw those conclusions? How much can you say about another religion if you've never been a practitioner or been close to someone who is? How well can you assert a point of view if you've never spent time with people who are negatively impacted by that view?

Let's take a deep dive into how these three avenues—reading, experience, and encounter—grow critical thinkers. Yes, you're about to use reading to learn. If you want the benefits of the insights I offer here, however, I urge you to do the activities along the way. They'll deepen your own learning through experience and encounter.

CHAPTER 7

Reading: Up Close and Personal

Close reading, then, should not imply that we ignore the reader's experience and attend closely to the text and nothing else. It should imply that we bring the text and the reader *close* together.

—Kylene Beers, Robert E. Probst, *Notice and Note*

When I was a girl, my mother instituted a bedtime policy: I could stay up as late as I liked, if I stayed in bed reading. Even if she kissed me good night at eight thirty, I could keep the lights on and read until midnight, if I could stay awake. Countless nights I woke at 2:00 a.m. with a book slumped open on my chest. I'd rouse myself enough to tuck the bookmark between the pages, flip the light switch, and fall back to sleep. I grew a love of reading in the comfort of my own bed, under a well-lit lamp, tucked in with a comforter and fluffy pillow, room temperature an even seventy degrees year-round.

We're told again and again that the heart of a good education is found in books. As long as we can read, we're on the path to a vibrant intellect and becoming an informed person, right?

I'm here to explode that myth. You're welcome.

Reading is powerful, but it's also safe. Did you catch the context of my "love of reading" life? I could read about the snowy Alps while snuggling under warm covers, without experiencing the slightest chill. I could read about Jews escaping Germany to Denmark during the Holocaust, safely in my suburban, twentieth-century, California bedroom. With reading, the risks are low—both physically (barring the odd papercut) and intellectually. Hear me out. It's not that reading material can't be emotionally raw, subversive, or political. When we allow our imaginations to include the intimate revelations of the writer, we may in fact be moved deeply. It's just that the reader decides whether to *keep reading*. The reader decides what credit to give to the content, how receptive to be to the point of view. Readers can create distance between themselves and the writer and topic, or they can invite them in and receive their message.

For instance, when I read, I can compartmentalize the troubling ideas and give greater weight to what I support. I can skip statistics (by the way, I *frequently* do—numbers don't stick with me easily, and I find it difficult to imagine the scope of them). But my skipping them does pose a good question: What is the net impact when a writer uses statistics to make a case? Will I miss the point, go unpersuaded? When we read, we bring our personalities and preferences, our current circumstances and needs with us no matter the goal and agenda of the author.

I can ignore a well-made argument or double down on the ones I like. I can read earnestly or skeptically. Not sure that's true? Hop on your favorite social media space. How do you read the people who align with your politics? What about the ones who don't? Do you trust them and their "facts" equally? Why or why not? My point: reading is fully under our control, and what we choose to absorb or adopt as true is up to us, no matter how well the researcher provides peer-reviewed studies and data.

Reading allows us to explore (at a safe distance) all kinds of information. For instance, readers can travel through historical fiction to India and learn about the time of the partition with Pakistan while rooting for the lead characters to fall in love. Kids can read about the five-hundred-year history of the Roman Empire in a two-hundred-page comic book. A friend might send you a *New York Times* article about the Rohingya, a Muslim ethnic group from Myanmar who are victims of genocide, yet you decide how to value it: whether to scan, read, or file it. You might become passionate about their plight and critical of organizations not doing enough to help alleviate their suffering, all without traveling to Asia or having sent a single dollar to support those human rights activists. We assert opinions based on what we read, without fully understanding the complex dynamics firsthand. Reading allows all of us to consume (to become consumers of) a wide variety of information but requires no action on our parts. In the worst cases, reading enables us to feel smugly well informed with a right to strong opinions, even when we haven't put anything of ourselves at risk.

Today, the bulk of most people's reading happens online—snippets of opinion released in unending real time on Twitter, Facebook status updates of people you haven't cared about in years prompting you to care, Instagram photos paired with captions, news articles and opinion pieces on websites you select because you "like" them, the ever-changing Wikipedia pages with their helpful summaries and inevitable inaccuracies indistinguishable from each other at first glance. I pop through blog articles checking publication dates hoping to read essays written within the last year. My mind naturally resists content that's more than a year or two old—information glut is real, and an article from five years ago already feels out of date. Meanwhile, the tech industry designs algorithms that are meant to engage us with content they select, based on their analysis of what might draw our attention and keep us on their social media sites.

Our children are even less equipped to evaluate what they read.

Socrates said all those years ago before most people were literate, and long before the printing press and the internet: "The unexamined life is not worth living." I want to tweak Socrates's timeless wisdom to say: "The unexamined life ought not read books or surf the internet." An examined life allows us to read critically, with more awareness, with healthy skepticism, with an openness to being changed by what we read. The skill called "examination" is the ability to discern or differentiate, to identify what is useful and what is rubbish—or even more, the ability to say truthfully, "I don't know which is which." That's the essence of critical thought.

Literacy gives a person agency—the chance to become informed by choice, to gain perspective, to shape opinions—if we read with critical awareness. In a thinker's diet, reading makes up the largest percentage of our input and sources. Reading matters, in both its vastness and its limits. What we want to bring to reading is a curious mind, an expansive imagination, and a hunger to know. Reading and writing are not merely about deciphering text and transcribing thoughts, then, but the power to matter to self and to others.

Literacy

Right now, you're reading text. If you use your eyes to read a book or a screen, you're in the act of what literacy specialists call "decoding." Once readers get a word sounded out, their minds shuffle through possible meanings of the word and what it is meant to do in this new, unfamiliar context. For new readers, sometimes the struggle to sound out is so taxing that by the time the word is formed in the mouth, the brain no longer has the energy or working memory to make it make sense. The little reader can't answer a question about the story—our student has only successfully decoded the words. Once the reader has put in the disciplined work to learn how to decode language and achieved the necessary level of speed and accuracy, the next level of literacy is available:

making meaning of the sentences when taken together. Comprehension at this level means the ability to restate information after reading. The next level of reading comprehension, however, is a more sophisticated still: "A reader must call upon both word knowledge and world knowledge (including experience) to make sense of any text." In this sense, the reader is joining a conversation in progress. The reader can decode both the words and the world of ideas.

Literacy can be understood more broadly as well. For instance, visual literacy includes images and symbols. What's the difference for a new baby between "that person in the green scrubs" and "the person in the bed cuddling me"? We know that one is a nurse and the other is a new mother. From the moment of birth, a baby is confronted with interpreting her visually accessed world, learning symbols and signals that will help her make sense of living among people. According to Brian Kennedy, the director of the Toledo Museum of Art, "Visual literacy is the ability to construct meaning from images. It's not a skill. It uses skills as a toolbox. It's a form of critical thinking that enhances your intellectual capacity." To decode an image or a symbol *is* to apply critical thinking skills to reading. Today, we use the term "literacy" to refer to a wide range of disciplines that require basic knowledge, too. For instance, we might talk about "computer literacy" or "math literacy" or "workplace literacy." These word pairs expand the definition of literacy to go beyond decoding letters to sounds and basic meaning. Instead, they point to a larger scope or broader context—literacy is having fluency in the vocabulary, symbols, and practices of a specific domain.

Let me share a story about symbol literacy that I experienced as an adult that reminded me of both a fluency and lack of fluency of mine. I flew to Japan on Singapore Airlines decades ago. I made my way to the tiny bathroom at the back of the plane. I pushed open the accordion door, slid my pants down my legs, and paused mid-bend at the waist to notice a pair of images explaining how to use the toilet. My initial reaction was surprise. Were there people who didn't know how to use a toilet? One image showed the shape of a person squatting—both feet on the toilet seat. This image had a red X over it. The next image showed a shape of a person sitting on the toilet seat with both feet on the ground. No X. I read these images left to right.

One level of image literacy: the ability to decode illustrations. The pictures were a bit like cartoons—hand-drawings of body shapes, not photographs. Literate image readers recognize the two-dimensional shapes as representing real-world items and people. I easily understood that the drawings corresponded to the toilet and a human being. I'm used to seeing shapes that represent real-world items and people. But that skill has to be learned; it's not automatic. Have you ever been to a pair of bathrooms in a themed restaurant, for instance, and the owners have been too clever in their illustrations, perhaps using hats to indicate men and women? If your western hat literacy is not up to snuff, you may wonder which bathroom is for "cowgirls" and which is for "cowboys"! That's what I'm getting at here.

Another feature of image literacy in that cabin was the ability to interpret the big red X over the first image. I knew that if there was an X, it meant "not this way" or "this is forbidden." I wondered: *What if the person in the cabin was from Thailand or India or another country that used a different orthography? Did readers of Thai or Hindi use the roman letter X in this way to indicate "forbidden"?* I understood the color red to mean "don't do this." I wondered again: *Does everyone know that? Is red a globally recognized interdiction color?* Perhaps the stop sign has made it universally understood. Truth be told: a stop sign could have been blue or even green. At some point the collective "we" decided to associate the color "red" with the meaning "stop"—a color literacy that has to be learned.

A third aspect of image literacy, then, was the ability to interpret meaning. These toilet signs were not decorations. I was meant to apply a lesson. The first posture on the toilet was forbidden, and the second posture was correct. I asked myself *who* needed this gentle instruction?

It was the first time I realized that some people in the world were not "western toilet" literate. They had a different method of handling their business. The images were meant to instruct wordlessly. I was nonplussed since I understood the symbols and had used a western toilet all my life. (As fate would have it, I moved to Morocco that year, and my first apartment provided a squat toilet—and I had to learn how to use it without helpful images to instruct me!)

Hours later, our plane landed in Japan. In Tokyo, I entered Narita International Airport and a high-tech toilet experience I still don't know how to interpret. The stalls were mini cabins with floor-to-ceiling doors. The space-age toilet gleamed white and had a multitude of buttons with Japanese characters next to them that I couldn't decipher. There were buttons on the wall, on the toilet itself, and no obvious knobs or flushing handles. I knew to sit down but was alarmed that there was no seat cover. I couldn't figure out how to flush. I spent several minutes in awe of all the buttons, afraid to push them, and then realized I'd only learn what they did if I took a risk and pressed them. Five minutes of carefree button pushing, water movement, and surprised laughter followed. One button triggered a toilet cover zinging around the seat with a loud whizzing sound—too late to be used. I pushed another button that made a flushing sound but did not dispense water. I learned later that the Japanese are a modest people. They like to flush twice in public places to cover the sound of urinating. To save water, this flushing sound effect had been added to public bathrooms to give the Japanese a provision for their modesty. After several other random button pushes, the water suddenly flushed—surprise! I burst out laughing. I'm pretty sure I still don't have toilet fluency in Japan. That said, I knew enough to press buttons. I had learned early in life that buttons were for pressing! A literacy that bailed me out that day.

My confident toilet use on the plane was dethroned (ha!) in Tokyo. It occurs to me now as I think back on the two toilet experiences that our sense of power and powerlessness has a lot to do with how well we can *read* in any circumstance—reading people, signs, language, faces, machines, traffic, viewpoints, and more. Perhaps culture stress is merely exhaustion from learning to "sound out" and interpret a new culture, language, food system, currency, set of mannerisms, and place when reading in a new environment. Imagine how exhausting it is to be a child, then, to become literate in so many areas all day, every day, on top of lessons from school. As young kids grow up, they learn to read and interpret a parent's face, voice, body language, and intonation—when to relax and when to get that butt in gear! Now imagine being a child with a learning disability. A whole other level of challenge.

Decoding faces, behaviors, social cues, tone of voice—these are literacies we build from very early in our lives to help us get along with each other. Think about how your toddler doesn't always recognize your urgency or insistence. It takes time to realize that tone of voice, not just the words, is communication. Next time a child whiffs on responding to your irritation, ask yourself: *How fluent is my child in my irritated tone of voice?* Maybe he needs a little crash course in "Hey! Follow through, little man!" Similarly, how frequently does a teen misinterpret a text message from a parent and vice versa? The younger generation has revolutionized how we express tone of voice in writing because of texting— yet another literacy to master!

The point is, we have to decode all varieties of language and images in order to operate in our increasingly symbol-dependent world. While the term "literacy" is more frequently associated with decoding alphabets for reading, I'm broadening its use here to include the way we also decipher an ever-increasing array of images to build a lexicon of meanings for those symbols. For driving, we decode traffic signs, lights, and paint lines on the road. We read gauges on the dashboard of a car. A previous experience with one make and model of car allows us to make better guesses each time we climb into another one. Assembly instructions for furniture and laundering directions for clothing must be deciphered (pause and notice the word: de-ciphered—literally undoing the cipher—decoding the pictograph) in order to build the table or avoid ruining a *dry-clean-only* blouse.

What other "literacies and lexicons" do you and/or your kids use every day?

- Managing your life on a smartphone
- Computer programming
- Online searching
- Remote control use and recording programs on a DVR
- Navigating streaming services on a variety of devices
- Operating machines like a dishwasher or leaf blower
- Reading a recipe and making the food
- Playing card, board, and online games
- Following the directions for a LEGO set or furniture from IKEA
- Interpreting emoticons in a text message
- Telling time on an analog clock
- Navigating an airport in a foreign country
- Sewing on a machine and following a pattern
- Reading the scoreboard for a sporting event
- Recognizing a profession by uniform
- Understanding receipts and ticket stubs
- Interpreting financial charts from an investment account

I like to think of these as "little literacies and lexicons," all the ways we learn to read our environment and everything in it. Each time your kids learn how to follow a pattern of information, they've mastered another "reading" skill, and they've applied their critical thinking powers to it. In today's technological landscape, the number of literacies and lexicons we're expected to master is exponentially exploding. Our globalized drive for sameness has created the perfect environment for symbols to thrive, bypassing the need for language translations. Our children are digital natives who are able to use technology without an accent. For people my age, we call the nearest teenager to bail us out of technical troubles.

As you raise kids, it's useful to note the variety of literacies and lexicons they call on to interpret their world, and to value them. It's taxing to both decode and interpret all day long. Each time they succeed, they've added another data set to their ability to better read and interpret. The truth is, these literacies and lexicons are deeply connected to our sense of place, our religious or nonreligious backgrounds, and our experiences in life. The interpretations we give to what we "read" shapes our identities and our worldviews. It takes deliberate effort to make space for someone else's quite different background as they report how they see the world from where they stand. We're all interpreting all the time, and we don't all have the same level of skill in every subject domain. Moreover, we don't all interpret the same information the same ways. It's possible to use the same words or identical symbols and intend entirely different meanings. "Deeper literacy is metacognitive," explains Rita Cevasco, speech and language pathologist (SLP) and founder of Rooted in Language. "We can recognize and appreciate that multiple interpretations can coexist." In fact, it takes humility to recognize that within our carefully created sameness, a rich, vibrant variety of experiences exists and leads to various interpretations. We can admire this variety rather than judge it.

Our little literacies and lexicons lay the foundation for critical thinking. Our assumptions about terminology, for instance, can get in the way of grasping the message of a writer. One of the goals of education is to grow our students' domain-specific vocabulary in each subject area so that by the time they get to college, they have a working knowledge of how to talk about literature or how the government works or how to work a proof or what makes up the structure of a cell. Students gain access to the great conversation in a domain when they've spent enough time learning the background information that enables them to interpret what they read and learn. Ultimately, comprehension is tied to background knowledge, linguistic concepts, and underlying oral language skills.

When students are assigned reading without a foundational grasp of the underlying law, or a historical context, or the religious tenets that frame the worldview of the writer, they're as hampered as I was in that Japanese bathroom with hiragana-labeled buttons! It takes time and dedication to become a skillful reader—and our skill levels vary depending on which subject is in focus. The more our children learn to be curious to interpret what they don't understand and take the time to build that lexicon, the more skillfully they will use their minds to think well. To help you help your children grow the ability to read closely and carefully, I've designed a series of activities that will make reading a more powerful tool in critical thinking. Each activity can be applied to any family member at any age (including parents and teachers) and is made up of a variety of activities. Feel free to take them a few at a time.

✳ ACTIVITY 1: LITTLE LITERACIES AND LEXICONS

The first activity is to value little literacies—all the ways your children and teens are "code-breakers" already. You're training your children to see that the world is filled with secret messages waiting to be deciphered. Our task is to be like a spy with a kit of tools, identifying the messages as intended by the sender. These activities are organized developmentally starting with your youngest prereaders all the way up to teens.

Bright-Eyed (5 to 9): Prereading Literacies

Notice literacies that support the activity of reading. Your children don't realize *how much reading* they're already doing right now! Some of these activities may be challenging to struggling readers. If the difficulty persists, seeking professional support is a gift you can give your children!

- Turn pages left to right.
- Flip a book to right-side up.
- Point to an image and says its name.
- Count items on a page.
- Say the alphabet (naming each one when looking at uppercase and then lowercase letters).
- Sound out the alphabet (saying the sounds when looking at uppercase and then lowercase letters).
- Notice font differentiation (cursive, sans serif, serif; a.k.a. curvy, boxy, extra squiggles).
- Put words in alphabetical order.
- Put items in alphabetical order (more difficult).
- Name colors.
- Identify punctuation.
- Name numbers.
- Identify mathematic symbols ($+, -, =, \times, \neq, \div$).

Bright-Eyed (5 to 9): Visual Literacy in Reading

Some children may find visual literacy challenging, particularly autistic kids. Be patient. This isn't a test, but a set of practices to try. These activities help kids with the metacognitive tasks that support interpretation.

- Differentiate images: faces, animals, plants, machines, buildings.
- Tie facial expressions to emotions.

- Understand the difference between photographs and illustrations.
- Sort a collection of items, like LEGO bricks, or office supplies, or toys, by color.
- Recognize and name an item/person/animal seen from behind or above or at profile.
- Identify the weather and seasons by visual clues.
- Recognize buildings and places: post office, schools, apartments, grocery stores, houses of worship, gyms, homes, parks, beaches.

Funny story: when my oldest son was four years old, we attended a church that met in a school gymnasium. One day while we were driving along in a different neighborhood, he pointed out the window at a school and declared, "Look, Mom, a church!" A great example of how personal experiences form our perceptions that shape how we interpret our world.

Quick-Witted (10 to 12): Collect Symbols and Make Your Own Dictionary

- Collect symbols for a week from traffic signs, supermarkets, buttons on the remote control, online gaming icons, trading card game symbols, appliance buttons, and so on.
- Make a lexicon of them, having the child provide definitions in their own words. Use a cell phone to snap photos of the symbols, print them, and put them into a little dictionary.
- Applaud your child's ability to decode the meaning. Talk about how your child was able to interpret the symbols. Notice which symbols are not immediately

clear. Discuss why. Have your child suggest better symbols!

Quick-Witted (10 to 12): Create Your Own Household Symbol Vocabulary

- Create symbols for daily activities.
- Make note cards for each one.
- Discuss why you picked each symbol: a symbol for vacuuming, cooking, teeth-brushing, playing piano, going online, and so on.
- Use the cards (rather than words) to communicate for a day.

Quick-Witted (10 to 12): Practice Tone of Voice Lessons

In the following series, have adults and kids take turns both as speaker and as interpreter.

- Create a sentence: "I don't want to go." Say it with as many intonations as possible, to switch the meanings. Guess what is meant.
- Convey sarcasm, annoyance, enthusiasm, worry, fear, anger, and more. Talk about why one tone tells one story and another tone tells a different one.
- Get analytical: Did the volume change? Did the voice move up or down the scale in tone? Is there any word that gets exaggerated? If you exaggerate another, does it change the meaning of the tone? Experiment!

Nimble-Minded (13 to 18): Try the Orthography of Another Writing System

The goal of this experiment is to simply recognize that language has been transcribed in lots of ways and that there is no "right" way (a subtle lesson in recognizing the diversity within a universal practice).

- Using Google translate, take an English phrase and translate it into another language that uses the same alphabet as English, like Dutch. You and your kids will now copy it longhand. Ask your kids to notice the quality of attention they give to Dutch versus when they copy a sentence in English.
- Try a different alphabet, like Russian or Hindi. Translate the same phrase into Chinese characters. How much more difficult did the task get? What don't we know about how to handwrite the Hindi alphabet or Chinese characters? What strategies did your kids use? Which helped? Which didn't?
- Watch a YouTube video about how to write in these languages to compare.
- Try writing English right to left or top to bottom. How do they look? Which is more difficult to read?
- Does anything change in how you understand what you read? Does a word stand out? Does a concept shift in its importance?

Nimble-Minded (13 to 18): Name the Wildlife in Your Yard or Neighboring Park or Tide Pool

Botanist Robin Kimmerer notes that children are able to identify up to one hundred corporate logos and fewer than five plants. Let's fix that!

- Grab a field guide and go! Name the world outside your door.
- Learn to differentiate various species of barks (trees), mosses, birds, and flowers.
- Keep track of these differences in a personal notebook. Pro tip: photograph an image, and copy the information from a field guide.
- Have your child set an objective: How many species will your child learn to identify in each category?

Nimble-Minded (13 to 18): Create a Word Pool of Domain-Specific Vocabulary

Get really nerdy with this one. Whether indoor rock climbing, macramé, hip-hop, the physics of flight, or computer programming—list all associated terminology. Try a STEAM topic (science, technology, engineering, art, mathematics).

- Pick a subject or interest. Collect terms for a week. Jot them on a whiteboard as you think of them.
- Sort them by category: items, verbs to do the activity, equipment, locations, famous people, skills, slang, descriptive terms, and so on.
- Note terms that are specific to the field (e.g., "bouldering" in the practice of rock climbing). Note

terms that can double to describe activities in other contexts (e.g., "harness" has other uses besides rock climbing from different domains).

- Search online: enter the topic plus the word "vocabulary" to see how many other terms go with the topic.

The better a child's vocabulary and background knowledge in any arena, the better reader that person becomes. Precise vocabulary and accurate decoding of symbols and language allow a person to be nuanced when forming an opinion. When you read about a subject with your children, do a crash course in related vocabulary before reading to prepare them to think well. For teens: once you've had a chance to explore domain-specific vocabulary for a hobby, try the same activity with a social issue.

✳ ACTIVITY 2: LIBRARY OF VARIETY

At the top of the chapter, I explained that reading is under our control. We can get a lot out of what we read, choosing to be influenced by it, or we can dismiss an author's message without a second thought. One of the ways we control what we read is to limit our sources to ones we like or that appeal to our style of thinking. For example, if you're the kind of person who loves historical fiction (I mean, who doesn't?), you may not be in the habit of straining the facts from the romantic context. Historical fiction takes liberties with the historical record for the sake of the story, which is fine, since it's fiction. But if that is the only way you learn about history, you may be misled into error about the facts.

Similarly, if you're used to reading biographies to learn about an era of history, you may become overly familiar with a single "celebrity" voice (historical figure, well-known politician) and miss the effect of that figure's policies on a common citizen or a victim of that leader's legislation or military choices. Naturally, it's difficult to find the point of view of a common person in writing as fewer texts exist. How do we go about expanding what we know, then, if we're short on resources? Readers can read across genres for additional insight by seventh grade. In the field of history, for example, that means drawing from a wider range of materials to understand an era, including primary source documents, like letters, legal papers, and records that are contemporaneous with the era. It might mean looking in other fields, like religious writings, diaries, and fiction. Historical criticism, news reports, treatises by subject-area experts, advertisements from the time period, archaeological records, poetry, song lyrics, and artistic artifacts can help to bridge that gap as well.

A "one-off" experience with a single writer in a single genre fails to get us to a well-rounded understanding of any issue. By the way, this is the trouble with the internet era: we want quick answers and rely on the same kinds of source material again and again, such as news sites, blogs, personal testimonies on social media, Wikipedia, YouTube. But if we're deliberate and explore the same ideas written in a variety of styles, we get a fuller picture. For instance, reading a government record of an event, then reading a journalist's report, followed by several first-person accounts is much more likely to give a realistic understanding of political consequence than reading editorial after editorial from the same point of view. Poetry, stories, and songs help create a well-rounded experience of a historical event, too. For instance, tall tales and camp songs were an expression of the folklore of the westward expansion of the United States. Merely reading about the construction of the transnational railroad without those literary works creates a shallow impression of the history. Imagine how satisfying it would be to immerse yourself across sources and styles of information! It's truly one of the thrills of reading widely.

Let's take a more contemporary example. What are all the ways to learn about the historic wildfires in the West during the twenty-first century? We could scroll all day reading tweets. We could limit ourselves to one media channel or one online source of news. We might read personal accounts via email from relatives. The goal, though, is to take in a variety of perspectives that include both factual details (how the fire started, where it's burning, what the firefighting response has been, where to go if you've lost your home, what the government is doing in the crisis) and anecdotal accounts (how the fire is impacting individuals, the firsthand reports of firefighters, the descriptions of trauma from the hospital workers who care for the victims, and so on). Reading the factual details from several sources while also reading a variety of personal experience accounts leads to a fuller picture of the wildfire's impact.

We want to teach our kids to know that they need *more* information, to be patient to find it, and to include it in their analysis. One writing project for children that I teach is to create a "mini-book" that focuses on a single topic, like sharks. Then I suggest that the child collect information from a variety of sources in order to paint a rich portrait. Facts about sharks, jokes, poetry, expert comments, a saying or proverb, scientific information, and any personal experiences provide the content. Illustrations, maps, and photographs add additional detail. This kind of writing project teaches children at an early age that there are lots of places to look when wanting to become intimate with a subject of study. The following activity helps your kids grow these skills. In all our reading, we want to curate a "library of variety." Variety is expressed in two ways: (1) genre and (2) representation. Both aspects of the library of variety can be cultivated for all ages of children and teens.

Library of Variety: Genre

What makes a text a fairy tale versus a report? What's the difference between a poem and a dialogue? How do we identify a news article reported by a journalist versus an editorial written by an opinion writer? How many different ways are there to write about a topic? What are the differences among them? Identifying the *genre* of a piece of writing is part of the critical thinking task. Knowing its characteristics helps the reader understand the mission of the writer.

Instructions

Collect ten different examples of various writing genres. Consult the list of twenty-five listed here if you need help thinking of ten. (Pro tip: You may need to get books from a library if you don't have a wide enough variety at home. Print online articles.)

- Picture book
- Fiction
- Historical fiction
- Fantasy
- Nonfiction
- Field guide
- Poetry
- Fable
- Letter

- Fairy tale
- Tall tale
- Folk tale
- Sacred text (Bible, Torah, Qur'an, Upanishads, the Tao Te Ching . . .)
- Newspaper
- Magazine article
- Encyclopedia
- Play
- Comic book/graphic novel
- Biography
- Review
- Memoir
- Myth/legend
- Textbook
- Speech
- Song lyric

Stack them (books and articles). Next, use one sheet of paper per genre, putting the name of the genre at the top of the page. Answer the following questions, and jot your notes on the correct pages. This project can take several days.

1. What's on the cover?

    (a) Images? Abstract designs? Which colors? What's your impression? Will you be entertained or informed or startled into new insight?

2. Notice the font styles: Whimsical? Large or small? Part of the design or not? More than one font? What's the largest font on the page (author or title)? Can you guess what the book is about from the title? Have you read anything by this

author before? What expectations do you have about what's in the book based on the title, author, and look of the cover?

3. Open to the first page of text in each book. Read each one aloud, one at a time. Invite your kids to compare and contrast.

4. How does the piece of writing open? Background information? Dialogue? Factual data? Lyrical lines? Which one "hooked" your attention the most? The least? Can you explain why?

5. Which genre is the shortest in length? Why? Notice the thickness of the books—then page counts. Stack them shortest to longest and then identify which books contain which kind of information. Learn anything new that surprised you?

6. Are the contents telling a story or reporting information? How can you tell?

Next select two books of very different genres. Let's identify the cadence of the language in each.

1. Photocopy one or two pages of each text.

2. Read them aloud, while the children follow along.

3. Ask questions of each one: Formal or informal language? Rhyming or not rhyming? Factual and informational? Persuasive or explanatory? Official or personal?

4. Apply math (you can create a graph or spreadsheet, if you like):

    (a) How many words per paragraph or stanza? (Calculate the average by tallying a page or two.)

    (b) How long is the average word?

(c) How many are words that describe in one paragraph? (Even if children select nonadjectives, list them in the descriptor category. This is a chance to see your children's minds search for description, not to identify parts of speech perfectly.)

(d) How many words are over six letters?

(e) How many words are new to your child (may vary by child)? What are they?

5. Make a list of all the verbs in one paragraph. Mark them as actions you can do with your body versus verbs that relate to a way of thinking or perceiving. Which category has more verbs in it?

6. Who are the "characters" in this type of writing? People? Animals? Artifacts? Statistics? Agencies? Experts? Everyday people? Historical figures? Scientific details? Information? Athletes? Children or adults?

7. What is the purpose of the first genre? What about the second? Which would you read for pleasure? Which for information? Why?

8. Notice punctuation and capitalization. Which marks are used the most? Are any missing? (Do you see any semicolons or colons?) If you're looking at poetry, does the poet bother with capital letters, for instance? How does an absence of capitals or colons or any other punctuation mark change how you read the writing?

9. Notice the writers. Are they writing in first-person or some other point of view? Does the author's biography have anything to do with the topic? What credentials support the author's ability to write this story or to write about this topic or to write this poem?

10. What purpose do you think the author had in mind? Humorous? Entertaining? Informative? Persuasive? Descriptive?

Your kids can ask questions to get you to do some hunting, too. They may ask: How many words start with the letter "b"? How many sentences are in each paragraph? You may notice quickly that the old rules (paragraphs have at least four sentences) are broken and that the writer defaults to using masculine pronouns to mean all people. When we look closely and ask questions, we discover what is actually *there* rather than telling our kids what they should find.

One way to grow a student's familiarity with a variety of writing genres is to include more selections during a daily read aloud time. Pick a poem or tall tale to start. Follow it with a bit of nonfiction. Read a current news article about a topic of interest. Look at a graph together. Then read a chapter from a novel. Each day, vary the sources to give your children a slew of writing styles to enjoy and eventually emulate.

Library of Variety: Representation

The next feature of the library of variety is what is called *representation*. Each of our families is unique. Cultural heritage, learning differences, spiritual and political beliefs, married or not, adoption, births, sexual orientation, and a whole host of other factors create a family's vibrant tapestry. In the end, no two families are exactly alike. Yet, for most of the twentieth century, children's books in English have featured the dominant culture, authored by the dominant culture.

Today, one of the important trends in publishing is to prioritize what are called "own voices" books. In 2015, Corinne

Duybis, an author of young-adult books, coined the Twitter hashtag #OwnVoices to refer to authors from groups under-represented in publishing, who use their personal experiences to write their stories (https://www.readbrightly.com/why-we-need-diverse-authors-in-kids-ya-lit/).

For instance, instead of reading a book by a white American author writing about Native American history, Corinne suggests children read a book by a Native American writer. OwnVoices books have come to represent a dynamic literary movement. The rich language, insight into traditions and habits, and description of the emotional impact of historical events are expressed by people within the communities who are at the center of those experiences. OwnVoices in publishing implies the difference between *learning about* and *learning from*. A helpful analogy: instead of reading a travel guide to *learn about* a place written by people without firsthand lived experience, you choose to *learn from* a person who grew up in that place who writes a travel guide about it.

Today's new authors are expanding how we hear the English language (cadence, nuance, and vocabulary) and how we relate to people we know but may not understand. They also offer members of their communities role models that validate their communities' unique constellation of experiences and beliefs. In turn, they provide commentary on our shared history. A variety of perspectives fosters breakthrough insights, too. To raise critical thinkers, always look for more to think about, more to consider. Here are some useful questions to ask yourself:

- When I look at our bookshelves, what world do I see reflected in our book choices?
- Which books reflect our experiences to my children?

- Which books help my child know and learn about experiences different from ours?
- Have I included books that explore music, science, history, geography, food, math, and art?
- Do I have books written based in research as well as those written with firsthand experience?

    Note: Neither firsthand experience nor research-based writing automatically qualifies or disqualifies a book. It's important to read reviews from members of the community. How was the book received by those represented in this story? Is it accurate in portraying the community/time period?

- Are there alternative books available that better represent the community/event/time period?
- Is there a mix of authors (gender, nationality, race, abilities, socioeconomic status, political affiliations, and so on)?
- Is there a mix of protagonists (gender, nationality, race, abilities, socioeconomic status, political affiliations, and so on)?
- Is there a mix of perspectives (historical, personal, statistical, editorial, artistic, factual)?

By curating a library of variety in both genre and representation, you enrich the soil of your students' understanding. Reading closely enhances critical thinking. Your kids will assemble a better tool kit for decoding information, separating fact from fiction, and including an author's firsthand experience as a source of authority on a topic.

In the next chapter, we talk about how to read these books *deeply*.

CHAPTER 8

Reading: Go Slow to Go Deep

As we go ever deeper into our own insights, we sometimes reach epiphanies beyond any information from the author. These insights are the basis for new thoughts that were not there before us and, perhaps, anyone else. In essence, we move during expert reading from the surface to the deepest level of thought.

—Maryanne Wolf

I can't imagine life without books. It seems like it would be a special kind of torture to have lived in an era without the solitary pleasure of cracking the spine, lowering my gaze, and curling up with a writer who will take me on a private journey. Yet reading as we enjoy it—reading in silence to ourselves—is late on the scene of human existence. Most people for almost all of time have not been able to pop open the pages of a book to bring themselves the intimate revelations of a writer—whether romance novel or careful explanation of how our planets orbit the sun.

Oral storytelling around a campfire and debate in the public square came first. They are the well-known ancient communication practices found in human societies in every nook and cranny of our globe. Reading and writing are new, by that measure. Did you realize, though, that not everyone saw the advent of the written word as a boon to our development as people? Plato, in his work *The Phaedrus*, records dialogues conducted between Socrates and his disciple. Socrates warns his charge about writing the way most parents today lecture their kids about video games—*Look out! Danger ahead that will rot your brain!*

Here's what he said: "[T]his discovery of yours [writing] will create forgetfulness in the learners' souls, because they will not use their memories; they will trust to the external written characters and not remember of themselves . . . they will be hearers of many things and will have learned nothing; they will appear to be omniscient and will generally know nothing; they will be tiresome company, having the show of wisdom without the reality."

Boom! Mic drop, Socrates! Can you imagine his reaction to Facebook? "Hearers of many things, having learned nothing, tiresome company. . . ." I shudder to keep typing. Am I contributing to the "show of wisdom without the reality" by writing books? Oral culture was prized for its liveliness, its unpredictability, the way wisdom was constructed as a community project, and for the communities themselves that it fostered. Native cultures continue to value their oral traditions in order to revitalize their heart languages, to remember their shared identity, and to protect communal bonds. The internet has similarly galvanized the project of reading together and forming communities. There's a liveliness and volatility in blogging and social media, online comments underneath news articles, discussion boards, and chat rooms that's invigorating and provocative. Are we seeing a blend of two modes of reading and thinking in this brave new age: namely, hyper- and deep-focus-attention states?

The Busy Brain

Back at the dawn of time, to make it in a hostile world with oversized brains and blunt teeth, human beings relied on a neurological habit of attention called "hyper focus." The brain adopts a hyper focus in order to flit from one threat to the next, always alert, multitasking for self-preservation. A swish in the trees, a faint growl, the downtick in temperature—these experiences act like "pings" of notification that we've got incoming data to check and manage *right now*, in order to stay safe. Our dynamic oral cultures are a reflection of that style of attention. Oral tradition is cocreated and responsive to the moment. Members of a community rehearse the shared story and express it in their own ways, modifying and expanding the narratives, adding traditions, rhythms, and rituals to underscore the meaning generated by the group and to promote memorization.

As oral language found its way into the written word (whether painted on cave walls or handwritten on papyrus or carefully copied into codices), stories and histories solidified into unified narratives. The resulting manuscripts were most frequently read as recitals or in public readings (like at church or a town hall). In fact, even literate people who had the privilege of being able to read alone still read aloud to themselves! St. Augustine in 380 CE showed genuine surprise when he saw St. Ambrose reading a text silently (without even moving his lips!). As writing became more and more popular as a way to record and transfer information, by the Middle Ages lots of people who weren't members of the elite class could read. Reading began to be used as a private tool for self-instruction and record-keeping rather than a public performance by leaders for the communities they guided.

Language took on new shapes, too—spaces between words, punctuation marks added. Writers could now edit their own writing. This led writers to make better arguments that were more nuanced and complex. Reading and writing had begun to shift how human beings thought.

People needed time alone to read an idea, to consider it, and to associate it with other ideas. A seismic shift from our brain's *hyper* focus to *deep* focus was in the offing. Katherine Hayles, professor of English at UCLA, describes these two states of attention well: "Deep attention is superb for solving complex problems represented by a single medium, but comes at the price of environmental alertness and flexibility of response. Hyper attention excels at negotiating rapidly in changing environments in which multiple foci compete for attention; its disadvantage is impatience for focusing for long periods on a noninteractive object such as a Victorian novel or complicated math problems."

The printing press burst on the scene in the fifteenth century and accelerated the brain's shift to an attention state of deep focus. "The development of knowledge became an increasingly private act, with each reader creating, in his own mind, a personal synthesis of the ideas and information passed down through the writings of other thinkers." This ability to read alone, to sit with ideas, and to draw conclusions for ourselves powerfully altered our conception of education. Students were expected to make learning meaningful for themselves through deep focused engagement. Our academic institutions have thoroughly adopted the "deep focus" format. Hayles recognizes this trend: "In an evolutionary context, no doubt hyper focus developed first; deep attention is a relative luxury, requiring a group environment in which one does not have to be constantly alert to danger." With that in mind, we've designed our school buildings and libraries to support quiet, private spaces, protected from noise and interruptions, that allow for concentration while reading. We've trained our educators to believe in *deep focus* learning as the key habit of a well-educated student. In practice, though, the emphasis is often on quiet learning rather than depth. Parents, consequently, expect children to be quietly thoughtful when they do their homework to prove they're paying attention.

Yet here we are in the twenty-first century, and another seismic shift for our brains is underway. With the advent of the internet on our phones, we've been thrown back into the habit of attention of our earliest impulses: hyper focus. This primal need to monitor the environment and to stay alert to intrusions is back in our digital lives with a vengeance. FOMO (fear of missing out) is real! We may not be interrupted by the grunt of a warthog about to ambush us, but God forbid we miss a comment on Instagram! Red dots, dings, and vibrations on our multiple devices catch the corner of our eyes or jolt our ears or tingle our pockets. We feel compelled to interrupt ourselves. It's old, old, old programming, yet you must know—technology companies are happy to exploit it.

Social media corporations, like Facebook, design their platforms for maximum psychological pressure to stay logged in. "The seemingly innocuous features . . . —the 'like' and 'heart' buttons that signal appreciation and affection, the swipe gestures that refresh the screen with new information, the 'streak' counts that tally exchanges with friends, the infinite scrolls of stuff—are variations on psychological-conditioning techniques pioneered by slot-machine makers. They promise emotional and social rewards, and they deliver those rewards in an unpredictable fashion." The consequence of this algorithmic stress is that we're being trained to read quickly, react instantly without reflection, all day every day—activating the hyper, ever-vigilant alert system of our brains. Combine this pressure to react immediately to online content with our memory of the multiple-choice test with its timed pressure and correct answers, and we start to see why so many of us are obsessed with responding to every tweet or Facebook update instantly, declaring our most right positions!

But the kind of reading that enables critical thinking requires depth, and that's the kind of reading we don't do as easily anymore because our smartphones are literally rewiring our brains. Nicholas Carr asserts in his book *The Shallows: What the Internet Is Doing to Our Brains* that "As a society, we devote ever less time to reading printed words, and even when we do read them, we do so in the busy shadow of the Internet." After a hundred plus pages of data and research in his book, Carr explains, "One thing is very clear: if, knowing what we know today about the brain's neuroplasticity, you were to set out to invent a medium that would rewire our mental circuits as quickly and thoroughly as possible, you would probably end up designing something that looks and works a lot like the Internet."

I don't know about you, but I'm a distracted reader in today's digital environment. I scroll through articles (skimming the content), looking for what I hope to find, more often than I want to admit. I treat my print copies of books like websites: flipping through them, skipping around until a concept catches my eye, rather than letting a single author make a sustained case, chronologically, one chapter after another. I last three to five minutes on a website before I click through a hyperlink to another one. I've been on a "fast-food" information diet for more than a decade. That troubles me now. Rita Cevasco, SLP, described this style of reading as "squirreling." Our eyes and attention hop around the page, scanning for bits of information to tuck away, rather than tracking and carefully reading the text.

Maryanne Wolf, noted literacy expert, studies this shift in how we read. What I appreciate about her perspective is that she doesn't shame us for the way our internet use has changed our reading habits. Instead, she's interested in how we can embrace both book-learning and digital scrolling. Wolf suggests that by fourth grade, children can become what she calls *biliterate*. "Until I am convinced by research to the contrary, I am convinced that what we need is to build a carefully considered trajectory for the development of a truly *biliterate* child who knows what is best for different kinds of reading for them. Just like you and me, we can turn to books. We can print out things when we need slower attention." Wolf recognizes that today's adults who grew up with a habit of deep focus reading have greater facility calling on it when needed, even when they receive information digitally. She continues: "It's ultimately about quality of attention. We want the best forms of attention for our children over time. You and I don't need deep reading for most of our email. But we do want it for whatever requires our best thought." It's our job to help our kids experience the power of the two systems, helping them develop and balance both.

The shift that's well underway, however, is clearly a return to hyper focus. It's become our dominant way of interacting with any text—whether on- or offline. The problem with today's hyper-focus reading is that the words we consume often stay at a surface level of intellectual engagement. What we want to cultivate is the ability to connect various ideas to each other while making meaning for ourselves, and that requires deep-focus-attention states.

Textual Healing

Our kids are being raised on this fast-food digital diet. Books almost feel arcane or quaint by contrast. I've even "swiped" my finger on a physical page to turn it! Whether book or poem, article or tweet, reading is like pulling up a chair in the mental living room of the writer. I remember the early days of online discussion boards—how the introverts came out of the woodwork! These shy souls could put their ideas in conversation by typing and never have to worry about extroverts interrupting or shouting over their carefully formed thoughts. Reading allows us to get to know each other's insides. Glorious. The internet was heralded as a golden age of mutual sharing and understanding. The more access we had to one another, hate would dissipate, and kumbaya love would bloom! Aaaaand . . . scene. That dream blew up in pixels of trolling! Reading went from a solitary pleasure to risky (often public) two-way communication that either brought about the euphoria of connection or the devastation of being called out. Something meaningful about reading had been gained, but just as surely, something else had been lost online.

Today's digital environment is more like a party with many rooms and countless people. Conversations are in progress, people are chatting everywhere, and you may feel like a pinball being swatted around as you try to find a place to drop in. We can learn a lot by popping in and out of those conversations. But unlike the original optimistic utopia many of us (raising my hand here) imagined, a sinister result surfaced decades into this global publishing project: human beings were more interested in being broadcasters than listeners. Having a platform where you get to publish your thoughts for an unending array of readers is an intoxicating experience. Being able to give feedback in real time to those who publish is just as enticing—and too often, that feedback is off the cuff and blunt, the work of a moment of thought. Our kids are entering those rapids when they join the online world of conversations in progress. In fact, they don't know a world without it! This pressure-filled, react-to-everything style of engagement can weaken a love of reading offline where there's no pushback or performance incentive. Reading alone is not "party-like" at all.

The antidote to this untended, overgrown garden of global writing is to make the choice to read deeply, choosing to engage in a sustained way. Reading for depth—giving patient consideration to an idea—is like sneaking off to a quiet corner of the party with one other person where you won't be interrupted. Reading as listening means building *your* understanding, not correcting or cheerleading the writer. By giving the writer the floor—the full measure of space to make their case or share their story—the reader has the maximum chance to be impacted by the writer. Isn't that why any of us writes? We want to be heard and known, to be taken seriously. Deep reading means no one is expecting you to comment—at least, not right away. The internal dialogue, however, between text and reader can be rich and unedited.

For reading to be the educational powerhouse it can be for our kids, we adults need to create the conditions that enable deep reading to flourish. Books (offline, not on digital devices) are best for training our kids to be deep readers. Critically thinking about the content of what they read can only come after that immersive, slower-moving, undistracting experience. Naturally, reading proficiency is key here. If a child is still struggling with decoding, deep, silent reading will come later. What's beautiful about a deep-reading practice is the way it accumulates over a child's lifetime. The connections and observations your child will make happen internally, often invisible to you. Yet it's that patient posture toward the writer that allows the reader to be thoughtful and eventually to think deeply and well.

Deep reading heals us and gives us gifts, such as igniting our imaginations, connecting background knowledge to new concepts, delighting us with word play and inference, toying with syntax, and causing epiphanies of insight. Deep reading means "listening" to one voice at a time, over time, letting the writer have their way with you, until you have your way with the writer. It's an act of trust. When we read and allow a writer the floor, we create a space inside ourselves for that writer's viewpoint and story to be. We aren't obligated to render a thumbs-up or thumbs-down. We can live alongside the new information and let it settle before we make judgments about it. It's this slower-moving engagement with ideas that leads to the intellectual aliveness we crave for ourselves and our kids.

In fact, a deep-reading practice can help a child struggling with any concept. A child confused by a mathematic operation or a particular idea in science may need more time to sit with the concept before being asked to perform. One way to help that child is to print the information and encourage the child to read it silently, without interruption, before trying again. Sometimes in our rush to "get through and get done," we short-circuit the internal work that comes from simply giving full attention to the written word, without any other distraction (including you!). Alternatively, Cevasco recommends having your child read aloud, which offers multiple additional benefits: (1) it slows down the reader, (2) it gives auditory feedback, and (3) it recruits attention. Think of how adults tend to read driving directions aloud. Reading aloud creates that additional focus for better comprehension.

One way we measure whether a reader has read deeply is to ask the reader to restate the writer's perspective accurately (not necessarily agreeing but also not criticizing just yet). This is the psychology behind the practice of "narration"—retelling the writer's message, retaining its original flavor in the reader's own words. Think of narration like couples therapy. The therapist expects you to listen to your partner without interrupting. You restate what you heard (without assigning a bunch of motives). It's harder than it sounds because we're so efficient at making assumptions that suit our own perspectives.

Listening through reading can be a sustained agony (also like therapy!) when the viewpoint contradicts what you want to be true or the story line is disturbing. Reading is not always enjoyable. But to hear the author means to sit quietly, to listen faithfully, and to restate accurately before rushing to your own opinion. Offline reading gives us a better chance to sit with an uncomfortable perspective. This kind of reading starts with believing the writer is a rational being, or at least that the ideas the writer conveys hang together meaningfully for the writer, even if they challenge established facts or reek of bias. Tall order when you read a conspiracy theory or writing that accuses you of being a part of a systemic problem.

The opportunity of deep reading, however, is that we can take that pause if we need to, we can sit with an idea or someone's experience, without being called on to evaluate it. We can allow our emotions to follow a longer narrative arc than a few choice shock-jock-style phrases or a short-form blog rant. Deep reading also allows us to develop a healthy dividing line between the writer and the reader. When we are on a social media site, we might feel pressure to declare a position as an act of personal integrity in our community. Reading privately and deeply enables the reader to take a look at ideas without making a declaration or submitting to the scrutiny of others.

The illusion of the internet is that everything we could possibly ever want to know is housed on our behalf through no effort of our own. As a result, we learn to remember *where* to find information more than we remember the information itself. That's a net loss for thinking—because our minds can't make the connections that generate insight as easily. Our kids know how to be responsive to the multiple inputs of digital life: gaming, texting, video-making. I remember my daughter having six windows of instant messages open while she did her math homework, managing all of them at once. She harnessed this incredible flexibility of attention that hyper focus allows. That said, to master a new mathematical process, this style of study couldn't cut it. She needed to give exclusive focus. It's on us as parents and teachers to foster these two skill sets, teaching our kids what it feels like to make that cognitive shift from hyper focus to deep attention that helps them drop into immersive learning.

Exercising the Mind

The habit of deep reading is rapidly being lost. To benefit from deep-focus learning, we have to cultivate the habit anew. I've had to retrain myself to value sustained offline reading. I see deep reading as akin to exercising. We choose to enroll in spin classes or train for marathons for the sake of our health—even though the first five minutes or miles feel like a slog. If we want our brains to stay in shape, we exercise them by training ourselves to slow down and deliberately focus on one text for a sustained period of time, even though the first five minutes will also feel like a slog. We can create conditions that support deep attention states (like libraries have done for us) and then build our tolerance for that quiet, patient reading.

 **ACTIVITY: DEEP READING**

Sustain focused attention on *one* source of information (book, article, essay) at a time for a minimum of ten to fifteen minutes, with a goal of twenty minutes uninterrupted. To grow this practice, it helps to use physical books rather than e-readers. It takes about seven to ten minutes to settle down and fifteen to sink into a deep-focused state. A goal of twenty minutes of silent reading several days a week is a great routine to establish with your family or students. Feel free, however, to set a much shorter goal for struggling readers or children who are easily restless. Some children benefit from "partnership reading" where they take turns reading aloud with a parent alternating paragraphs.

There's research that shows that having a phone or computer device in the room with you sucks your attention away from what you are reading even if it is turned off. It helps to not only turn off your phone, but to put it in another room so that you can't even see it. If you can see your phone, it's still a distraction for your mind—similar to leaving a bag of chips on the counter versus putting them in the cupboard. Out of sight really is out of mind. Political commentator Ezra Klein shared on his podcast that he had to buy a safe with an alarm clock timer to house his cell phone when he decided to read a book so that his mind *knew* absolutely that he could not access it even if he wanted to. That's how powerful the brain drain can be if we rely on our devices eight plus hours a day.

All your kids and at least one adult ought to be a part of the following deep-reading training. Have each family member or student in the classroom put their phones in a basket, and move the basket to another room. Set a timer and find cozy places to sit in the same room. Read silently to yourselves until the timer goes off. For small children who are not yet reading, they can page through library books in an adult's lap if they are too young to sustain paging through them alone. One trick: younger children respond well to seeing a candle lit while they read silently. It's a quiet visual signal that while the candle is lit, everyone reads without talking. Once the reading time is over, invite your child to blow it out!

Deep-Reading Steps

1. Turn off distractions. (Phones go in a basket in the other room.)
2. Read the pages in the book in order.
3. Read them at a comfortable pace. (This isn't a race.)
4. Read without asking questions or getting up to snack.
5. Read with family together (training wheels).
6. After some sustained reading skill is attained, encourage reading at night in bed (expert level).
7. Gradually increase the reading time, starting with five to seven minutes. (Set a timer.)

Goal: To read for twenty minutes without interruption several days a week.

Once the timer goes off, you're done. There's no need to fire off a bunch of comprehension questions at that point either. Let each person enjoy the privacy of their own reactions and feelings. Once the silent deep-reading habit is natural, take it up a notch. Suggest bringing a book rather than an iPad to the dentist's waiting room or any place that will require wait time.

Activities to Go with Deep Reading

Deep reading enables students to make connections to a wide variety of ideas and points of personal meaning. Adults read literature and nonfiction both for pleasure and to be informed. The relaxed posture allows them more space to make personal meaning and to compare what they read to their personal experiences and their adopted worldview. Students can make these deep connections, too, if we shift how they think about their reading and give them space to connect what they read to the meanings they make for themselves.

Stanford researcher Sarah Levine recommends giving children and teens questions that draw out polarities. She suggests using a thumbs-up, thumbs-down approach to catalyze a personal response to literature, what she calls "Up, Down, Both, Why?" In this practice, the reading partner (parent, teacher) will ask a provocative question like, "Does this scene in the story seem more positive or more negative?" The students will then give a thumbs-up for positive, thumbs-down for negative, or both up and down thumbs if the scene is a little of each. Then the students are invited to explain their answers. In a family, the thumbs-up and -down may feel a little forced. That said, the concept is helpful. The goal is to draw out a child's relationship to the contents of the book, not merely to restate information from the text.

Other sorts of questions you might ask to provoke this kind of reflection are:

- Are you more or less sympathetic to this character?
- Does the weather in this scene seem a sign of good things to come, or is it foreboding?
- How does this repeating letter "p" sound feel in your mouth?

Questions that draw out a student's visceral reaction to reading help foster personal meaning. In graduate school, my professors assigned readings and then asked us to write five-hundred-word reflection essays each week about what we had read. I loved that practice! The dialogue with myself after reading led to some of the most fruitful thinking in my adult life. To raise critical thinkers, then, we don't want to lose the gift of deep reading, nor do we want to forget that reading benefits from some writing and discussion to make the meanings apparent and personally valuable. Writing is a form of deep attention and learning, too. The following practices expand the value of deep reading and enable some of those interconnections to be formed. Try these practices once or twice a month.

Bright-Eyed (5 to 9): Copy Work

Today's homeschool movement and many schools in Europe have adopted a practice called copy work as a way to preserve meaningful passages from a book or play or poem. Copy work (transcription) is gaining popularity in literacy research as well.

Here's how it works: the student copies a passage of choice, usually longhand (though typewritten copy work is also acceptable) into a notebook (or digital file that can then be printed and saved). Students select passages that are personally meaningful. In my family, we called these passages "golden lines." After copying a golden line, the child adds a sentence or two explaining their choice. Include the date. Over time, the reader has a valuable "album" of what they've read and their chief takeaways. Copy work helps a writer to appreciate literary beauty and power. Encourage rereading entries, too. Themes appear and connections are formed that might not have been immediately obvious while reading.

Quick-Witted (10 to 12): Commonplace Books

Many writers and scholars like to keep what are known as "commonplace books." These are personally curated notebooks that house thoughts and reactions, correlative ideas and powerful quotes. Think of a scrapbook, but for ideas rather than events. The entries are not meant to be like a cohesive journal, but a collection of assorted thoughts and quotes. For our modern-day young scholars, I recommend making entries as they read a book. No need to do so every day, but every few chapters might be a good place to start. They can also include a quick sketch of a character, a map, a list of new vocabulary words, and their own questions or reactions. The book often becomes a treasured diary of a season in your child's life. This practice is like taking a photograph every few weeks of your child's mind. Eventually, you'll have a full album of mental snapshots.

Nimble-Minded (13 to 18): Reflection Pieces

For teen readers, now's a great time to get in the habit of writing after finishing a chapter or a book. Freewriting is the tool that will be the most valuable initially. (Students will learn to write literary analysis essays in high school as well.) Freewriting means choosing a predetermined length of time to write. Set the timer and then write whatever comes to mind during that time period, without regard for spelling or punctuation. Just transcribe the ticker tape of thought as it occurs. Because we're using freewriting as a response to reading, I recommend targeting an aspect of what was read.

Here are a couple of ideas. (These prompts are written to be read by your teen writers.)

Freewriting Prompts for Reflection Pieces

- Select a single word from today's reading and write about it. For instance, the reading may be about "individuality" or "injustice." Put the key term at the top of the page and write. Each time you feel stuck, rewrite the word at the start of another line and go again. It may also be helpful to turn the page landscape view, using a blank sheet of paper without lines, and write inside balloons or bubbles as a way to cluster various thoughts.

- For fiction, write about a literary device, the motivation of a character, the impact of the most recent scene, or a quote from the text.
- For nonfiction, restate an argument or the data in your own words. Alternatively, rewrite the ideas/argument as if you're writing to a five-year-old. Or, write about what strikes you as new information or a fresh perspective to consider.

The next step is to polish one of these freewrites into a five-hundred-word personal reflection piece. The goal is to wrestle with or identify the idea that has "stuck." Get it on paper and tell your teens to let their minds go in any direction they want to go. Deep reading and open-ended reflection lay a great foundation for the deeper work of critical thinking.

Once your kids have discovered the power of reading, it's time to deepen their connection to the subject they're studying through direct and indirect experiences and the power of their imagination.

CHAPTER 9

Experience: Entering
More Intimate Territory

It's easier to act your way into a new way of thinking, than to think your way into a new way of acting.

—Jerry Sternin

Nearly everyone agrees that reading is key to a great education. Not as many people admit that reading can be dangerous to academic growth. Heresy, I know! Reading can provide detail you can't get through direct experience. However, it's easy to draw tidy, self-assured conclusions without having tested them in the world where they must prove themselves—flapping in the breeze, unsupported by great website design. Experience puts ideas to the test.

Like this: You have a thought in the shower. You like your thought. Then you go to put that thought into writing. The words vanish. The attempt to type them immediately clarifies your lack of clarity. That's the power of experience—it drives you to precision. It reveals what you know and don't know. Just as writing makes thought visible, experience makes learning visible. It moves us from confidence (I understand the information) to novice (actually, I don't understand) and then, over time, to aptitude (I get it now, with skill).

It's like reading piano music and then putting your hands on the keyboard. Initially, you can't remember what it is that you thought you understood when you read the line of music. Your hands won't obey what your mind is telling them to do. You know you're supposed to arch the fingers and keep an allegro pace, yet you fumble, hitting that one errant white key on your way back to a black one. The experience is both infuriating and instructive simultaneously. Practice reshapes the neural pathways of your mind to help your hands know what to do, how to do it, and when to do it. Direct experiences are learned in the body, by the body, for the body. If you learn to play the piano, however, when you read about music—for the rest of your life—you will have a different level of appreciation for it. Your insight will be built from direct experience, not from books you've read.

Indirect experiences also have an impact on how well we think. Historical fiction (films, plays, musicals), documentaries, news reports, concerts, and interviews give us access to people, places, and processes we won't ever get to experience firsthand. A film in period costume and setting can do a lot to enrich how you think about an era in history. Watching an interview with a world leader gives information (body language, intonation) that's not available in a newspaper article. Indirect experiences add complexity and detail to our reflections.

Calling on a student's imagination is a third way to deepen critical thinking. When we can't have a direct or an indirect experience, our imaginations can cut through our vague impressions if we know how to use them respectfully. Novels, for instance, help readers imagine another person's point of view deeply. British novelist E. M. Forster says in his series of lectures, *Aspects of the Novel*, "In daily life we never understand each other, neither complete clairvoyance nor confessional exists. . . . But people in a novel can be understood completely by the reader, if the novelist wishes; their inner as well as their outer life can be exposed." It is in the experience of intimacy with the characters through our imaginations (shared by the writer with us, re-created by us in our minds) that we gain more than a straight record of history. Experiences—direct, indirect, and imaginative—add depth to understanding.

Our kids (and let's face it, adults, too) are naturally myopic. We see the world through the lens that is created by our identities (as discussed in chapter 6). Experiences allow us to expand to include the perceptions and logic stories of others. No matter how you slice and dice it, experience is the spirited second leg of the trifecta that *is* the critical thinking journey. Essential, in fact.

Your Brain on Experience

At first glance, a few school subjects lend themselves to experiences more readily than others—like chemistry in a lab. The majority of the core subjects, though, aren't taught that way. Perhaps that's why science fairs and math competitions, history reenactments and literary magazines are popular. These experience-based activities are designed to bring the core subjects to life. If you ask teenagers for their favorite school subjects, however, they're likely to cite band, photography, art, shop, computer programming, theater, or sports. What makes these subjects different from social studies, math, and English? Electives encourage kids to do stuff. Students are trusted with the tools (they play the tuba, they pass the football, they write code, they throw a clay pot, they hang stage lights). Kids naturally gravitate to thinking that's *applied*. Ironically, most of the subjects they love are seen as "extracurricular." It's almost as if we've decided that *real* education must be dull. Everything else is entertainment.

As it turns out, electives get to the heart of what it means to be well educated. Direct experiences rewire brains for quality attention and skill mastery. You may recall the feeling of having studied for a test, passing it, and realizing two weeks later that if you had to take the test again, you couldn't do it. Yet a kid who plays the flute in a marching band competition is likely to be able to play the same piece of music a month or more later. What's the difference?

Whatever you "memorize" is stored temporarily in working memory, not necessarily preserved in the archive of long-term memory. I like Nicholas Carr's definition of the two types of memory: "If working memory is the mind's scratch pad, then long-term memory is its filing system." Kids with strong working memories get good grades and have an advantage over those who don't. They're able to memorize information and retrieve it easily the next day for the test. They can get those lecture notes onto the Etch A Sketch of their minds for a test tomorrow, but to make the insights meaningful and lasting, what's been learned needs to move to long-term memory. Long-term memory enables us to form complex concepts (what researchers call "schemas") that create links between a variety of associations—subject matter, memories, relationships, language, skills, and personal perceptions. In fact, this is one of the reasons why *visual* experiences aid the retention of what students read. "One of the most effective ways to encourage information to make that important jump from the limited short-term memory to the more powerful long-term memory is to pair text with images. Studies show that we retain approximately 10–20% of written or spoken information, but around 65% of information when it is presented visually." We even remember the look of a page and thickness of the book where the information was read: the upper-right corner, a third of the way in. That's an example of how the *experience* of reading helps us store what we learn *through* reading. It's one of the reasons, in fact, why many people prefer to read books in print rather than on e-readers. Our minds use visual memory of the information on the pages of the book to help us retain what is read.

Experience enables a student to make the meaning of what is learned personal, relevant, and active. The irony is, today's kids (and adults!) often don't feel required to hang on to the information they read. All the data we could ever need is an online search away. Because we *know* our phones hold everything we may ever want to know, we are less attentive to trapping details. We know we don't have to retain it all. So we don't. Instead of becoming smarter, as the internet gods promised, we're becoming more dependent and less focused.

This insight reminded me of how I feel when I watch a live high school football game. I notice that I often don't *see* the touchdown, even while my eyes are directed to the field. My mind wants a replay the moment the touchdown is made. It's hard for me to process action in real time. I've trained my brain to know that the camera operator will pay better attention. When I watch the NFL, I rely on the television replay to *really see* the touchdown. Because most high school stadiums don't have video replay, if you miss the score as it happens, you miss it! In fact, you can even miss it while watching. That's the point. We expect someone else to pay attention for us.

Kids ask: "Why do I have to pay attention? It's all in my phone, my calculator, my laptop, or my cloud storage." And while those are fantastic inventions (storing data in a real-time, updateable way for all of humanity), we're also faced with a dilemma. The stored information stays dissociated from our daily lives until we need to *use* it. On the one hand, the information may be readily available (hello, tax questions and answers). On the other hand, the information may still be completely opaque (hello, tax questions and answers). If I don't have enough *experience* in the field to apply what I'm reading, what good is the information to me? While I find it difficult to navigate tax information online, I'm much better at reading recipes. I know which ones will taste good and which ones won't simply by reading the ingredients and baking process. There's a reason why. I'm a thirty-year veteran in the kitchen. All that hands-on experience informs how I read recipes, which in turn, helps me make good judgments.

Neuroscientist Dave Eagleman explains that each time we have an experience, we alter the circuitry of our brains. The goal? To encode the most efficient way to perform an action. In fact, the more talented you are, he argues, the more likely it is that you've spent thousands of hours practicing, which is why your efforts improve and appear effortless. In truth, practice reshapes the brain to both *learn* and then *know*. Our most talented athletes, members of the military, and performers are often the most disciplined. They train rigorously, shuttling information derived from their experiences along the neurological pathways in the brain so that their actions come automatically when needed. The same rewiring of the mind occurs in mathematics and the arts, writing and the study of economics. Every subject has an experience component, if we're deliberate about finding it. Practice makes progress real. Top performers have brains to match.

According to brain researcher Dr. Barbara Oakley, children tend to fall into two types of learners. There are those she dubs "race-car" students, and others she refers to as "hikers."

The challenge is, some students do indeed have something akin to race-car brains: they can think very quickly, and in class, they are often the first ones with their hands up. But as we'll see, *speed is* not *necessarily an advantage*. Think about it this way. The race-car driver gets to the finish line quickly—but everything goes by in a blur. The hiker, on the other hand, is much slower. But the hiker can reach out and touch the leaves on the trees, smell the pine in the air, see the little rabbit trails, and hear the birds. It's an entirely different experience from that of the race-car driver—and in some ways, much richer and deeper.

The race-car student is typically rewarded in school. Quick learners are seen as intelligent. Slower learners, however, are not rewarded for their plodding pace. In fact, they're often pathologized as behind or less intelligent. Oakley points out that the difference between these two sorts of learners may merely be how they use their working and long-term memories. "The terms *working memory* and *intelligence* describe related underlying processes . . . if the person with a lesser-capacity working memory creates and strengthens neural links in long-term memory, those links can extend their working memory on that topic."

What Oakley demonstrates is that those kids with stronger working memories may not be as good at critical thinking. They see their education through a prism of right answers, more than as a tool for depth and breadth. Because they spend less effort storing information, they may not ponder all the implications as thoroughly. We saw this with the multiple-choice test scenarios in chapter 3. This is why experience is crucial. Students of all kinds, but particularly those with poorer working memories, need a multipronged approach. Reading combined with experience gives learners the best chance to form the neural links that make what is being learned available when needed.

Oakley warns against too much repetition without meaningful use: "Of course, no one wants to create and strengthen links via poorly designed 'drill and kill' approaches. . . . Given additional time and well-designed practice, people with lesser-capacity working memories can become as good as those with larger-capacity working memories in their areas of expertise—or even better." Oakley does see value in certain types of drill that provide a foundation for later learning—scales are useful for piano, memorization of times tables can provide ease to the math student. Drill without context is what leads to drudgery and disconnection when learning.

Elective classes level this playing field effectively. Everyone has to perform their answers, not merely remember the right information. Frequently adults who underperformed in high school courses remember with pride being trusted to stage-manage a talent show or to be the team leader for their volleyball squad. Somehow a lack of skill in test-taking had no bearing on their skillful participation and leadership in extra-curricular activities.

Direct Experience

We learn best through a combination of quality reading and direct experiences. To learn to garden or to play a musical instrument, to become a great chef or surgeon, to repair cars or to test the safety of shaving cream formulas, to fly planes or to convert wind into energy, book-learning is never enough. Higher education admits this. Trainings, internships, residencies, and certification programs are required to make sure that after book and classroom education comes the *real* training—hands-on! I didn't want a surgeon to repair my broken ankle after only having gotten an A on an exam. I needed my doctor to have cut open a few ankles first, successfully putting them back together.

You, a layperson, may understand the words on a website that explain how to conduct a "repipe" for your kitchen plumbing, but we'll find out how well you've understood once you attempt that repair and turn on the faucet! Passing a test on paper is not the same as passing the test under the sink. Critical thinking is activated when kids put what they're learning to the experience test, not merely the paper one.

I'm reminded of David C. Roy, an artisan in Connecticut. Roy has a background in physics, and his wife is a sculptor. With help from his wife, Roy has created over three hundred different designs of kinetic sculptures: wooden art pieces that are mechanically powered to rotate in visually pleasing patterns—all without electronics. His most successful windup mechanism allowed a sculpture to stay in motion for forty-eight hours. Roy explained that the goal was to create a design that was a "controlled release of energy that's self-sustaining." The sculptures are mesmerizing. Roy shared with *Wired* magazine that most of his work is trial and error, which blew my mind. It struck me that all his physics training did not automatically provide him all the answers before putting the mechanisms to the test. I love watching him work—there's a dance between his imagination, his education, and his ability to problem-solve. Background education and experience make powerful partners. Together, they provoke experimentation, insight, and better solutions.

Have you ever watched children set up a snaking line of dominoes to knock them over with one tap? I've treated that activity as an enjoyable pastime—something fun to do on a rainy day. But after watching David Roy, I had a flashback to my son and his obsession with dominoes. There's a painstaking process of setting them the right distance apart, the trial and error of adding curves, and the choice to have the dominoes go up or down a ramp. The theories, the guesswork, the testing of one portion of the sequence before connecting it to the rest—these were decisions my son had to make. The proof of how well he grasped what he'd learned through each attempt wasn't revealed until he set the dominoes in motion. I remember many moments of frustration—accidentally knocking over a big sequence too soon, or two dominoes being too far apart and causing the chain reaction to fail. Sometimes the curve was too sharp or the ramp too steep. There's a moment of held breath until the child taps that first domino. As the rush of clicks follow, onlookers hope for a swift decimation of the snaking line until the last triumphant clack of the final falling domino. That's the power of direct experience.

Perhaps you're asking how to bring this powerhouse of critical thinking into the traditional school subjects. For any information to become personally meaningful—hooked to countless other associations—direct experiences are the way to go.

Core Subjects

When I taught math to my children as a home educator, I worried if I would pass along my own weak math skills. I researched hands-on methods to teach basic computations. I tried one terrific idea with my daughter. It went like this:

- Select a countable item (like seashells)
- Regroup them to represent each of the times tables
  - Three groups of two shells each becomes six shells
  - Regroup them into two groups of three shells each, and so on . . .

I suggested my daughter show me the times tables for the "twos" using a jar of seashells. I headed off to change a baby's diaper while she set to the task. When I returned, I discovered that my nine-year-old had created a beautiful arrangement of seashells that looked like the shape of the number 2, followed by a beautifully designed X, followed by yet another 2 shape, followed by two straight lines, and finally the numeral for 4. She had not understood what I wanted her to do. Instead, she reproduced the image of the math problem using shells instead of a pencil. Her explanation to me at the time? This is what times tables *look like*. She had memorized the appearance of the problem, yet still didn't understand the mathematics.

The beauty of this "failed" exercise, however, is that we discovered together the gap lurking in her mind about multiplication. I would've missed it if she had successfully answered the questions in her workbook. By giving her a task, she uncovered a missing link between how math *looks* and how math *works*. We played with lots of countable items together (still away from the page) until she had a solid sense of how this addition shortcut actually worked. In fact, we put the processes on note cards, using reading as a backup system. In hindsight, I realized this was exactly the missing step in my own math education. My daughter strengthened her math competency through practical experience and reading, both.

"Help Me Do It Alone"

Maria Montessori says that in a traditional classroom setting, students can often be heard shouting, "I want to do it alone." Yet in the Montessori school space, children are heard to ask, "Help me do it alone." Adults are the best friends our kids can have! How many of you fondly remember a coach or theater teacher from your youth? Those adults who believed in you enough to trust you to do big things are often considered the best teachers (ironic!). These educators focus on helping kids to be successful. The soundboard is either hooked up to the microphones and speakers for the play or it's not. The marching band is either prepared to follow the drum major's directions or they aren't.

A child says, "I want to use a power drill." What do you do? Hand them a book about power drills? The request is a chance to collaborate with your child. Today's children are bubble-wrapped and protected from all kinds of harm (a.k.a. experience). It's no wonder the video gaming world is enticing. It's still a frontier of uncharted adventures using grown-up tools to have meaningful, practical experiences under their own control. Just like a microscope. Just like a saxophone. Just like a hatchet. Just like a motherboard and graphics card. Direct experiences are a shortcut to critical thinking. They require students to modify and adapt their thoughts and choices to the real-world feedback.

Kids naturally fall in love with some direct experiences, which we often refer to as their interests or passions. Passions teach your children and teens countless critical thinking skills the more they delve into the nuances of that particular hobby or activity. Yet to grow a wide array of critical thinking skills, sometimes it's the novel experience that becomes a robust teacher. A kid who is attracted to the fast-paced, quick reflexes of skateboarding may learn a whole other set of critical thinking skills when learning to garden. The slower pace; the patience to see results; the daily ritual of weeding and watering; and the regular involvement with nature, weather, and the seasons lead to skills like persistence, detailed observation, keeping a schedule, being responsive to the environment, and caretaking. Imagine how helpful it would be to a student to complement the body-based flexibility, depth perception, and high-speed navigation of skateboarding with a contemplative gardening experience. When you identify skills you'd like your child to have, consider introducing a new direct experience that can facilitate that growth. The best way to introduce a novel experience is to do the activity *with* your child. Borrow from what they know to help them navigate the new: "Remember how you practiced that one skateboarding trick for an hour straight? Patience to weed your garden is similar—a repeated action over time that gets you a wonderful result."

Indirect Experience

Another way to bring experience to learning is via indirect participation. Not everything we want to know can be experienced firsthand (like history). Not only that, we don't have time to turn everything we want to know into a firsthand experience. Who can learn to play every instrument in an orchestra just to know the xylophone and cymbals better? We turn to experts in various fields because they have the experience necessary to educate us, help us, or entertain us. An indirect experience can offer more nuance, awareness, and appreciation for a topic.

Indirect experiences fall into two categories:

- Watching an expert
- Approximating the experience for yourself

You may never learn to play an instrument. Going to a concert allows you to watch expert musicians in action, which deepens your appreciation of music and musicianship. Documentaries provide expert insight into any number of subjects, from glassblowing as art, to religious festivals in other countries, to how the criminal justice system works in our own. Visits to places such as a capitol building, a factory, a farm, a homeless shelter, a place of worship, or a sports arena put students in contact with experts in action.

Another way to indirectly participate in a subject of study is to approximate an experience. When my family became birding enthusiasts, my kids wondered how birds stay warm in icy waters. We learned that birds have an oil gland above their tails that secretes a protective coating to prevent hypothermia. I found an experiment that approximated how that protection would feel. Here's what we did: First, we filled a bucket with water and ice. Next, we coated one hand in shortening. Then we dipped the uncoated hand into the bucket to feel the icy chill. We timed how long we could stand having that hand in the bucket until we had to pull it out. Next, we inserted the shortening-coated hand. We again measured how long we could bear the cold. What followed was startling. Our shortening-coated hands stayed warm, indefinitely (beyond what we had the patience to measure). We understood our backyard birds much better!

There are lots of ways to approximate experiences. Reading does give access to historical events, remote places, and people we'll never meet. Historical fiction provides setting details and gives a more intimate experience of a character's motivations, habits of thought, and personal challenges in a bygone era. Barring a time-travel machine, however, we can't create a direct experience of history. We have to use facsimiles—visiting the Colosseum in Rome, going to a museum, watching a period-piece film. We might try living by candlelight for an evening to approximate what it was like to live in a time without electricity. Walking over a battlefield or visiting a cemetery where war veterans are buried makes the statistics of the dead far more real. Performing in a play, like *Les Misérables*, can give a student a more intimate sense of what was at stake in the French Revolution. The wildly popular musical *Hamilton* did that for modern American students. The songs became a key card into the various documents that were written during the founding of the United States.

Most kitchen chemistry experiments are designed as indirect experiences: tornados in a bottle, carnations that change colors, and the ever-popular baking soda volcano. Games (both on- and offline) are especially good at giving indirect experiences—buying and selling, navigating a map, caring for a pet or family, building a world, being a detective, creating an identity, learning about other cultures. Indirect experiences call on critical thinking in meaningful ways—upending preconceived ideas, taking a simple understanding and "complexifying" it, adding nuance and appreciation for the scale of the topic.

Participation Through Imagination

Another way to bring experience to life in learning is through our children's powerful imaginations. Recent research on long-term memory suggests that memory-making is active—not merely storing a bunch of facts in a set of mental file folders. There's a dynamism that is sometimes lost in the conversation about memory and learning. As Edmund Blair Bolles notes in his seminal work, *Remembering and Forgetting*, "Emotions, perceptions, and reminders all stir the imagination, and imagination, not storage, is the basis of memory." When we stir our emotions and use our imaginations, we are quicker to retain and make use of what we've stored in our long-term memories.

Our children naturally use their imaginations to increase their intimacy with any subject they love. Little kids dress up like their favorite superheroes. They pretend to have special powers. When I read *Robin Hood* to my oldest son, he wanted a green cape and a hat. He wore them for months, popping in and out of his fantasy identity. Theater programs offer the same kind of experience; play-acting allows you to inhabit a viewpoint that isn't your own by virtue of imagination. Young kids who dress up and older kids who play-act have discovered a little-known secret to the power of imagination: they can meaningfully separate their own identities from the identities of the people they pretend to be.

That means that if my child, as Robin Hood, robs the rich (my pantry) to feed the poor (his baby sister), I don't worry that my son is, in fact, likely to rob people out in the "real world." Instead, it's as if he's cast a temporary spell on himself to see how it feels to inhabit that point of view. Kids pretend to be dogs by crawling on all fours and eating food from a bowl just to see the world from a dog's eye level. They pretend to be schoolteachers and queens, war orphans and famous athletes. As adults, we endorse this kind of play. It's experiential, rooted in imagination, and not a threat to the values we teach in our families.

When teens become stage actors, they take this kind of pretend play to the next level. They enter the story of a script, identify the motivations of the character, and perform a disappearing act: the teen is no longer present in the choices and motivations of the character that get expressed onstage. Now the actor is a pathological liar, a disabled person, a greedy autocrat, an ingenue, or a member of the resistance. Acting allows the actor to create a wall inside that divides the person who is acting from the character being performed. No one leaves the performance thinking that the teen actor holds the same beliefs as the character he played. Yet because of acting, the student becomes more intimately acquainted with the logic story of another point of view.

Similarly, video games come in a wide variety of styles that let kids inhabit alternate worlds, create original identities, and at times, experience empathy. Even games like *Grand Theft Auto*, known for its complete disregard for law and order, allows players to experience a world without rules from a safe distance. Some games excel at inviting children to inhabit a worldview that is brand-new to them. The video game *Never Alone*, for instance, is known as a "World Game." It features Native Alaskan storytellers who present the life and values of the Iñupiat people to players. "It takes the traditions of a people not celebrated in the global spotlight and holds them aloft, confident in their intrinsic value." The game gives non-Iñupiat players access through their imaginations, which enables them to experience a worldview that may be new to them.

Alternatively, for Iñupiat game players, they get to experience being represented in a video game, which allows them to feel seen and known.

Imagination-driven experiences give students a chance to inhabit a viewpoint without fear that they're betraying their own identity to do so. When we read a historical record, we typically stay rooted in our own identities, reacting emotionally to the content. When we enter our imaginations to inhabit someone else's way of seeing the world (whether through film, historical fiction, or play-acting), however, we suspend our need to approve or disapprove. We simply gain access to another way of being. Imagination allows a person to try on a viewpoint, seeing the landscape from another vantage point (as covered in chapter 2, when we discussed perspective in painting).

Magic Tricks

There's another side to the power of imagination and experience in critical thinking. Kids are smart. Their persistent unvoiced question is: *Can I count on this—this experience, this swing set, this adult, this feeling, this belief, this home, this data, this hand, this teacher, this viewpoint, this community?* Remember, a key critical thinking skill is the "ability to vet" for trustworthiness. Early experiences with deception have a powerful impact on how a child thinks as well. Consider card tricks and sleight of hand. These baffle and delight kids. Reliable ways of knowing are confounded by what simply *can't* be true! *There was no quarter behind my ear (I didn't feel one) and yet there it is! You've produced it before my eyes.* Suddenly, there's "more than meets the eye." The Western concepts of Santa Claus and the tooth fairy are examples of culturally acceptable deceptions that capitalize on a child's imagination. Children find these story lines and beliefs magical, delightful, and believable at first. Eventually they are disillusioned. That is, the illusion of Santa Claus and the tooth fairy are dispelled and shown to be fantasies. The first exposure to reality not matching a child's sensory observations or belief system is a powerful cognitive moment. What's hidden from view or what pops into view creates a lasting impression on a child. Their brains scramble to fit this new information into their worldview: *Not everything I see or believe is reliable.*

When a student studies any subject, a capable thinker wants to know what's hidden from view in this discussion. They want to understand if the report is credible. Can a student identify what's being excluded in a discussion? Will a student get curious about other, unnamed perspectives? Can a child vet the quality of an experience? Is the child or teen able to notice manipulative statistics to call them out? These are the magic tricks of the skilled critical thinker. Academic training in the humanities in particular—history, social science, literature, political science, psychology, theology, communications, linguistics, philosophy—requires this exact skill set.

The Challenge of Experience in Learning

The tricky part of relying on experience is that our own subjectivity is wrapped up in our perceptions and the meaning we make for ourselves. Anyone's ability to think critically is impacted by both positive and traumatic events. The experiences we create for our kids should be identity-affirming for the student and should not trivialize others. The best foundation for healthy learning honors the dignity of each person. Many significant historical moments were traumatic to the people who lived through them. That trauma continues today in their descendants.

I noted earlier that acting in a play can be a good way to bring experience to students' education. There's a different kind of "play-acting," however, that can be dangerous. Reenactments of historical events in a classroom risk disrespect and a dangerous misinterpretation of the historical record. For instance, in 1971, my fifth-grade teacher organized my class into a mock Nuremberg trial. Barely twenty-six years after World War II had ended, my teacher assigned me the role of the defense attorney for Hermann Göring, one of Hitler's chief henchmen. At age ten, I had to find justification for his participation in the Holocaust. I discussed the history of the war with my dad, who was a lawyer, and I spent hours poring over our *World Book* encyclopedias. I tried to "put myself in the shoes of my client." (I wither remembering it.) I built a defense. Göring was following orders. He was unable to make rational decisions because of a twenty-year morphine addiction. The students in the mock jury found Göring guilty for his participation in the murder of six million Jews. If I'm honest, a part of me was disappointed that I failed to get him off. I was a kid. I had put in a lot of work. It took me several more years to understand how misguided that whole enterprise had been, particularly since 80 percent of the students in our school district were Jewish. Can you imagine Jewish students sitting on that jury while I hurled my weak-sauce defense at them, knowing that some of those very children were heirs to family members who'd been killed in concentration camps? What a misguided learning experience!

The 1619 Project commissioned by *The New York Times* found similar disturbing attempts to make lessons about slavery experiential. One adult remembers a class debate. Jane Zhi, thirty-three, writes: "I was on the antislavery side, so I got up and talked to the class about families being torn apart and babies ripped out of mothers' arms. I remember this activity so clearly because I thought we had the easier argument and we should have won by default. I was shocked when the judges voted against us." Is it even ethical to put slavery up for a vote among children? Another teacher from Indiana wanted her eighth-grade students to experience what is called the "Middle Passage" (the transatlantic trip enslaved people made in the belly of slave ships—more than two million Africans died in that journey). She put her students on the floor curled up beneath their desks in the fetal position and then flipped the lights on and off while playing "crashing waves and spooky thunderbolts." She told her students that this is what Black people must have felt on that treacherous voyage. Such minimization of the very real trauma experienced by Africans who were kidnapped, violently mistreated, and forcibly sold into slavery is unacceptable.

In the winter of 2021, a middle school teacher in Mississippi gave a writing assignment to students. They were instructed to write letters as though they were enslaved. The directions suggested they tell family members back in Africa about their lives on the plantation and the family they worked for, describing "day-to-day" tasks and their pastimes when they weren't working, as well as their memory of the Middle Passage. Never mind that enslaved people were prohibited from learning to read and write, this letter-writing assignment grossly misrepresented the lived experiences of enslaved people as well. Classrooms that create mock-ups endanger turning those historical events into a mockery. In fact, it's imperative that our students be taught moral outrage, without having to center their personal relatable experiences as the departure point to understanding. (More on that in the next chapter.) We risk an "everything has two sides" approach to history. Not everything does. Slavery and genocide are always, emphatically wrong. Attempts to imagine oneself in those experiences trivialize them at the least, and grossly misunderstand them at the worst.

The movement that suggests these types of classroom experiences and reenactments is called "living history." It gained popularity in education in recent decades but has come under criticism in the last several years. Experience teaches, but we have to be careful about what is learned. It's important to ask what's hidden from view in this exercise, and which viewpoints are not being considered.

While researching the effects of re-creating traumatic events in history, I ran across an article by a living history enthusiast. The teacher described a student creating an experience for her classmates about a Native American nation. The student constructed a fake campfire, dressed in what the teacher described as "a homemade native shirt and headgear," and passed around a pretend peace pipe to her classmates while she retold aspects of "her" tribe's life. The teacher recalled that the students were riveted, which led him to conclude that the lesson had been a success.

Native Americans have expressed that their traditions are sacred. Their peace pipes, their headdresses, the feathers they use in ceremonies are not meant for imitation or use by people outside their tribes. This example is a living history experience gone awry. Imagine a student who is not Catholic, for instance, re-creating the experience of church by wearing homemade vestments. Then picture that student consecrating a pretend host and serving it to classmates. Most Catholics would find this offensive and sacrilegious. Reenactments run the risk of taking what is holy or traumatic in one community and devaluing it for another, even if the goal is well meaning. There are other ways to have experiences that protect and preserve a culture's dignity. One way is to visit historic locations.

Historic Sites

My kids and I read books about slavery and abolition together when they were homeschooled while we lived in California. When we were new to Cincinnati, my husband and I saw a chance to give our kids an experience to enrich that reading. We took our family on a drive in southern Ohio one wintry day in January. We visited the Rankin House, a first stop in the North on the Underground Railroad—a series of benevolent way stations provided by abolitionists. The Rankin House is located above the Ohio River, with a clear view of Kentucky on the other side. John Rankin and his family are remembered as among the most active "conductors" on the Underground Railroad.

The day we visited the historic site, the temperature was 16° Fahrenheit outside. As Californians, we didn't know that you stay home in weather below 20°. We bundled up in borrowed coats and mismatching mittens. We curled up the long drive to our destination. We felt the wind whip our cheeks as we walked from the parking lot to the unremarkable brick home. It impressed us as being extremely small, given that John Rankin sired thirteen children! We walked to the lookout at the end of the yard, snow beginning to fall. From the top of that steep hill, our family looked down at the ice floes on the pulsing massive river. One of my kids exclaimed, "How could anyone cross the Ohio and survive?" Shivering, in awe, we wondered how these same brave people then climbed the face of the hill, soaking wet, without freezing to death, to arrive at this lifesaving house.

We were floored by the courage and the lengths to which our fellow Americans had to go to escape slavery. We were equally humbled by the risks the Rankins took to ensure that safe transition to freedom, and the generous way they used their tiny home in service of people who had traveled a great distance in great peril on foot. All the reading, all the films about abolition—none of them had the impact of that frigid day in January. Experiences provoke critical thinking because they engage our emotions, our skills, and our imaginations. We find the familiar and the mysterious when we add experience to our critical thinking tool kit.

✳ ACTIVITY: REFLECTION QUESTIONS

A good question to ask anyone who expresses a strong opinion is:

- What experience do you have with that (issue, person, topic, institution)?

Two good questions to ask ourselves when teaching are:

- Have I added a direct or indirect experience to this topic?
- Is there a respectful way to use the imagination to gain more intimacy with the topic?

Reading and experiences are both essential methods for gaining more access to a subject of study. In the trifecta of promoting quality thinking, the next tool in the kit powerfully overturns preconceptions and assumptions. Encounter is the most potent means of growing a mind!

CHAPTER 10

Encounter: Overwhelm That Overturns

Love and compassion have to be stretched wide enough to
include both the victim and the victimizer. . . . The ethics of
encounter relies upon changing one's social location,
interrupting social separation and polarization in order to share
life with others across differences.

—Marcus Mescher, *The Ethics of Encounter*

When I was in graduate school, I took a class that changed my life. The
professor offered a remarkable lecture on the first day (approximation of
what he shared follows):

The story of America begins like this: three boats—the *Niña*,
the *Pinta*, and the *Santa María*—crossed treacherous seas car-
rying Christopher Columbus and his crew to the new world,
a land of opportunity. Years later, another boat called the

Mayflower crossed the Atlantic with more Europeans and laid the foundation for a free society in the new world. These pilgrims fled religious persecution and built the foundation for a new kind of government that treated all people as equals, given unalienable rights by God, promoting religious liberty.

I listened. I thought, *Okay, so here we go again, talking about the story of the United States.*

Then the professor paused and said, "Who wasn't on those boats? Whose story was not being told? Who is sitting in this classroom right now knowing that this is not their story?"

Bam! A hit to my solar plexus. I had never considered those questions. And the truth was, even my ancestors were not on those boats. My family is Irish, and they didn't make it to the United States until the potato famine centuries later. Yet somehow, I still identified with the pilgrims.

Professor Clark continued. There were other boats. Slave ships, like the *Amistad*, in which enslaved Africans were transported across the ocean against their wills. They mutinied for self-preservation. They resisted being enslaved. They were brutalized. Who's telling that story? At what age did any of us hear it in school?

I knew I hadn't ever heard that story put that way in school.

Dr. Clark paused. Then he continued:

My people didn't get here on the first set of boats or the *Mayflower*. I sat in my second-grade class knowing that the story my teacher told was not my story. My people came on those other ships. My people were enslaved, yes, but they also actively resisted enslavement. The white settlers did not come to an empty wilderness, or a new world. People already lived in North America and had built their own societies. These natives were overtaken, many times killed, and forced off their land.

Meanwhile, descendants of all these people sit in our American classrooms without hearing their stories.

His language was sharply different from how I'd ever heard the history of the founding of the United States. Similar to how we looked at the story of the *Three Little Pigs* in chapter 1, I was faced with a point-of-view shift. I had one controlling narrative in my head that I thought was the truest version of US history because it had been repeated so frequently. I was being invited to listen to other storytellers—to expand to include additional viewpoints and to reconsider the one I had taken for granted. That day is a pivot point in my life. It wasn't reading that changed how I thought. It wasn't a field trip or a reenactment of history. Instead, I was being invited to confront—to encounter—the completely different experience of my professor and his memories of second grade. Encounter is like that.

The path to becoming a skillful critical thinker includes reading closely and deeply to broaden our base of knowledge. It engages the whole body in experiences, which imprint themselves in long-term memory. There's a third way to expand our critical thinking function, though, and I consider it the most essential. It's a powerful and dangerous tool. Like a knife, it cuts through the tedium of study and the vague certainties we take for granted. Encounter is that knife—it slices through our conventional understanding. The result? Revelation, epiphanies, and aha moments. Encounter accomplishes its work through "firsts"—the first time we hear a viewpoint or have an experience. Sometimes, breaking a rule causes an encounter. The most potent encounters, however, are when we get to know other people and listen to how they tell their own stories.

The familiar definition of the word "encounter" is to meet with an adversary. This reminds me of the classic fairy tale story line where an ingenue confronts a witch or a wolf. She may even be confounded by a fairy godmother—quizzically assessing if the lady with a wand is good or evil. An encounter is coming "face-to-face" with the unknown. There's a quality of danger. Encounters evict us from our certainty with sudden force, our ineptitude and ignorance on display. Who likes those feelings? Yet if we stick with the encounter, and live through it, oh the stories we have to tell! An encounter creates a treasury of insights: new awareness, intimacy, aptitude, humility, and deep appreciation for what we know now that we didn't know before. What's learned is not only memorable but becomes personally meaningful. Encounters do two things well: they challenge our personal perceptions, and they require us to evaluate community narratives. An encounter is transformational.

Encounters push learners to their limits. Sometimes it feels like taking a bold step backward in both understanding and skill. Think about learning another language. Day one, you move from fluent in your native tongue to babbling like a toddler in another. An encounter can be disorienting and sometimes crushing. What felt natural is awkward. What we knew is up for review. Encounters grow additional critical thinking strategies such as learning to take responsible risks, developing tolerance for our discomfort, thinking about our own thinking, accessing empathy for another way of being or seeing, and unlearning what we thought we knew.

In her book *Braiding Sweetgrass*, botanist and Native American Robin Wall Kimmerer describes a perfect illustration of what I mean by encounter. Once a semester, Kimmerer takes groups of college students into the forest for a weekend of camping without modern supplies. The young adults are called on to build a shelter from plants, find sources of food drawn from cattails, identify natural medicines to treat scrapes and sunburns, and dig roots to weave baskets. For city-dwellers, the trip is daunting. Students anticipate a confrontation with nature. Kimmerer reassures them: "[T]he woods are just about the safest place in the world." Yet at the instruction to wade thigh-deep into a mucky marsh, her students recoil. Kimmerer ticks through a list of what the college kids will not find in the pond to reassure them: water snakes, quicksand,

and unfriendly snapping turtles (who hide when they detect the presence of people).

With shouts of support, the brave ones tiptoe into the murky waters, then call the others to follow. They harvest cattails and learn how to cook them as patties over a fire. They build a shelter from what they can gather from the forest floor. They treat each other's scrapes and burns naturally using plants. As the weekend goes on, they become more and more comfortable. Their personal perceptions are challenged—it's not dangerous here, the forest does have enough provision for them. Their community identity is realigned. Now they are not only city-dwellers, but survivalists, too. They learn practical skills from their wise professor who has spent thousands of hours in the wild. They move from dread to exhilaration and fascination. Upon returning to the classroom, their perspectives are transformed. Before the weekend, many reported that they had been indifferent to the natural world. After the camping trip, they felt intimate with and protective of it. The students' initial fears were not tethered to reality but to their individual imagined perceptions (scary woods) and the city-dweller logic story (nature is for creatures, not people). The encounter at first overwhelmed and frightened them, but by the end of the weekend, the encounter overturned what they thought they knew about camping. It left them with a transformed relationship to nature. Encounter is like that.

An encounter flips you out of your comfort zone directly into your unknowing, your lack of skill, and the awareness that what you knew prior to that moment in time is not enough to save you. Where experience centers you (I'm a tourist looking for tourist attractions designed for me), an encounter decenters you (I'm an expatriate living abroad, butchering the language, and trying to fit into the local customs). You get to choose your experiences. You don't always get to choose your encounters. An ordinary experience is built from a cache of skills you already have. There will be challenges, certainly. Yet the experience is something you can envision. For instance, once you've learned to read music, you can imagine playing many instruments. If you find joy in the kitchen, you may choose to bake pastry as a bigger challenge. This is the premise of school—information is introduced incrementally so that a child can build on prior success and weave it together with new material.

Encounters, on the other hand, provoke a different kind of thinking and learning. They drive students to what I call "epiphanies of insight" through the destabilization of what they've taken for granted. In the example of the weekend of camping, Kimmerer's students presumably had been in nature prior to college. What they hadn't done was depend on it. They had seen ponds and forests as a blur of outdoorsy scenery, not as participants in their survival. By spending a full weekend deliberately relying on the forest and marsh to feed and care for them, these grown-up kids encountered nature. Their epiphany? The forest was a gift; it was supportive to human life, not a threat to it. They felt an intimacy with the forest that overturned their previous indifference. Encounters are frequently dramatic, mood-altering, and destabilizing. Many first experiences (like surviving a weekend in the woods) fall into this category. Firsts have a way of stamping themselves onto our identities. They are memorable because they're startlingly new. Other encounters provide a steady drip, drip, drip of provocation sustained over a period of time—like raising a child or performing a longitudinal research study or moving overseas. Encounters provoke us to think again, to expand to include, to appreciate more, and to reconsider.

Sometimes you fling yourself into an encounter (getting pregnant, getting married, speaking another language, joining a protest movement, changing religions, going to therapy, fostering a baby, learning from someone's perspective that's new to you). Sometimes you're flung into one (getting pregnant, getting a divorce, a cancer diagnosis, a child with a disability, a lawsuit, sudden fame, falling in love, a tornado). Encounters alter the way we understand our current reality. What we take for granted is suddenly upended, and we're called on to realign our point of view with a new paradigm.

A Culture of Encounter

In the critical thinking tool kit, encounter deepens our relationship to any subject or person. Marcus Mescher, in his book *The Ethics of Encounter*, explores the properties of what he calls a "culture of encounter." He defines encounter this way: "Encounters offer a glimpse that there is always more to learn about ourselves, others, and the world." He goes on to say, "Every encounter involves a choice: to engage or ignore, to accept or reject." The concept of "encounter" implies a power dynamic that's about to shift. That moment of realization that our current resources aren't a match for the challenge *is* the key moment of an encounter. The power shift puts us in direct contact with new ways to see. When my professor recast the history of the United States through his personal story, my eyes were opened to an entirely different perspective. What's exciting is that we can train ourselves and our kids to *recognize* when we're in an encounter moment so that we'll be alert to what it wants to teach us (rather than trapped in our heads—dreading, resisting, and judging it).

In chapter 2, I referred to a book called *The Overview Effect*. The principle by the same name is an effective method for provoking an encounter. In the book, when astronauts were able to look back on our planet from space, they were liberated from the only perspective they had ever known as earth-bound human beings. The astronauts *encountered* the earth newly, despite having lived on it their entire lives. In a similar way we can call for an "overview effect" in school subjects and relationships—helping our kids get outside of themselves long enough to provoke a new way of seeing. Not all encounters are of the magnitude of flying into space. Some are tiny tremors of insight. My daughter had a breakthrough when she used the seashell strategy to learn multiplication—a math encounter. What about language arts? When I work with children's writing, I offer a strategy to help kids see their own writing with fresh eyes. I recommend triple-spacing and printing their drafts. Then I suggest cutting the writing into sentence strips, laying them on the floor, and having the student literally stand over the body of work, looking down at it. Seeing their writing from above, individual sentences liberated from the screen or a solid page, gives them a gestalt. They see their writing as malleable. They're pushed into an editor's mind naturally, automatically. They *encounter* their writing with fresh eyes. An encounter is a deliberate act to provoke a new way of seeing that leads to epiphanies of insight.

Encounters come in many varieties, but let's look at three ways to provoke an encounter.

- Tackle a first
- Break a rule
- Meet a person

Tackle a First

Never discount the power of the new. Our brains *love love love* novelty! Newness is the key to provoking all kinds of delicious internal reflection. Our firsts are memory-makers. They require us to screw up our courage and enter into the unknown. Preparation for a first encounter is helpful, whether through reading, conversations, or related experiences. Once prepared, however, it's time to introduce the novelty encounter that pushes a child to draw on new resources. Any "first" ups the ante and leads to powerful problem-solving skills. Not only that, tackling new endeavors increases a student's willingness to face the next challenge.

The critical thinking tool that helps us embrace the new is a willingness to be daring. In his sixteen habits of mind, educator Arthur Costa describes quality thinkers as those who push themselves to the limits of their competence. They take what he calls "responsible risks." These thinkers will select experiences for themselves that require a high degree of flexibility, spontaneity, and possible failure. They use previous experiences and background information to help them assess the safety of the risk. They improvise, innovate, and stretch their imaginations. Most video game play falls nicely into this category. New challenges and levels keep the encounter going. The skills needed to level up are both challenging and yet within reach because they build on previous skills.

A few examples of other powerful firsts are earning a scuba license, rescuing animals, joining an open-source gaming community that writes code, becoming an exchange student, participating in the Model UN, learning to play a musical instrument, backpacking, starting a business, performing on a stage, building a backyard rocket... The adventure-seeking child cultivates the ability to manage risk successfully. The results of these risks vary in the specific skills learned, but the fruits are increased confidence, troubleshooting under pressure, working cooperatively with others, and a willingness to test new ideas and strategies.

There's a caveat to consider when embarking on a first, however. Firsts that are singular—onetime occurrences—may give a misimpression. What causes an encounter to become a powerful rethinking tool is the opportunity to sustain it over time. My son gave me a great illustration of this exact scenario. One of his friends served as a Luce Scholar in India. On this scholar's first day living in New Delhi, he saw an elephant walk down the middle of the street in the city. His first thought? *That's so India.* He formed an immediate impression based on previous stereotypes he'd heard during his years as an American. Ironically, after living in India for a year, he never saw another elephant parade down a street again. His sustained encounter with India led to all sorts of complex understandings about what is common and what isn't. Elephants walking down the street turned out to be rare. A single snapshot is not an encounter; it's a moment of disorientation and might contribute to a hidden prejudice or bias if left unchecked. When our kids tackle a first, it's important to remind them that a single event is not the extent of the encounter. No need to draw conclusions right away. Day one is the start of a relationship—an encounter over time.

Break a Rule

As I asserted earlier in the chapter, encounters reveal our personal perceptions while we confront community narratives. The common core can be seen as our culture's logic story about what should be learned by the time a kid grows up. The thinking goes that if students know what they're meant to learn, and then are taught the rules or processes, they'll become well educated. Yet what happens if the student never connects the dots of the explicit teaching to internal meaning-making? What if their perceptions go unchecked? For instance, a child may be able to complete a worksheet putting commas in all the right places but may fail to include them in their original writing. Retention of what is learned and insight into why it matters are not as likely when the primary strategy is studying, memorizing, and test-taking.

As I watched my kids struggle to remember to use capital letters or to find common denominators, I asked myself: *Why aren't they retaining what I'm teaching?* I thought about the fact that most adults rely on their ability to be reflective and self-corrective as they go. They aren't applying rules as much as they're applying habits, personally created meaning, and a sense of what fits and what doesn't. I wanted that for my kids, now.

My mission became: *How can I provoke meaning-generation in my kids?*

I wondered: *What would happen if we broke the rules first—got wrong answers or explored wildly unpopular theories?*

I began with punctuation. One way to think about punctuation is as another language that needs to be learned *as a language*. Punctuation fluctuates depending on each language and writing system. In English, it's a series of dots, curves, and dashes that communicate with readers. Sometimes they are singular (one dot is a period, one curve is a comma or an apostrophe). Sometimes they come in multiples (two curves to indicate quotations, or three dots for an ellipsis, or two dots stacked on top of each other for a colon). Sometimes they are mixed together (the semicolon is a dot on top of a curve, an exclamation point is a vertical dash stacked on top of a dot). And one of the common marks is a curve attached to a dash, hovering over a dot—the question mark. The rules for punctuation are nearly impossible to master (ask any copyeditor who consults *The Chicago Manual of Style* for guidance). That said, most of us are comfortable enough to sprinkle our writing with those marks with pretty good results. Why? Because adults have developed a personal relationship to punctuation over a lifetime that is meaningful to them.

Our usual method of instruction is to teach punctuation as a series of rules. Then, we hold kids accountable by pointing out the missing punctuation in a child's original writing, often with red marks. Frequently, kids go on making the same mistakes. By adulthood, there are plenty of us who are still a little iffy about the rules for commas and semicolons.

I decided to try an experiment with my kids.

Rather than teaching the times and places commas ought to appear in sentences, I prepared a lesson that would break the rules. I began like this: I read a sentence with commas (like this one from *Children of the Longhouse* by Joseph Bruchac) to my children.

"He stood and made the motions of catching the ball, cradling it, and then throwing."

I paused naturally at the commas. I asked, "What did you notice when I read?" None of them noticed anything. To them, I was merely reading aloud as I always had. So my next step was to add commas after each word. I handed the page to one of the kids and asked him to read it aloud, *obeying* the commas.

He read, without pausing at the additional commas, in his natural cadence. I stopped him and modeled the first three words with a pause where each comma occurred.

"He, stood, and,"

Then I handed the paper back to him to read it again, obeying the commas.

> "He, stood, and, made, the, motions, of, catching, the, ball, cradling, it, and, then, throwing."

This time, giggles bubbled up. The sentence sounded so funny with all those extra pauses. It felt unnatural. I suggested that my son erase any comma he'd like and read it, again obeying the commas. He eliminated a few in random places and read it once more. It sounded funny still! We continued to play with comma placements until it became clear that the best place for the commas turned out to be where they had been originally. We reread the sentence aloud, aware that we were, in fact, obeying the commas this time, pausing in the right places.

We moved on to another sentence where I removed all the commas first. We read the sentence, racing along without any pauses. I asked, "How did that feel? Did you want to pause anywhere?" We read the sentence again, noticing when that natural breath interrupted the flow. We tested putting commas in between those words. At the end, we compared our choices to the original. In fact, we made a different comma choice from the original writer that worked. That opened a whole other discussion about authorial control and intonation, and even grammatical uses of the comma that are not dictated by a need to take a breath. By *encountering* the comma—getting to know it in all its facets, experiencing its personality and power—we got to *know* how to use one.

This activity could be expanded further in this digital era. I'll never forget my college-aged daughter reacting to a text I sent her. She went from warm and friendly, sprinkling happy face emojis throughout her communication, to stiff and formal. When I asked what was wrong, she told me, "You ended your last text with a period. Why are you mad at me?" I called her. Apparently, to show that the relationship is still open for more conversation, her peers never end a text with a period. Periods indicate irritation or an end to the discussion. I thought periods demonstrated good punctuation! Today's digital natives are reinventing how we use punctuation because they spend so much time online. Twitter and Instagram have character counts, discussion forums include a slew of emojis in their text editors as alternatives to words, and habits of communication are established to convey good manners versus trolling.

If I were to apply the "break a rule" encounter methodology today, I'd get my family onto our instant message devices and send all kinds of oddly punctuated communiqués and discuss which felt what way! If I start a sentence with an exclamation point, does that register differently than ending with one? Can I communicate without any words at all, relying only on emojis? I remember a digital challenge years ago to retell the plot of a novel only using emojis. My friend Patrice's daughter, Montana, sent the entire plot of *Les Misérables* in a paragraph of French flags, loaves of bread, rifles, and faces. If you knew the story, you could follow it perfectly just by looking at each tiny image.

We can ask other questions, too: What role can a GIF play in getting my message across? What changes do I wish were widespread in how people punctuate text messages? What are the differences in style between generations? This "break a rule" style of instruction provokes reflection and self-correction. It makes the meanings personal.

Here are a few other "break a rule" encounters you might provoke:

- Create new punctuation marks. How about a squiggle to indicate that the reader should raise an eyebrow? What about a loop that requires the reader to reread a sentence or a word?
- Read the last page of a picture book first. Then ask, "What do we understand about the story by knowing the last page before the beginning? What do you expect this book to be about?" Then read the book and compare. Try it again with another book, only pick any random page

to read first. Ask again: "What can be known about the story from this one glimpse?" Read the book. Ask: "Were we right?"

- Read a book last page first, moving page by page from the back all the way to the beginning of the book. What was that like?

- Flip the script. Can your child create a dialogue on sticky notes for a picture book you've read to them, turning it into a script (or graphic novel with bubble captions)? How does that change how the story reads (dialogue only)?

- Turn a movie villain into a hero. Retell the story. Turn the hero into a villain. Retell the story.

- Try adding fractions without common denominators. Try dividing fractions without inverting the second fraction. Try to perform a fraction problem using flour and measuring cups. What do your kids learn when they compare these "break a rule" methods with the conventional processes?

- Imagine alternate histories. What if there had never been a slave trade? What if the Allies had lost World War II? What if women had written the Constitution? What might be different? These may require some research.

- Find new ways to lose a game (board or online). How many can you find?

- Think about social issues: What would happen if we decided that equal pay for equal work was not important? What if a business owner decided to pay people based on their family size, so a person with five kids gets more money than an employee who is childless? How might that change the size of families or the way workers see their jobs?

- Turn a poem into prose. Take a passage of prose and turn it into a poem.
- Bake a recipe, doubling only some of the ingredients and halving others. What do you learn?
- Change the point values for a sport like basketball. A bank shot gets five points, a dunk gets one point, a free throw gets four. How does that alter the strategy of the game play?
- Find an opinion piece the child agrees with online. Have the student rewrite it from the opposite point of view, never revealing the child's real beliefs.
- Change all the pronouns in a piece of writing to the opposite gender. Up the ante. Now do the same practice with a religious text. What does your child discover?

To break a rule is to provoke a different relationship to the original practice or thought pattern. These encounters are great disruptors of habits of thinking.

Meet a Person

I like to say that other people are "free radicals." They don't submit to our constructs for who they are or how they should behave. They have their own complex identities, community narratives, and perceptions to juggle. They respond to the same stimuli I do with a different set of beliefs. They make meanings that may seem to align with mine but, upon closer examination, do not draw on the same resources. The quickest way to grow a mind is to meet a variety of people. Give them the full measure of space to be who they are. An easy way to do that is first through indirect experiences—like reading a novel, following a personal blog, watching actors in a film, or listening to a TED Talk or lecture. When we witness a person's story or worldview, there's a chance to watch how life unfolds for them without having to also manage our reactivity. We can listen and notice our dismissive attitudes or the way the storytelling lands without worrying that we might offend them. There's privacy and time to adapt to what feels unsettling or new.

If you have the chance for a direct encounter, however, with a real person, take it. If you want to know more about what it's like to be religious, if you want to understand the experience of being a refugee, if you wonder how an astrophysicist works, the best, most direct way to do that is to befriend a person. There are countless people with just as many points of view waiting to be known. One of the key ways to increase your children's global understanding is to resist the temptation to shelter your children away from people who think differently than your family and community. Rather, by establishing relationships with others, we reduce the tendency to perpetuate stereotypes. We also gain new skills for living (for instance, learning how to make someone's cuisine, or discovering a belief that brings you comfort).

In raising kids, we can make the mistake of giving them such a strong sense of their own identities, they're ill-prepared for the day they meet people who see the world in a vastly different way. It's important for children and teens to learn about lifestyles and beliefs different from theirs before you toss them into encounters with other people. I remember when my own homeschooled kids joined a Shakespeare acting troupe for teens. They came home that first day with a slew of questions about their new friends who came from different ethnicities, religious and political perspectives, and a range of gender identities. That ongoing encounter over four years became an enormous touchstone of growth as a result. Our agreement or disagreement is not relevant when we're with people in person. Our relationships are not subjects for essays. The key to encountering others is developing the critical thinking tool called "tolerance." But let me say this first: I use that term differently than you may have heard it expressed before.

Tolerance

In the game of life, one of the cards we'd like others to draw when they spend time with us is "tolerance." We want to be understood, to not be judged, and to find acceptance. Yet humans are not as quick to extend that same grace when they meet people outside their chosen communities. Even so, when Americans are polled, they long for a little generosity of spirit between the polarities. They cite tolerance or compassion as the key missing national character qualities. Our uneasiness with difference would be blunted, the thinking goes, if we were just willing to be less critical of each other. Parents urge children to be more tolerant of the disadvantaged or people from other religions or that kid who looks "weird." Educators create an array of experiences to help children develop empathy. They teach teens to become better informed of alternative viewpoints. The polarization of political, cultural, and religious identity has caused such deep rifts and distrust, the one solution we cling to is tolerance. It's as if we're hanging on by our fingernails to be civil to each other in spite of our deeper irritation and frustration with *those* same people.

And yet, that objective seems off target to me. What is the skill we need in order to get to know someone who is different? It's not the ability to tolerate *them*; it's the ability to tolerate *our own discomfort*. That means noticing our body's reaction, the immediate defensive thoughts, and the stereotypes we generate for self-protection. Self-awareness is key.

I experienced a great example of the transforming power of encounter in Morocco. Naturally, living abroad itself is one extended encounter, from language to foods to shopping habits to how to make friends. One experience in particular comes to mind as an example of how tolerating my own discomfort led to a breakthrough of insight. I lived in a neighborhood that was several miles from town. The handiest way to get downtown was to take a taxi. To catch a ride, neighbors gathered under a taxi sign. The first time I approached the taxi stand, I stood in what I thought was the line. There were three or four people clustered in front of me. When the cab arrived, what followed blew my mind. The person who seemed to be at the front of the line did not get into the taxi. She was pushed aside, and another woman who had been standing well behind, leaped forward, grabbed the handle of the door, and dragged her daughter into the taxi all while shouting at everyone to stand back. I was shell-shocked. My immediate reaction was dismay and outrage. *Why can't these people stand in line taking turns? How will I, a five-foot, two-inch woman, ever get a taxi?* I backed away from the curb and stood at that taxi stand for an hour, watching person after person hurl themselves at the doors of the arriving taxis, stuffing themselves inside before someone else could get in.

I was a mess. I couldn't work up the courage to battle with the crowd. But I needed to get to town. Encounter. Completely in over my head. My objections to the method of keeping lines? Pointless. I waged the same battle again and again in my mind and lost each time: *This makes no sense. Someone needs to stop this chaos.* Yet if I wanted to take taxis in the future, I had to grapple with the reality, never mind my opinions about it. As I stood in my shell-shocked reverie, a Moroccan friend suddenly grabbed me by the arm and shoved me into the cab with her, even while my mind shouted that this taxi-acquisition strategy was ludicrous. You might be thinking that right now, too, if you are from a wait-in-line culture.

What I had to learn wasn't to be tolerant of the Moroccan system, nodding with kindness at their "odd-to-me" way of living. That system, for better or worse, was how my neighbors handled taxis. What I had to learn was how to tolerate *my* discomfort with their methods. I tolerated my flash of anger, my judgment of the "illogical system," and my self-righteousness about the superiority of the "wait-in-line" method. And then, I learned how to catch a cab, which meant tolerating additional discomforts: being aggressive, bumping against other people's bodies, shouting, and getting my way.

Months went by. I got better at it. My sister visited. We walked to the taxi stand, and I forgot to prepare her. A cluster of people gathered. I had learned over the months that there was an invisible order to the system, after all. You never took the first cab that arrived. That said, you also didn't wait for someone to give you a turn. I had discovered the sweet spot: you lunged for a cab after two or three people had gone before you. When I sensed that it was my time to lunge, I yanked my sister's arm and stuffed her into the taxi while she shouted, "What are you doing?" I held open the door while blocking anyone else from getting in. I yelled in Arabic: "Stand back! It's my turn!" With that, the crowd relented, and we were happily seated and on our way downtown. Erin was in the same shock I had been in only months earlier. She was quick to question what had happened. I was stunned at how I no longer saw this system as terrible.

In fact, I discovered something through repeated encounters with the taxi stand. If you were running late, you could shout your need to go first while launching yourself at the door handle, and frequently the crowd would withdraw to let you "jump ahead" of those who "deserved" that taxi. It was a little thing, but something that rarely, if ever, happens in the United States. Regardless of personal circumstances, we, Americans, must wait our turn, even if it means being late. Not only that, I came to admire the women, many wearing face-coverings, who took up space, yelled for their turns, and pushed men out of their way. That realization alone completely contradicted everything I thought I knew about being a Muslim woman.

Tolerance, I found out, is not about condescending to others with a beatific attitude. It's becoming self-aware enough to tolerate your own discomfort long enough to actually see what you see and to learn from it. Tolerance of your own out-of-control feelings and thoughts allows an encounter to have a transforming impact. I'm reminded of Pope Francis, who launched his papacy with a campaign he called a "Revolution of Tenderness." The crux of his message is that we've become accustomed to indifference. That indifference is supported by distance—choosing to be remote from the other, making up stories about groups of people, reading about them instead of meeting them. We might declare that we're "tolerant" without even knowing them. In order to deepen our sense of responsibility and connection to one another, we need a culture of encounter (not ideological tolerance) that puts us face-to-face with each other. As the pope shared in his TED Talk, "If I do not stop, if I do not look, if I do not touch, if I do not speak, I cannot create an encounter and I cannot help to create a culture of encounter." Our willingness to tolerate our discomfort while we pause, look, listen, and learn is what facilitates encounters between ourselves and others. Encounters are not about affirmation or rejection of someone's way of life. Rather, they are opportunities to generate insight and gain understanding.

✳ ACTIVITIES: PROVOCATIVE QUESTIONS AND COMMUNITY OF VARIETY

These practices can be done with bright-eyed (5 to 9), quick-witted (10 to 12), and nimble-minded (13 to 18) kids. Adjust the level of maturity for the questions according to your best understanding of your children and use resources accordingly.

Provocative Questions

When my homeschooled daughter prepared to study American history, she declared that she was tired of hearing the story of the United States told from men's point of view. She wondered what role women played in its founding and continued development. No doubt her love of American Girl dolls led to this awareness that women even mattered in the retelling of US history. I found a book that compiled original letters written by American women from the Revolutionary War until the twenty-first century called

Women's Letters, edited by Lisa Grunwald and Stephen Adler. These letters were direct reports—a critical tool in any historical inquiry. We read letters from many women, including Abigail Adams, Sojourner Truth, and a Cherokee woman writing to a government official in 1818. We were able to ask important questions like: "What might women have wanted that they didn't get at the founding?" And "How did women of color and Native women factor into the women's rights movement?" These letters transcended time—it felt like they were speaking directly to us.

Our kids have a chance to meet a wide variety of people in the stories we tell about history or in literature, through politics or social movements. We can provoke an encounter with them by posing questions that challenge the status-quo community narratives. For instance, imagine teaching the European settlement period of the United States. There's no "one story that is always true" and all other versions are less true. Start by reciting the story as you currently know it, and then ask these viewpoint questions.

> **Ask:** *"Who's telling this version of the story? Who are the major players?"*
> **Follow-up:** *"Who isn't named in this version of the story? What do we know about them?"*
> **Wonder:** *"What were the goals of the original explorers? Who had the authority to commission the settlement of North America? Who recognizes that authority, and who doesn't?"*
> **Ask:** *"What was the mission of the first settlers? Who benefitted, and who didn't?"*
> **Consider:** *"Who decides which people are heroes in history, using what criteria? Who decides which people are the villains of history, using what criteria?"*

Ask: *"Whose voice is ignored in this story? Whose voice is amplified?"*
Wonder: *"What is the underlying value being promoted in this version of the story? By whom? What is good about that value? What is limiting about it?"*

In addition to asking viewpoint questions, students can monitor their reactions—tolerating their discomfort or even their sense of triumph. Here are some questions to ask to help them stay self-aware in their thinking.

Wonder: *"What do you hope is true? Why do you hope that?"*
Consider: *"What are you afraid is the truth? Why do you fear that version of the story?"*
Ask: *"How does this version of the story affirm or harm your self-concept?"*
Check in: *"Do you notice any body sensations or emotions now? What are they?"*
Connect: *"What do you think caused that sensation or emotion? How do you explain it?"*

These sorts of questions provoke an encounter with the topic. It might be a good time to revisit the worldview grid in chapter 6 as well. Ask your kids to notice whether their reactions and thoughts are coming from personal perceptions or a community narrative.

Next, retell the history from a different point of view. By shifting to other storytellers, even the structure of the story may change. For instance, Native Americans don't have a "discovery of America" story. They frame their relationship to what they call Turtle Island differently. Using the questions above as a model, craft questions that address this version of the story.

Community of Variety

Encounters are best delivered in first-person point of view, when possible—whether in original writings, via televised interviews, or through in-person meetings. In chapter 7, I recommended building a library of variety. In this chapter, I recommend that you populate your children's lives with a "community of variety."

- Letters, diaries, manuscripts, navigational logs, records, and reports are valuable sources when studying history. Even if you only pepper your students' education with a few of these, they do a great job of helping students see *real* people in history. Take advantage of the internet to help you find photographs of those records. There's something about seeing the handwriting (in most cases) that personalizes the power of those historic communiqués. I well remember the impact of seeing the direct facsimile of the Declaration of Independence in person in Washington, DC. I had no idea how large the manuscript was, and the John Hancock signature was far larger than I had ever seen it. That direct experience has a psychological impact worth unpacking with your kids.
- Documentaries are an effective tool to encounter a person or an event of history. Seek documentaries that offer original footage when possible or archaeological digs. These provide visual context for the events of

history. It's important to keep in mind your children's ages—some footage can be traumatic.

- Make friends with people who are unlike you. Meet families from other countries. Visit houses of worship. Take in an exchange student. Join community activities that are not centered on your political or religious beliefs. Travel. Learn a new language.

The quickest way to provoke new thinking is to encounter difference directly. When you help your kids navigate complexity and difference, you show them how to grow their capacity for participating in a world populated with variety. The better able they are to greet difference (which is not the same as agreeing with it), the more skillful their thinking will become. Which leads us to part 3. It's time to tackle the complexity of those differences that surface during reading, experiences, and encounters. How do we evaluate the ideas and perspectives that are in conflict with our own values, habits, and beliefs? What does the academic task require of our kids? Let's find out.

PART 3

. . . .

The Rhetorical Imagination

Much intellectual work embraces the art of the possible; it is like an archaeological process where one goes deep in search of truths that may constantly change as new information comes to light.

—bell hooks, *Teaching Critical Thinking*

Imagination: dress-up clothes, face paints, child's play. Imagination evokes a sentimental feeling for a simpler time of life. How often is imagination mentioned when talking about research papers or lab reports? Less. Much less. And yet, shouldn't it be more often?

bell hooks, an education reformer who challenges status-quo thinking about learning, is especially insightful about the role of imagination in education: "We live in a world where small children are encouraged to imagine, to draw, to paint pictures, create imaginary friends, new identities, go wherever the mind takes them. Then as the child begins to grow, imagination is seen as dangerous, a force that could possibly impede knowledge acquisition. *The higher one goes up the ladder of learning, the more one is asked to forget about imagination* (unless a creative path has been chosen, the study of art, filmmaking, etc.)." Might this shrinking space for imagination in academics be a result of Paulo Freire's "narration sickness" that we discussed in chapter 3, the phenomenon in which academic success has been most often based on the ability to repeat, rehash, and opine (argue)?

Yet here we are. Thinking critically about critical thinking. What else goes into the intellectual stew?

Parts 1 and 2 walked us through the foundational aspects of critical thinking: the vocabulary, the storytellers, keen observation, caring to vet data and sources, identity formation, reading, experience, and encounter. The next essential feature of an active self-aware critical thinker is what I call the *rhetorical imagination*. Students who exercise it examine academic subjects creatively, analytically, and empathetically. They hypothesize, evaluate, interpret, problem-solve, and consider a variety of competing perspectives at once and dispassionately. These imaginative thinkers rise to the ten-thousand-foot view of an issue, taking in the meaning of a trend in interpretation or research, not only the most current findings. Even the sciences benefit from a rhetorical imagination: "Creativity and critical thinking are of particular importance in scientific research," because breakthroughs and insight come from taking the data and imagining its uses and effects. Science is not merely a set of facts to be proven but a method of exploration and discovery.

The other term badly in need of redefinition is "rhetorical." Rhetoric is supposed to imply sophistication in academics—better vocabulary, arguments, and acumen. One definition I ran across in a quick Google search cracked me up, honestly: "Rhetoric: Language designed to have a persuasive or impressive effect on its audience, but often regarded as *lacking in sincerity* or meaningful content" (italics mine).

What's that now? "Lacking in sincerity"?

I couldn't resist. I found myself scribbling on a notepad with maximum snark: *The rhetoric stage of education—when learning lacks sincerity.* I hate to admit it, but that's how it sometimes feels. High school and college treat learning like big hoops to jump through regardless of how anyone feels about what's being taught. The pressure to argue persuasively is overemphasized to the point of squeezing out the possibility of insight. Too often, students "learn" without any emotional, intellectual, or ethical engagement. Instead, they crank through papers arguing for positions they already hold or that are easiest to prove. The rhetoric stage of development might be the most jaded of the stages—the one that says, "Get information, express it as if you care, finish your education, get a job."

I'm *not* okay with that! I bet you aren't, either.

When I work with teens, I'm repeatedly astonished by the power of their insights when they *do* care. Because they've spent less time on the planet, they frequently serve up innovative ideas and fresh takes when they invest themselves in a topic by exercising imaginative thought. What enables students to tap into that mindful exploration? In my own research over the last two decades, I looped back to the arts. As discussed in chapter 4, I discovered through drawing that to accurately illustrate an image on a page, I had to learn to see differently. Betty Edwards, author of *Drawing on the Right Side of the Brain*, explains that we each have an "I already know what it should look like" mechanism at work in our minds that prevents us from actually *seeing* what's in front of us. Betty asks those who want to draw representationally to discard what they believe they know in order to *see* or *perceive* what's actually there. Edwards recommends that her students flip the image the student means to draw upside down to provoke a new way of seeing it. I noticed as I applied her method that I became fascinated by the nameless lines and contours—noting their relationships rather than labeling them as "mouth" or "nose." Amazingly, my accuracy rocketed. I had flipped out of my "right answers" mind into my "perceiving, insight-generating" mind.

This is what we're asking of students each time they read a book or learn a story from history. We ask them to shed what they think they know to be open to something new. That something new is not meant necessarily as a corrective to wrong thinking. Rather, it's an opportunity to enrich and expand what can be known, as well as noticing correlations between subjects and thinkers. Our goal is to help our children, and particularly our teens, pop out of what they assume is true or expect to find. We're inviting them into their rhetorical imaginations. Part 3 offers a variety of processes to help them have that experience.

Students at this stage of education will grow best if they're encouraged to imagine all kinds of relationships as they learn. For example:

- Imagine life from the writer's perspective.
- Imagine the era.
- Imagine ordinary life and royal life and the disparity.
- Imagine suffering.
- Imagine being *from* that place rather than merely reading about it.
- Imagine body sensations, the weather, the season of the year.
- Imagine that one concept can be related to another.
- Imagine that the opponent's view is as sacred to that person as my own viewpoint is to me.
- Imagine that statistics can be both accurate and misleading at the same time.
- Imagine that early childhood experiences play a role in adult choices.
- Imagine limits to what can be known.
- Imagine the impact of a viewpoint—its benefits and liabilities.
- Imagine an audience.
- Imagine that my way is not the only or best way.
- Imagine that the writer is wrong or mistaken.

- Imagine that the writer is right or sincere.
- Imagine that more can be known.
- Imagine that the era held superstitions.
- Imagine that the era had access to truths we've lost over time.
- Imagine a research project to test a theory.
- Imagine new methods to solve old problems.
- Imagine the intersection between two disciplines to create new solutions.
- Imagine fictions and stories to bring dull facts to life.
- Imagine history in living color.

A rhetorical imagination is key to critical thinking. It's what allows us to drop a partition in our minds between what we believe and what we're willing to entertain while studying. The rhetorical imagination allows us to "root" for the writer to make their case, even if we don't wind up agreeing with the conclusions the writer draws. The first step in reading any opinion becomes understanding it, not rendering a verdict.

To help our awesome young people grow their critical thinking skills, I shifted away from looking at the scope and sequence diagrams of high school academics. I got interested instead in how human beings form perspectives. What are the forces that animate thinking? What leads us to conclude we're right and others are wrong? I became curious about perception over evaluation. I wondered about the influence of community loyalty and our need to belong. I delved into intuition, generating insight, creating correspondence between ideas, and the ramifications of following a hunch.

I wondered how to help students become *fascinated* rather than *convinced*. What shapes anyone's opinions—what is persuasive, after all? How can we guide students to find metaphors and similes, analogies and comparisons? Could they interpret an original text (like my Bapa's letter described in the introduction to this book) without bringing their automatic preconceptions with them? Could they read a viewpoint without searching to confirm their biases? How might they conduct research with curiosity about a variety of perspectives rather than defensiveness about a single point of view? Would they be able to interpret what they read, experience, and encounter with nuance and self-awareness?

Naturally, these skills develop over time. Our youngest children are less adept at perspective-taking than our teens and young adults. That said, little kids can be encouraged to consider multiple ways of seeing and knowing through the age-appropriate activities I offer in part 3. The primary focus of the next several chapters are processes to use with teens, however, to prepare them for high school and beyond.

As you embrace the academic task with your students, remember that the goal of learning is not to merely get accepted into college or to find a paying job. A vibrant education is about the search for meaning, the sorting hat of our personal views measured against community values, the evaluation of scientific research and data, and the hunt for more information to consider, not less. To be a thoughtful person means being aware of the dynamic exchange between self and subject matter. I see a rhetorical imagination as the wind in the sails of invention and insight—it frees thoughts that would get overlooked otherwise, and it allows empathy and awareness to grow. What subject area wouldn't benefit? A rhetorical imagination lifts us out of what is into what could be. Until we see it or can imagine it, we can't apprehend, appreciate, or appraise it. Let's follow bell hooks's injunction: "When a teacher lets loose an unfettered imagination in the classroom, the space for transformative learning is expanded."

CHAPTER 11

The Surprising Role of Self-Awareness in Critical Thinking

The body knows things a long time before the mind catches up to them.

—Sue Monk Kidd, *The Secret Life of Bees*

It happens like this. You're in a conversation, believing yourself to be open to learning more about a topic. Then, your conversation partner launches an idea at you that contradicts one of your convictions. What happens? Tense jaw? Pit in your stomach? Hot lava shame rolling over you? If that person says, "Have an open mind," can you? In that moment? Most of the time, we ignore our body's reactions while our minds rush to the set of points we use to defend our way of seeing the topic.

When your viewpoint is under assault, what happens? Does your heart race? Are you flushed with anger? Do you experience a shot of adrenaline? What stories does your mind make up about the evidence the other person presents? Do you doubt their sources automatically? If you take the extra step to actually examine the evidence, and by some gift of integrity conclude that it is accurate and your conversation partner was right, now what? Can you quiet your nerves? Do you admit your error? Will you revise your thinking? What if you've already invested a lot of heart and time into that now-errant position? Imagine what that error means if you've made lifestyle and financial decisions based on those ideas. Suppose you're a member of a community dedicated to beliefs in conflict with this new evidence. Can you easily move on, revising your opinions and practices to align with this new data?

Back when I was an undergraduate at UCLA, I wrote a paper that thrust me into this dilemma. I expected to find validation for my thesis and did . . . until I stumbled on one important source that contradicted my argument. My face burned. I felt exposed. I didn't want these new facts to intrude on my convictions. Did I change my thesis or rewrite my essay to address this challenge? Nope. I simply pretended that the contrary evidence didn't exist. I wrote the paper without it. Researchers call this kind of bias the "ostrich effect." I chose to stick my head in the sand, ignoring the data I didn't like. Why would I do that? Wasn't the goal of the paper to learn? What drove me to deliberately *not* learn? That's the question we want to explore in this chapter. What blocks our ability to give a fair hearing to all sorts of data about any topic?

Full Minds

One of the most commonly cited critical thinking tools I've found on nearly every list I've examined is to be "open-minded." I scoff each time I see it. Is there such a thing? To be open implies spaciousness. Yet our minds are crammed full of self-protecting perspectives. It takes real work to sort through that overstuffed library of our emotions, thoughts, ideas, experiences, and beliefs for a new concept to find space on our mental shelves—particularly one that challenges a beloved viewpoint. A better injunction would be: be mindful of *your full mind*!

To have an open mind suggests that we can meaningfully separate our emotions, our thoughts, our body sensations, our community identity and loyalty to that group, and our well-established sense of right and wrong from what we study. The truth is, human beings are not good at it—at all. Our biases, unchecked, control our thinking. An injunction to do better doesn't fix it. We're bad at convincing ourselves to be open to ideas that contradict what we expect to be true. It takes some other disposition to crack open our minds.

In the landscape of critical thinking, then, the key practice that allows us to benefit from all the skills we've talked about so far isn't open-mindedness. It's *self-awareness*. Without turning the camera lens on ourselves, all our researching, caring, identity observing, and encountering can wind up reinforcing our preconceived ideas. Why does that happen? Because we're loyal to our own habits of thought. We've decorated our thinking room with our favorite colors, and we've got a big comfy chair to sit in while we enjoy our well-formed opinions. Asking anyone to open their mind is like asking them to remodel their favorite study.

Have you ever watched a sporting event with rabid fans? The moment a referee makes a questionable call, it's easy to predict with great accuracy which fans will approve the call and which will disapprove of it. Logic has little to do with it. The drive to be identified with the winning team overrides the ability to be open-minded about the evidence. The fans will make up an instant logic story to passionately explain why the evidence goes with or against the referee's ruling. Asking a fan to be open-minded? Please! An exercise in futility.

Naturally, there are those souls who pride themselves on being objective, who will say, "Yes, the referee got it right," or "That fact is true, despite how I feel about it," even when that fact harms their "team." Most of us can relent to the evidence when the stakes are low—that cleaning product *does* brighten my whites better than the one I currently use. When the stakes are high, however, it's a whole other ball game. If your family owns the white-brightener company and you've used their product since childhood, your own eyes may not be able to tell you that the other cleaning agent is more effective. It's enormously difficult to allow an assaulting fact to overturn what you *want* to be true and what your community asserts *is the truth*! Research even points to the idea that our in-group attachments release oxytocin, a powerful hormone of pleasure and bonding.

If you've made behavior commitments to match your "truth," you'll be even *more* resistant to contradictory evidence. The "escalation of commitment" (commitment bias) interferes with your ability to accept challenges to your beliefs. No admonition to "have an open mind" will solve it for you. In fact, you'll see having an open mind as dangerous. Communities double down on their version of the truth all the time—whether an official group, like members of a religious faith, or people who share the same ideological posture, like "marriage is best." The faithful will see any challenge as heresy, not new evidence to consider.

When people double down, sometimes they do so to their own detriment. I watched a friend who was a holistic health teacher wind up in the hospital with malnutrition, denying the evidence that he was slowly starving himself in his desire to detoxify his system. I've seen home-educators cling to a belief that their child would eventually catch on to reading rather than hire a specialist to help them. I've known women of religious faith who choose to stay in marriages that aren't good for them long after they've understood their husbands to be abusive or philandering. The greater the stake we have in our communities and beliefs, the harder it is to have an "open mind" to dissenting facts. To change viewpoints often requires a corresponding change in practice and outing yourself to your community who may, in turn, reject you. Kids experience this same zero-sum dilemma in their own families. They experience the twinge of anxiety when they get too close to a parent's sacred belief when asking a dissenting question.

In the critical thinking literature, there's another idea that's floated as an antidote to all the ways bias prevents us from thinking well. In addition to the recommendation to open our minds, we're enjoined to think like a scientist. The idea is to be more interested in *getting it right* than *being right*. By being interested in getting it right, the thinking goes, we'll follow wherever the evidence takes us. Noble ideal. Does it work, though? Certainly the activities that rely on math and science like engineering and surgery require precision and accuracy. Yet in this context of critical thinking, we're examining the arena of debatable ideas in particular. As we've already discovered in these pages, research and interpretations of the findings fluctuate year to year, era to era. "Getting it right" can imply that our dilemmas have a single correct answer for all time. (Remember our multiple-choice test dilemma?) Yet on closer inspection, most provocative questions are complex, with nuances to appreciate, not just right answers to get. "Getting it right" may not help kids, in particular, when faced with multiple sources that contradict each other. For instance, when studying whether or not zoos are valuable to animal conservation, it's easy to find studies that conflict with each other. Which study is right? How does a student reconcile those contradictions, particularly if told to "get it right"? It's easier to exclude the research we don't like, and to return to our original position, rather than learn anything new.

Insight

In the self-awareness skill set, let's first talk about the queen bee herself: Lady Insight. According to Renate and Geoffrey Caine, education experts who write about how the brain constructs meaning, "Insight is much more important in education than is memorization. Felt meaning begins as an unarticulated general sense of relationship and culminates in an 'aha' experience that accompanies insight." Insight, they explain, evokes joy, awe, delight, relief, and energy. What if instead of urging our students to *get it right*, we shifted our attention to *generating insight*? To have insight is to be able to see into the inner nature of things, to have a penetrating mental vision of the subject (person, issue, topic, reading, experience, encounter). To have insight is a different experience than agreeing with clinical results or validating the viewpoint of a study. Insight is a felt sense of meaning derived from a relationship. Another way to think about insight is the moment when a new understanding clicks into place—what the Caines call a "gestalt." I like to call these "now I get it" moments, epiphanies of insight. We go from "What the heck?" to "Ah, I see it now." Insight is not necessarily about compassion or empathy, though it can be. We might get a window of insight into the horror of someone's motivation to commit despicable acts, for example. Insight doesn't primarily live in the mind. It's felt as a moment of clarity that registers as a ping. Insight might show up as chills, tingles, awe, relief, terror, or deeper curiosity. Insight is noncommittal because it fluctuates. It enables us to retain our identities while gathering appreciation for outstanding information and alternate experiences. Insight has the advantage of being temporary, and readily improved upon.

Imagine listening to a person with an opposing view and being alert to discovery rather than agreement or disagreement. The goal becomes: *I'm here for an epiphany of insight into how this particular person holds this particular view.* Your task isn't to find the hole in the argument. You don't have to like their position or find it rational. You don't even need to make their viewpoint make sense *to you.* Your only task is to "see it" with new eyes. The goal is to "get it," not "get it right." You might gain a flash of awareness of a victim's pain, or an increasing repulsion for the motivations of the perpetrator. You might better appreciate the background of the individual that led to that point of view or the historical context of the topic. You might discover an adjacent belief that acts as the controlling lens for why that person shows such commitment to an idea—even one you find repulsive or immoral. "Getting it" implies that what you learn *lands* with you. It moves the task of learning from mastery of information or perfected argument to impact. A more colloquial way to put it would be: *How is what I'm learning rocking my world?* That's an insight question. If you don't have an answer to that question, it's likely you haven't had an insight yet. The same disposition can be applied to research studies in conflict: *I'm reading this study to grasp the point the study wants to make.* Instead of rendering an immediate verdict, identify what the study offers as an important consideration in the discussion of this topic.

I had this experience when I first examined the value of zoos. In Cincinnati, we have one of the finest zoos in the United States (second only to the one in San Diego, which was my favorite growing up). My children were typical zoo enthusiasts. Yet as my kids got older, they also got curious. Are zoo animals treated well? Is this a good life for them? I did research; the findings were in conflict. On the one hand, some studies suggested that zoos protect endangered species by making humans care about their preservation, and that zoos are able to breed these rare animals in captivity away from predators. I remember being deeply impacted by one study that asserted that zoo animals led a much happier, carefree life in captivity than they ever did in the wild. Zoos eliminate threat and hunting for food. They provide their animals with regular meals and existential safety. In lots of cases, the individual animals live longer than they would in the wild.

Other research, however, contradicts these findings. There are reports that some species are less likely to procreate in captivity. Other studies show that when zoo animals harm humans (even misbehaving humans), they're killed. One of our best loved apes at the Cincinnati Zoo was shot after a toddler got through the fencing into the exhibit. To protect the baby, the ape was put down, even though not at fault. Additional studies show that the living conditions in zoos are unnatural, and often the local weather is dramatically different from the natural habitat of the species, impacting their welfare. These studies also point to the stress the animals experience based on how their enclosures are designed for the purpose of entertaining people.

My initial instinct was to want one view to be right and the other wrong. I slowed myself and shifted gears. I approached the research using the "overview effect." I considered them in a broader context. I noticed that both sides of the zoo discussion purported to want the same things: preservation of biodiversity and protection of endangered species. I didn't treat the research in either study as waiting for my approval or rejection. Once I had vetted the researchers as qualified professionals, I chose to allow the points the researchers wanted to make to impact me. I chose to feel what the arguments set out to do. That process also required time. I spent over a year thinking about these ideas, reading articles, and asking opinions of people who work in the field. Driving for insight allows this flexibility of mind. When I put the two seemingly contradictory positions together, I had an epiphany. I realized that the question on everyone's mind is how to motivate people to want to protect animal life on planet Earth. I became *more* interested in the controversy, yet *less* convinced.

Staying open to insight, I didn't pit the research results against each other, nor did I accept one and discard the other. To be sure, there are times when one study overturns the results of another, and it's important to admit that. But that's not always the case, nor is it the first assumption to make. Instead, by reading more than one side, you enter a Ping-Pong match of facts and assertions. It helps to transcend the debate and ask the larger question—whatever it may be. In this case: How can humans become motivated to both enjoy and protect animals?

Insight is fluid and energizing. It correlates one idea to another and fosters deeper reflection. You can help kids recognize insight by describing what it feels like when they're having one. It's often experienced in the body as a little zing or a sudden aha or sweeping relief. They might notice a brand-new thought that delights them. I remember at age eleven discovering the symbolism of a rose and its thorns—loveliness and pain, side by side. I was moved by my own sudden depth, never mind that poets had been making that correlation for centuries. I felt it as my own. That's the experience of insight. The multifaceted idea remains complex but is better appreciated and understood with more nuance. Insight isn't something an adult provides to kids. It comes from within each of us. All we can do is create the conditions for it to erupt.

Those conditions are:

- **Freedom** to draw tentative conclusions
- **Space** to feel deeply
- **Support** during the moment of crisis: "That finding ruins my thesis!"
- **Time** to mull over the ideas

Insight is the fruit of the self-awareness tools we're about to explore.

In working with students for the last twenty-five years, I've seen that it is, in fact, possible to show them how to be less defensive when they learn—getting past that initial resistance to new data, ideas, and viewpoints. There are practices that allow students to do that deeper work without the knee-jerk reactivity that makes them stop learning (hello, college paper, again). Sprinkled through the rest of this chapter are preparatory activities for younger children and provocative processes that are best suited to junior and senior high students. I recommend that you try them yourself, so that you can experience the subtle shifts in your emotions and body reactions that inform how you make meaning. You'll be better able to guide your kids. It's also wise for students to begin these practices with "low-stakes" topics for which a student's opinions are not well formed. They'll be able to pay attention to how their thinking can be influenced because they won't have adopted a firm opinion yet. I've identified these three key practices in self-aware critical thinking:

- Exposing our first impressions
- Recognizing our differences
- Identifying our loyalties

Expose First Impressions

Our bodies and minds work fast. They provoke emotions and deliver instant reactions, even if you try to restrain them. Our first impressions of a subject of study can quickly become the controlling lens for how we evaluate information. Insights have a difficult time bubbling up if your body is sending you a wave of anxiety or a surge of triumph. First thoughts include the vocabulary a person associates with the topic, familiar sayings and slogans, prejudices (or "prejudgments") the individual carries, and personal hunches. I like to define the term "hunch" this way: a hunch is a person's internal belief that if people could live up to their ideal perspective, the world would be a better place. Like this: "I have a hunch that if women were paid equally to men, the workplace would be a fairer environment." Our hunches are expressed as opinions often before we've had time to do the research to confirm what we expect or imagine to be true.

Let's call first impressions to center stage.

☀ TOOL: FIRST IMPRESSIONS

Bright-eyed (5 to 9) kids can answer these questions thinking about an item they love or strongly dislike, like a food item, or a toy, or something found in nature like a flower, a pinecone, the sun, or the ocean.

Quick-witted (10 to 12) kids can consider a concrete topic they enjoy or find tedious, like board games, astronomy, comics, math facts, fantasy novels, or robotics.

Nimble-minded (13 to 18) teens can focus on controversial issues, like driverless cars, vaping, hunting for sport, the draft for military service, and curfews.

Before Study

- When you think of your topic, what happens in your body?

  Are you aware of any sensations? What are they, and where are they happening?

  Are you relaxed and at ease? Happy and eager?

  Or are you nervous? Are you bracing yourself?

  Do you feel a tightness in your jaw or stomach?

  Are you aware of any other sensations?

  Alternatively, is there no physical sensation?

- Next, let's evaluate the thoughts you have.

  Identify vocabulary related to the topic (with or without definitions). Make a list.

  List slogans and sayings (for all viewpoints— positive, negative, indifferent). Even a concrete item like the ocean will call up sayings like "Surf's up" and "Life's a beach."

  Note prejudices (prejudgments) you make about people (both the people who agree with you and those who don't).

  Name your hunch. What about your current viewpoint would make life better for everyone if they adopted it?

    -Bright-eyed example for the sun: The sun makes it possible to play outside.

    -Quick-witted example for board games: Games bring families together.

-Nimble-minded example for curfews:
Teens should be trusted to get home when
they feel safe, not in a rush to beat a curfew.

Now read and explore the topic. For your youngest kids, help them consider the opposite of their impression. For example, if they are thinking about sunshine, ask them to think about when the sun is not pleasant or beneficial. Discover who might benefit and who might not benefit from lots of sunshine. The goal is to "complexify" their relationship to the sun. That will be enough investigation for your littler kids. For older kids, it's time to examine the topic using outside research (not only your current impressions). Select at least three articles to read so that you have more than one viewpoint to consider. Type the topic plus the term "controversy" in your internet browser search field to help bring up opinion pieces.

After Study

For each article your student reads, ask these questions:

- What in the article provoked body reactions in you? Can you tie what you learned in the article to specific emotions like fear, worry, anger, delight, or vindication?
- Was the initial vocabulary list before you studied the topic in more depth accurate to what you just read or learned? What new words were added to your understanding of this topic? What terms took on new meaning now that you've learned more?
- How do you see your previous "prejudgments" and hunches now? Any modifications you'd like to make?

No need to treat these questions like a questionnaire. They're just as powerful in conversation with you over a latte at a coffee shop. Once your student or child has had a chance to mull over their first impressions, ask these questions:

- What insights (an aha moment, any new thoughts, or provocative questions) have you generated?
- How do your insights alter what you understood about the topic before you began?

Exposing first impressions is a habit to cultivate. Checking in with what your body tells you and how that shifts based on new information is one way to track the impact of an argument. When I wrote my college paper and discovered contradictory evidence, my stomach dropped. My heart raced! To stop my panic, I deep-sixed the article and pretended it didn't exist. Then I worried that my professor would know I had ignored that material and would give me a poor grade. All of these sensations stood in the way of my learning more about the topic and growing a well-formed opinion. I was afraid to let go of my first impressions.

FRAMING

Another way we form first impressions is through the vehicle that delivers the information to us. Artwork is most often framed before it is hung on a wall. The frame gives the viewer a hint about its elegance, importance, style aesthetic, and how it fits with other paintings in the same room. The best frame highlights the artwork itself, enhancing it. The worst frame detracts from the story the painter wants to tell. Similarly, every source a student studies has a frame. The frame might be the perspective of an instructor, textbook, or academic journal. The frame might be a historical novel (fiction) or a nightly news story (television journalism). The frame may be the vehicle of delivery (style of artwork on the book cover, documentary in color or black and white, audio versus print). One way to get beyond the seductive power of the frame is to name it and identify how it steers first impressions. The questions that follow work best with kids who are quick-witted and nimble-minded (ages 10 to 18).

✳ TOOL: FRAMING

Try These Questions

- Is the source a human being? If so, what about this person shapes your reaction? Dress? Hair? Voice? Is the person in a position of authority or a close friend? Is the person expressing firsthand experiences or reporting what someone else experienced? Does the person have the credentials to speak with authority? Which credentials? What about the person causes you to either trust implicitly or react with initial distrust?
- If the source is material, what's the packaging? Sturdy book? Are the pages of the book edged in gold or roughly cut? Paperback? What's the cover design? Is the credentialed expert prominently displayed on the packaging? Publisher (or self-published)?
- If a digital or media source: Website for an advocacy group? Multimedia presentation? Interview with firsthand witness? Collection of handwritten letters? TED Talk? Radio show? Audio recording? Historic fragment from an archaeological dig?
- How does the framing predispose you to think about the content? Do you see it as credible? Why? What could cause you to either lose trust in its reliability or

to gain it? Can you compare it to other sources (websites of different viewpoints, books on the same topic, audio versus print version, other television stations)? How does that comparison impact your emotional reaction to the source? Which sources appear trustworthy and which don't? Why?

- What does this frame imply or hope to elicit?
    Objectivity?
    Emotional connection?
    Action?
    Reflection?
    Outrage?
    Respect?
    Awe?
    Empathy?
    Credibility?
    Protest?
    News?
    Something else?

- Does the frame support the status quo (how things are currently), or does it challenge it (how things could be instead)? For instance, if it's a petition, the goal is to create change. If the book is an exposé, it intends to upend the established narrative. If it's a report, the goal may be to affirm established findings. Which is it for this source? How does that understanding shape your expectations for when you consume it?

- Does the frame reference an authority figure? Someone with qualifications? Someone with direct experience? God? Celebrity? Political leader? Religious leader? PhD?

ONE TEXT, MANY FRAMES

A religious text, like the Christian Bible, is a great example of how frames influence our first impressions. The Bible is the most published book in history. The *Guinness World Records* book claims that more than five billion copies have been printed and distributed worldwide. The Bible is most often printed and read as a single book, even though the contents were composed over centuries and represent a collection of writings from an assortment of authors. The entire Bible has been translated into over seven hundred languages worldwide, not to mention many additional versions in single languages like English, Spanish, and German. Each translation is a frame—a way to convey the immediacy of the content to each group of people. Some translations focus on contemporary language and have bindings to match. In English, the modern translations of the Bible are often printed in paperback with contemporary designs on the cover. This presentation could be construed to convey that the religious information within is approachable and relevant today, despite having been written thousands of years ago. Other English versions of the Bible use the seventeenth-century King James translation. Many of these Bibles have pages edged in gold with leather covers. The old-style language combined with the elegant binding creates an impression of specialness and authority.

Contrast the framing of these modern-day Bibles with the Dead Sea Scrolls found in the West Bank region of Qumran. These nine hundred plus fragments of biblical texts, from what Jews call the Tanakh and Christians call the Old Testament, are handwritten on papyrus. Many are stained, incomplete scraps. There are no spaces between words, and "[t]he scrolls have shown how biblical texts are actually fungible: a few words re-ordered, and in some cases whole passages excised or re-written." Think about the impact of these two frames (modern and ancient) on similar content—how they drive first impressions and emotional responses. Consider how difficult it is to set aside a personal investment in a way of seeing the text before beginning the critical inquiry. Even if we find it challenging to set aside the initial impression, we can at least be made aware that we have one. Once you teach your kids to notice frames, they will have a leg up when they get to college and beyond. They will not be as easily swayed by how information is presented and will know how to cut to the heart of an argument.

Appreciate Radical Difference

The next tool for insight generation dives a little deeper. Many educators ask their students to use the skill called "empathy" to help them find common ground with how others perceive the world. Yet just as asking a student to be open-minded often leads to a dead end, so, too, the call for empathy. Iris Marion Young, professor of Public and International Affairs at the University of Pittsburgh, challenges the idea that we ought to develop reciprocal feelings with others—trying to understand one another by getting behind their eyes and imagining their experiences for ourselves. While imagination is a powerful tool, Young points out that our positions in life are not mirrors of each other (or as she puts it: they're not "reversible"). We each bring different life experiences, histories, emotional habits, and goals to our outlooks. When we believe we can walk in someone else's shoes, Young argues that too often, "[we] project onto them a perspective that complements [our] own" rather than one that is true to the individual in question. Instead of being able to imagine how it is for the other, we imagine how we believe it would be for *us* given *their* circumstances. She cites a powerful example of how this type of projection can result in dire consequences.

In the 1990s, the state of Oregon offered reimbursements for specific medical treatments to able-bodied individuals and denied reimbursement for the same procedures to people with disabilities. When challenged to address the inequity of this proposal, the justification was shocking. "Officials thought they had objective grounds for this judgment because they had conducted a telephone survey of Oregon citizens." The able-bodied people in the survey were asked to imagine themselves in the place of a person in a wheelchair or a person who was blind or deaf. "The majority of the respondents said that they would rather be dead than wheelchair bound or blind." The political judgment was made that the disabled, therefore, would not receive the same subsidies as able-bodied people. However, Young points out that studies demonstrate that disabled people have low rates of suicide and consider their lives very much worth living. The statute was overturned due to its violation of the Americans with Disabilities Act. Even so, Young's point reverberates: "When asked to put themselves in the position of a person in a wheelchair, they do not imagine the point of view of others; rather, they project onto those others their own fears and fantasies about themselves."

In order to offset this tendency, Young advises that we adopt an approach of "asymmetrical reciprocity." The goal is to make moral and academic judgments that come from our shared respect for the radical difference between us, not through conjuring what we perceive to be identical feelings. In fact, she argues that our commitment to one another ought to be grounded in moral solidarity, not the ability to fathom someone else's circumstance. As we work with our kids, this is a skill of particular value. Sometimes children and teens find it difficult to imagine how they impact other people. A teen might participate in cyberbullying, or a small child may punch a friend. Asking the perpetrators to imagine how it would feel if what they had done had happened to them may not be effective. The teen might say, "I wouldn't care! I would have laughed it off." The young child might say, "He deserved it. He stole my toy." The posture of asymmetrical reciprocity is valuable here. The goal is to help our children and teens hear how it really is for the other person, and to recognize that person's right to an entirely different perspective—even one they don't fully understand. To be a critical thinker in this context means growing the capacity to see that someone else's experience holds value intrinsically, not because it can be felt or understood by others. Their perspective is whole and not subject to diminishment by the person who caused pain or lacks access to a similar experience. The asymmetry of respect in this case is tilted toward the one who is suffering, not the one who is well or oblivious to the pain caused.

Young suggests two practices that help us in our quest to facilitate this asymmetry of respect. First, she recommends that we approach the other person with "wonder." The curiosity we show for another person's point of view is rooted in wondering how it is for them, not how we would feel in their place. Here's where Lady Insight helps us again. While learning, students can stay alert to the needs, interests, perceptions, and values of the thinker under consideration, rather than deciding if they can imagine themselves under similar conditions. The goal is to "get it," not to feel it. Young explains, "This implies that we have the moral humility to acknowledge that even though there may be much I do understand about the other person's perspective through her communication to me . . . there is always a remainder, much that I do not understand about the other person's experience and perspective." For instance, a disabled person can express their frustrations with the limits of their body and their dependency on a wheelchair. Hearing about those limits and even imagining them as an able-bodied person is not the same as having a direct experience of relying on a wheelchair. One side is weighted with a lived reality while the other with an attempt to imagine it. Part of this quest to understand more deeply, then, according to Young, is to admit up front that there is an asymmetry of experience when we embark on hearing someone else's point of view.

When confused or put off by an experience or perspective, students can be reminded to adopt the "respectful stance of wonder" again, recognizing that their own position is just as mysterious to others as the one in question is to them. One way to express wonder is by asking questions rather than making assumptions. Even when reading, it's possible to form questions and then to look for the perspectives the writer takes in that reading. If given an opportunity to meet with a person (encounter), posing curious questions is even more powerful. Young explains: "Questions can express a distinctive form of respect for the other, that of showing interest in their expression and acknowledging that the questioner does not know what the issue looks like for them." That said, questions need not be fired at a person as some kind of drill or quiz. Each one of us ought to have the freedom to answer or not, according to our own criteria. "Respectful listening thus involves attentive and interested questioning. But answers are always gifts." The stance of wonder orders the relationship: it provides a bed of curiosity and interest that allows the fruit of insight to grow. It enables the participants to recognize any power differential (for instance, between parent and child, or older teen and younger sibling, or a status-quo point of view and a divergent one). Each encounter is seen as fresh, then, awaiting new insight. Wonder is not ideological. It allows for more than one experience to be unveiled and distilled.

The second way to respect our differences is through what Young calls "enlarged thought." The hallmark of the rhetorical imagination is the capacity to hold multiple points of view in one's mind without having to render immediate judgments. We enlarge our capacity to include divergent thoughts and perspectives when we do two things: (1) we scale back the importance of our own position, seeing it as one among many, and (2) we include more perspectives to consider than only two (getting away from binary thinking). Enlarged thought is characterized by "moral judgment." According to Young, "A moral point of view requires a person to think about a question or proposed action not only in terms of how an issue or action affects him or her, but also in terms of what others need and want or how they may be affected." Adding this purposeful approach to study keeps students centered on impact, not merely amassing more information or validation for their beliefs.

Rather than establishing support for a position that ensures protection of their own place in the world, moral judgment asks students to grow and develop a viewpoint that includes more people and takes into account additional experiences and circumstances. A well-formed opinion built from "enlarged thought" bridges these differences meaningfully (not just choosing "the lesser of two evils" or "the one that works best for me"). The more voices we teach our children to include, the more viewpoints they consider, the better they can understand our shared reality and make judgments that are good for the community, not only the individual—and vice versa: that are good for the individual, not only the community. An appreciation for radical difference allows anyone to transcend self-interest in order to stay curious and interested.

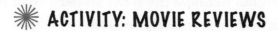 ## ACTIVITY: MOVIE REVIEWS

Quick-Witted (10 to 12) and
Nimble-Minded (13 to 18)

Talking about a political or social issue can raise the blood pressure quickly. One way I've helped students experience the power of multiple viewpoints on the same topic is to lower the stakes by examining movie reviews. Reviewers work with the same content (a film) and render different interpretive analyses of it. By reading both positive and negative reviews, students can experience the power of persuasive rhetoric firsthand without much of their identity at stake.

Have the student pick a favorite movie to rewatch. Rewatch it now.

Make a list of all the aspects of the film that your child appreciates and loves. Be specific. Here are a few categories for consideration:

- Acting by specific actors
- Dialogue

- Sets, costumes, makeup
- Action sequences
- Story arc
- Special effects

Next, go online and visit rottentomatoes.com. Read movie reviews that agree with your child's positive take first (healthy red tomatoes). Notice how they align with your child's viewpoint and how they expand reasons for that positive view of the film.

Now, select and read several negative reviews (green-splat tomatoes). Notice how these reviewers interpret the identical content using different criteria. See if your student can identify those criteria. For instance, perhaps the beloved story line is failing due to a sociological concern (like, how women are portrayed). Or perhaps a reviewer cites historical inaccuracies.

As your child reads, have them note any emotional reactivity.

- Are they defensive?
- Are there any reasons they want to use to offset the reviewer's perspective?
- Is there any single assertion the reviewer makes that knocks the student's position off-kilter? What comment or piece of analysis did that? Why?

Urge your child to take a stance of wonder.

- Can they be curious without entangling their own perceptions? It's okay if they can't yet. It's a difficult skill to cultivate. Go back to simply noting the reaction if it's too difficult to shift to wonder.

- How does your child's evaluation of the film shift as they consider negative reviews? Or does it?
- Can the child make room for both? Is there any reason not to? Can the child use "enlarged thought" to expand to include any of the criticisms of the film in their own love of the movie?

There's no right conclusion. The child doesn't have to come to a compromised view of the movie or ever agree with negative reviews. This tool is a method for monitoring individual reactivity when confronted with a viewpoint the student doesn't want to be true. It's also an opportunity to notice how the same source material can result in two entirely different "takes."

Identify Loyalties

The biggest barrier to critical thinking is often invisible to us. We're influenced by our loyalty to our communities and the valuable sense of belonging we gain from them. Communities share a similar paradigm, which can be defined as "patterns of thought that are destined to be compared with each other." Our social paradigms are often expressed as binaries: secular and religious, capitalist and socialist, rural and urban, homeschooling and public education. We know we're in or out based on how we align with the paradigm. No one wants to put at risk friendships or family or allies in a cause. To consider perspectives that challenge our community's well-established beliefs and values is to risk sabotaging that membership. Our craving to belong is as deep as it is wide. It's also ancient. Our biology is hard at work making us feel as though we'll lose everything if we lose our people.

To delve into the study of a topic that conflicts with our loyalties, students benefit from asking these questions first:

- What's at stake?
- What would I have to give up to change my mind?
- Who would be disappointed in me if I did change my mind?
- What values do I fear I'd have to betray to be fair to this topic?
- Who are the sources of authority in my group? How do they see this topic?
- How would my community see me if I changed my mind? Would my membership be at risk?
- Who are the people that think this way? Do I see them as friends, enemies, or a neutral party?
- What practices in my life are associated with my current view?
- What practices would I have to change if I adopted this other viewpoint?
- How are these ideas in conflict with the community logic stories I've been taught?

We can also ask questions about the community that sees differently:

- How do they characterize their viewpoint as moral or justifiable?
- What logic story drives their viewpoint?
- What hunch is at work in their perspective? (Remember, I define a hunch as the belief that if people adopted a person's particular viewpoint, the world would be a better place.)
- How does that community see my community? Friends, enemies, or neutral party? How does that knowledge impact how I see them?

- What practices characterize this community? Do these practices have social value or personal meaning? Can I identify what that is?
- Who are the sources of authority in this community? How does my community see their sources of authority? How did my community form those views?

We belong to a wide variety of communities, not just the ones that show up on a census review. Those communities, as we saw in chapter 6, help us interpret our personal perceptions and offer us logic stories to make sense of our place in the world. They provide us with people who want to do life with us—whether being the fan of a band or a member of a faith community, whether a skillful hobbyist or an unschooler. Anytime you name an identity for yourself, you're simultaneously naming the group that identifies with you! If you want to understand someone else, go to the source. Listen to the leaders and members of the community, not your own community's interpretation of the "other side."

Put Them All Together, and What Have You Got?

Self-awareness in critical thinking is an ongoing journey, not a once-for-all accounting. The habit to momentarily turn away from the topic in order to monitor personal perceptions and community logic stories is the beginning. Let's take a look at how to apply these tools in a group setting.

Picture a group of tenth-grade students. The teacher suggests that the students prepare to discuss the topic of gun control in the United States. They are given articles to read. Some of the questions they are to consider follow.

- What is meant by the concept of regulation in the Second Amendment ("a well-regulated militia")? Are we regulating people, guns, or both?

- How much regulation should the government be empowered to have? Should that control be federal or by state?
- Background checks: What kind, if any?
- Waiting periods for purchasing guns: How long, if at all?
- Right to purchase: Who can own a gun? Adults? Children? What about felons?
- Varieties of guns: Which types can be purchased? Any restrictions at all?
- Regulations for use: Open or conceal carry? "Stand your ground" laws that protect armed citizens who shoot when they feel under attack, or no?

The students are told to divide into two groups based on how they align with the gun control issue. Except, the first self-aware question you may already be asking is: How do they align? This wide array of considerations doesn't necessarily represent a simple pro–gun control or anti–gun control position. We're already aware that there's no way to "get it right." There are lots of "its"—details that need to be better understood and interpreted. Rather than debate, the teacher could instead instruct students to divide into two groups that have a mix of backgrounds and perspectives. The goal would be to *generate insight* to share rather than driving to persuade. How many ways of seeing these questions can they discover together? How many possible suggestions? Immediately those conditions lower the stakes and allow for much more space to critically think.

Imagine, now, students with wildly different backgrounds in these groups. One student comes from a family where a sibling has been killed in a school shooting, another comes from a family with generations of hunters, and yet another, with a family story of someone whose life was saved by the intervention of a person with a firearm. To tackle this topic and these ideas, these kids, in particular, will need to know that they can voice their strong feelings about guns without being shouted down or persuaded to feel differently. Their perspectives need to be seen as valuable to the discussion, not merely strong opinions to overcome or set aside. Their *personal perceptions* deserve to be fully heard (if not personally traumatic for them to do so). They may also have a better ability to narrate their *community logic story* about guns using the natural vocabulary of that community. Too often, we ask students to set aside their backgrounds to become objective. Yet in a community project of this nature, powerful viewpoints can and should be allowed to surface. These polarities often help unearth other student commitments as well. Those who have the most to risk in the discussion will need to be approached with wonder, with an awareness of the asymmetry between them and the other students who don't share their backgrounds, and it will be important for the community conversation to include possible solutions that take each of their experiences and communities into account.

Together, the two groups can list all the possible solutions and questions that arise when looking at these suggested considerations. Personal stories ought to be included. It's an exciting moment to hear from both groups and to see how the train of thought diverged in each one. Once every idea and thought is weighed and considered, the question to ask isn't: What side are you on now?

Rather, the groups can be asked these questions:

- What new insight did you gain?
- What do you understand differently now than before?
- What new questions emerged?
- What is one principle you find helpful in guiding this discussion now?

If the quest is generating insight rather than debate, the conversation stays focused on the complexity of the details rather than reducing differences in order to make persuasive arguments. Adam Grant, author of *Think Again*, put it well on his Instagram account: "The hallmark of a productive debate is not persuasion, but insight." The idea here is to identify the moral judgments that honor individual experience, yet also account for the impacts on various communities. Remembering that we're human beings first and students second helps.

In the next chapter, we look at how to deal with texts. What is the art of interpreting contemporary and ancient writings? How do we generate insights to make meaning from all the communications we're asked to evaluate?

CHAPTER 12

The Art of Interpretation

The issue therefore is not about finding the truth the author wrote about but realizing the truth it has for the reader, how it becomes alive for the interpreter.

—Paul Regan

Y ou've arrived at the apex of this book. All critical thinking drives for a single end: interpretation. We interpret our encounters with others, symbols we see, visual media, books and articles we read, expert opinion, eyewitness accounts, conversations, news reports, interactions in our families, and experiences we have. In other words, we're interpreting "texts"—the communications of others that we "read" and seek to understand. It's an inescapable practice. Human beings can't help but make meanings. Most of the interpreting we do happens intuitively, which means we do it without thinking about it. We read body language, intonation, volume, context, relationship, identity, grammar, and expectation in every interaction. If a friend tells you to "go jump in the lake," you're likely to stay dry because you know the friend, while rude, meant it metaphorically. If your triathlon coach, who's training you to swim long distances in naturally occurring bodies of water, tells you to "go jump in the lake," you strip off your sweats and dive in. His meaning, you understand, is literal.

Interpretation is an art! It's not a scientific exercise in exact measurements. Rather, all interpretations benefit from a spirit of play. There's a dance that happens between the messenger and the receiver. The message is sent with the writer's intentions in the writer's immediate context. The message is received in the new context of the interpreter. When these two perspectives collide, a fresh interpretation of the work is revealed. Interpretations are not once for all time. They're continuously renewed. This is why interpretation can be seen as an art, not a science.

Context Is Everything

Remember, in publishing, "content is king." But in critical thinking? Context is everything. Context is a multifaceted prism for reading. German philosopher Hans-Georg Gadamer explains how critical context is in the act of interpretation in his seminal work, *Truth and Method*. Each original text reveals two primary contexts, according to Gadamer: the horizon of the author (the worldview of the writer at the time of writing) and the horizon of the reader (the reader's contemporary worldview). The fusion of these two horizons impacts how we read and what meaning we take. Or as Gadamer elegantly summarizes it: "To understand [a text] does not mean primarily to reason one's way back into the past, but to have a present involvement in what is said. . . . To think historically always involves mediating between those ideas and one's own thinking." In other words: every reading requires us to tease apart our current context from the original one, in order to make a new, relevant interpretation.

Context matters because it's not what is or isn't true that has a lasting influence on us. It's what we *say* about what we read. The meanings we generate create our perceptions of reality, whatever the original writers intended. This dialogue between the two horizons can move in either direction. Sometimes original context is meaningfully informative and corrective to an errant popular view. For example, in ancient times, rain and sunshine are both seen as divine gifts of blessing because an agrarian culture needed both for survival. In today's agribusiness world not dependent on rainfall, our modern relationship to the weather leads us to see rain more as a nuisance or symbol of sadness. (Watch any romantic comedy.) If you are reading an ancient text, however, understanding that rain is not a symbol of persecution or retribution, but one of divine generosity and goodness, will impact the meaning you make.

Other times, the contemporary reading is a necessary evolution of the original concept. This is the tension we negotiate in the United States every time anyone debates the interpretation of the Constitution. Certainly there's no American today who believes that the right to vote is only for white landholding males. It's clear that the founding documents have needed amending. (There are now twenty-seven amendments—modifications—to what the original document specifies.) In fact, the Ninth Amendment specifically names that there are other rights citizens will understand themselves to have that are not enumerated in the Bill of Rights. What an insightful modification! Yet who decides which rights, for whom, and when? That's what interpretation is—that very act. The Supreme Court revisits old interpretations of the Constitution and its amendments, too. The Thirteenth Amendment abolished slavery and overturned Article 4, Section 2, Clause 3 of the Constitution—the Fugitive Slave Clause. The court removed rights previously granted, stating that slave owners had no rights of ownership and, therefore, could not retrieve formerly enslaved Americans from the free North. The original intentions and meanings may be accurately understood, even while the modern-day interpretation overturns the power of those very ideas. This is why when we talk about interpretation, we're looking at layers of understanding—and then fusing them together for now, for today.

Another way that context influences how we interpret goes back to the viewpoint of the writer. Jackson Katz, a social commentator, pointed out that in the United States, we use the passive voice to describe bad things that happen to women, as though there's no agent. He argues that how we speak about violence against women leads to an interpretation of that violence as less aggressive than it actually is. In this instance, the grammatical construction (passive voice) influences how we hear the message.

> We talk about how many women were raped last year, not about how many men raped women. We talk about how many girls in a school district were harassed last year, not about how many boys harassed girls. We talk about how many teenage girls in the state of Vermont got pregnant last year, rather than how many men and boys impregnated teenage girls. So you can see how the passive voice has a political effect. It shifts the focus off of men and boys and onto girls and women.

The passive voice here puts the emphasis on the victims rather than the perpetrators. This is the type of lens to note when interpreting any text.

Classic Literature

Let's look at how this dynamic plays out when we read classic literature, particularly with kids. Books routinely go in and out of favor based on context alone. A book that was popular in one era may be seen as racist in the next one. The Little House series by Laura Ingalls Wilder is a perfect example. Wilder's first book in the series, *Little House in the Big Woods*, was published in 1932. The series became an award-winning juggernaut, selling millions upon millions of copies, earning multiple Newbery Medal awards, and being honored with the creation of a children's literature award in Wilder's name. I own hardbound copies of the series, have read them countless times to myself and my children, and visited Laura's home in De Smet, South Dakota, with my family. For decades, Laura's books were heralded as exemplars of high-quality children's literature. I love Wilder's gentle, spare writing style and dry wit. And yet. Somehow readers (for decades) bypassed Wilder's firsthand matter-of-fact accounts of her era's racism. Quotes like "The only good Indian is a dead Indian" from *Little House on the Prairie* and the breathless buildup to a minstrel show featuring Pa and friends in black face in *Little Town on the Prairie* were accepted as reflecting the late nineteenth-century life on the frontier with precious little critique from twentieth-century readers.

Wilder's racist treatment of Indigenous and Black Americans flew under my radar as a child. I remember the shock of encountering those racist renderings as I read the books to my children in the twenty-first century. I chose to see those texts as opportunities to teach my white children about the evils of racism. Step one, to be sure. Today, our culture is undergoing a further revolution of awareness. Readers of all backgrounds are being challenged to consider the impact of that literature on Indigenous and Black children who read Wilder's stories that depict racism in their classrooms and homes. Additionally, white parents and teachers are being asked to think about the legacy these stereotypes create in very small children and how stories like these shape their early imaginations too forcefully. As our culture undergoes the self-examination of its history, our interpretation of what we read changes and what remains canon shifts. In other words, there's no once-for-all-time interpretation of any text.

In 2018, the American Library Association renamed the Laura

Ingalls Wilder Children's Literature Award to the Children's Literature Award, removing Wilder's name as an acknowledgment that her writings were no longer emblematic of the values contemporary readers expect to find in children's literature. It's worth noting that 2018 is eighty-six years after the first publication of *Little House in the Big Woods*. "Wilder's books are a product of her life experiences and perspective as a settler in America's 1800s," the association's president, Jim Neal, and the president of the children's division, Nina Lindsay, said in the statement. "Her works reflect dated cultural attitudes toward Indigenous people and people of color that contradict modern acceptance, celebration, and understanding of diverse communities."

When we interpret books, we are bound by both the horizon of the author (the setting in which the book was written) and the horizon of the interpreter (the time and place in which it is being read). It took nearly a century for interpreters of the *Little House* books to categorically change their perspective of the values on display in Wilder's series of novels, and consequently our interpretation of her work. We can read the books at a critical level, understanding that her writings represent an original perspective of white settlers on the frontier, certainly, and particularly as adults because we are better equipped to critically identify the political and social context of her life span. But it is this choice to read her books critically that is the fruit of fresh interpretations in this era. For nearly a century, the books were read benignly to children with little thought to the way they contributed to a sustained, unacknowledged racism.

The Art of Interpretation

All of us are interpreters. The tools we've looked at in this book so far give your students a fighting chance at being good at the task of interpretation. In this section, let's bring the skills of critical thinking to the interpretation of written texts. Once your kids get the hang of it, these skills can easily apply to TED Talks, college lectures, documentaries, films, plays, poetry, and conversations with friends. To interpret a text (particularly one divorced from the original context), the first step is to realize that decoding the words is not the same as understanding the intent of the author. The interpreter's current vocabulary, cultural values, expectations, personal perceptions, and community logic stories will initially exert influence on how a text is read. That first pass invariably leads to an inadequate interpretation.

One of the classes I taught to high school writing students asked them to interpret the famous feminist essay by Judy Brady called "Why I Want a Wife." The article is pure satire and focuses on the domestic role of wives from the mid-twentieth century. Brady portrays wives as domestic servants to their husbands, and the article quips that even wives would benefit from having wives themselves. When I asked this homeschooled population of kids to read the article in the early 2000s, many of them became defensive because they had mothers who had made the choice to stay home in a traditional role. That initial reading felt threatening, as though it was minimizing the value of their mothers' work. My students had not yet acquired a historical lens to understand how today's stay-at-home mother has many more choices compared with the wives being described in 1971. Interestingly, in the last five years, I've noticed that student reactions to the article have softened. Many stay-at-home mothers include work in their stay-at-home lives, and these kids see their fathers participating more readily in typical domestic duties. As a result, the teen reaction to the essay in the third decade of the twenty-first century is less antagonistic to the original text. How we understand any text is temporary and culturally controlled. Personal perception is a powerful controlling lens, particularly on a first read. As your students work through the interpretation of a text, remind them that they will form additional insights *after* the first reading. It takes a deliberate, second effort to dig a little deeper. The following process is meant for nimble-minded (13 to 18) students. These are challenging questions to answer that require your kids to have a good foundation in the other skills we've already addressed in this book.

✳ ACTIVITY: TASK OF INTERPRETATION INVENTORY

One of the best ways to learn how to interpret a text is to use a tool that poses reflection questions to the student as they read. Tell your kids: "Be honest and true! No one is watching." Some of my favorite books have wildly emotional margin notes where I let myself vent the full force of my uninformed ignorance. Later, once I did more research, it was a time capsule for me to see how far my thinking had come compared with that first blush. In the following activity, the work of Hans-Georg Gadamer has informed my own. I've adapted his three horizons of interpretation for teens specifically.

The inventory that follows is written *to* the interpreter—in this case, your student or teen. Select a written text for this process: novel, poetry, speech, historical record or document, religious manuscript, philosophical treatise, textbook, literary criticism, movie review, diary, newspaper article. Start with a text that is fewer than a thousand words.

Next, have your teen follow these instructions.

1. **Print or photocopy the text onto paper with large margins.**
   If at all possible, get the text out of a bookbinding. Photocopy it (shrink the text if necessary) and allow for wide (two- to three-inch) margins. If it is difficult to get the text out of the book for any reason, retype the text, triple space it, and then print.

2. **Ask questions of the text in the margins.**
    Highlight passages *and* pose questions to the text.
    Record your true reactions in your natural writing voice.
    It's perfectly acceptable to write things like "What on
    earth does this mean?" or "I can't believe this writer is so
    ignorant." These first impressions give you a clue about
    your bias as well as what is of interest to you. You may
    have feelings of confusion, or you may feel provoked. By
    the end, the reading may make more sense. Or
    conversely, you may find agreement initially, only to
    have your viewpoint challenged by the time you finish
    the reading. Note it all in the margins.

3. **Underline or highlight repeated terms, phrases,
    evidence, and literary devices.**
    In addition to asking questions of the text, notice writing
    craft. Does the writer repeat a certain term? Does the
    writer include substantiated evidence or credible
    research? Notice the effect of various literary devices,
    like alliteration or rhyme or assonance. Identify any
    metaphors or analogies. Asterisk the personal
    experiences of the writer or anecdotes used to make a
    point.

4. **Correlate your initial observations with other writings
    or data.**
    The margin notes and questions are a pathway back to
    the bits of the text that provoked a reaction in you. They
    can offer an excellent starting place for determining a
    thesis statement or an angle of focus for a paper. Make
    connections like, "Contrast this idea with Smith's theory
    in *X* book" or "Check out this statistic for validity."

These kinds of notes help you relocate an important piece of information for further reflection.

Once you've read the text and jotted questions, highlighted passages, and made margin notes, it's time to ask yourself some questions. For shorter texts like poetry, political speeches, or religious texts, rereading is critical. If using a longer text, you may not have time to reread, but you can scan and look for passages to support your answers.

Horizon of the Interpreter (You)

As you read the text, ask yourself these questions.

Your Disposition

- What do you hope to find in the text?
- What suspicions do you bring to it? Do you read "with" the text or "against" it? In other words, are you a receptive reader or a hostile reader? Simply note which.
- What angers you?
- What surprises you?
- What relieves you?

Your Reactions

- What images go with your reading? (See chapter 4 for the keen observation activity for nimble-minded students if you need image questions to prompt you.)
- How do you react to the language? Are there stereotypes, polemics (strident unsupported

assertions), name-calling? Does the writer show restraint, balance, or nuances, accounting for the opposing viewpoint?

- Do you trust the writer? Why or why not?
- What are your immediate reactions to the writing? (Remember the margin notes here. They may help you.)
- What do you wish to avoid?
- As you read, what other voices do you reference? Your family? Religious community? (If you need them, the previous chapter has additional questions about community identity and loyalty that you can use to probe further.)
- Whose voice is loudest in your head? A favorite writer? A friend? A leader of some kind?

The Impact

- How does the text relate to your personal experiences? Does it feel familiar or foreign?
- Who are you? Does the text affirm your place in the world (your identity, economic status, religious outlook, race, nationality, age group, gender, sexual orientation, education)? Or does it challenge it or say nothing to it? Remember, you are multifaceted, so there are several pieces of identity to consider.
- How does the text suggest a hopeful vision? Or does it?
- How does it suggest doom? Or does it?
- Why are you reading the text? (If for an assignment, what is the express reason for the assignment?) Get at a reason that goes beyond "for class," as usually there

is a purpose in the analysis that is meant to engage your critical thinking.

- What is your overall reaction to the text now that you've read it and thought about it a bit?

Once you've taken this inventory, it helps to freewrite for several minutes. Put your jumble of thoughts into a few free-flowing paragraphs of unedited thought. Then move on to the next inventory. You may want to take a break—even a day off—before you move to the next level of analysis.

Horizon of the Text (Author)

Each piece of writing grows in a specific context. The more recent the publication, the more likely it is that you'll have a firm grasp of the cultural, political, and linguistic world of the text. In most academic settings, however, we're often required to examine and comment on writing that is from a remote social, historical, and cultural place. Sometimes you'll be working with texts translated from other languages, even (a book or a film in another language with subtitles in your own). Knowing a thing or two about the historical, socioeconomic, racial, and political context is critical to accurate readings. Similarly, language and culture impact the writing as well. With these in mind, let's look at how to examine the text/ writing itself.

As you reread the text, consider the following.

The Text Itself

- What text are you working with? Determine if this is a work of literature, history, criticism, science, religious manuscript, research study, poem, news report, and so on. The genre (kind of text) determines what attitude one takes toward it. If you are working with legend, you will treat it differently than if you're reading historical records. Understand the properties of that genre of text before you go on. (Chapter 7 has a list of genres on pages 158–59 that may be helpful.)

- How does the text come to you? Why is it important? Who has considered it important?
- What language was it written in? What language are you reading it in? Are there any footnotes that clarify terms or images or references that are unfamiliar to you? Look these up and read them.

The Writing

- How is the text written? Is it meant to be an argument, a narrative, a poem, a record, a political screed, a religious message?
- Is the writing in active or passive voice? Can you identify the narrator?
- Do you sense an antagonistic audience? Is it written for the purpose of entertaining or persuading, warning or reassuring?
- How does the text play on the emotions? Do you notice any particular metaphors, images, or analogies that help the reader "feel" the writer's meaning? Can you identify how they were understood in that era and context? Do they work as well today as they did in the original era?
- Outline the logic of the piece. What kinds of support does the writer use to make the point? If literature,

describe the plot line and identify the climax. How does the writer get you there? Does it work? If poetry, what is the ironic moment or the moment of insight? How does the poet get you there? If a news report, what are the essential facts, and in what order of significance are they introduced?

The Audience

- Who was the original audience? Were they the "intended" audience? For instance, a speech may be intended for those not present because the speaker knows it will be reported. Can you detect the objective of the text? Was it commissioned by an authority (the pope, a queen)? Was the writer in danger for writing the text? Did the writer suffer for writing the text?
- How did the original audience receive this text? (For instance, in Shakespeare's day, his plays were well received and notable. Yet for some religious texts, they were completely ignored until years after the writer's death.)
- Was the text meant to consolidate power or subvert it? If fiction, does the text address a specific sociopolitical context? Which one and how?
- Are there cultural references that must be understood? What are they? Do you see myths, legends, metaphors, ideas, or motifs in this writing that should be lifted from the text and understood at a deeper level?

The Significance

- What questions does the text attempt to answer? What material from a previous era contributes to these answers?
- What is the historical context? What is the scientific worldview (Flat earth? Pre-Newtonian? Gods control the weather? Empiricism leads to truth?)? What is the political climate? Who is in power? Does the text support or criticize the prevailing powers?
- How does this text speak to the economic situation of the period?
- What is the situation of the author? Do we know the author's education, genealogy, economic condition, social standing, reputation at the time of writing and now historically?
- Has this text come to you with interpretive baggage? Who else has considered it worth interpreting, and how have these previous interpretations influenced our modern reading of the text?

Fusion of Horizons (You + Author)

It's time to interpret the text! Interpretation is a privilege. It's given to those who care enough to engage the material without making assumptions and who are willing to be transformed by what they read. Interpretation is an art form and, therefore, each interpreter's interpretation will bear the marks of unique insight. That means that there is no "one-size-fits-all" interpretation. Yet there can be overlapping consensus from a variety of interpreters, in many cases. The world of academia spends a lot of time debating who has a more compelling reading of a text at any given time, but they also realize that multiple readings can offer valid differences in perspective as well.

The art of interpretation is like throwing clay pots or assembling a crazy quilt or painting a landscape. There are many pieces to fuse together to create the resulting interpretation. What you create is an artful rendering of how you now understand the text in question. It will bear the marks of your uniqueness, even as you work to be objective and fair. Interpreting a text is deeply satisfying when engaged with patience, curiosity, and care. Answer the following questions in light of the two horizons you've already considered (yours and the writer's). You may not have answers to every question. Feel free to skip one if it doesn't relate to your text.

As you form your interpretation, consider these questions.

The Goals

- What's at stake? That's the crucial question for your entire interpretation. In *Pride and Prejudice*, for instance, the relationship between social convention and personal fulfillment is evaluated and critiqued. What is at stake? The structure of the class system in Britain and the importance of personal choice. Ask yourself: What is at stake in this text, story, poem, document? Also ask what is at stake for readers in this era? How does the text challenge your contemporaries?

- What questions does the text attempt to answer? Which questions can't it answer? Which answers have we found to these questions in the ensuing era (if applicable)?

- How does the text move you? What ideas do you find yourself considering? Are they subversive? Are they inspiring? Are they solution-driven or reflection-inducing?
- Summarize what you believe is the writer's intended message.
- What subplots or nuances are interesting to you?
- What does the text fail to address?
- How is your worldview or ideas about reality challenged by the text?

The Limits

- What prejudices are challenged? What prejudices remain unchallenged?
- How do you think this text influenced its era or spoke to it? How might it speak to ours?
- What community are you a part of, and how does the text relate to it? (This is where you would consider your faith community, nationality, race, economic status, gender, and so on.) Does the text hold an open future for you and your community, or does it subvert it? What loyalties surface for you as you interpret?
- What possibilities are foreclosed (limited) by the message of this text?
- If the writer were on a talk show, what do you think the writer would want to say to today's audience?

Your Reflections

- Have you changed during this process of interpretation?

- How has your initial hunch or agenda been modified
  or remained constant?
- Have you tried to control your interpretation
  throughout? Why?
- What is unsaid even after all this work? What more
  do you wonder?

Tentative Conclusions of the Interpreter

Once you've gathered your ideas through this guided question format, it's time to take a stab at an initial interpretation. There are a couple of principles to keep in mind:

1. You'll write a better interpretation if you sit with your reflections for a few days before you try to synthesize them.
2. You're allowed to change your mind. It may be that you thought you knew the direction you wanted to take with your response to the text when you began. If the inventory and rereadings have altered that initial hunch, note that. Identify what provoked those changes. Identifying how a text transforms understanding is a powerful way to form an interpretation.

How to Begin

For your kids who are tasked with writing a paper or articulating an opinion, here's the process to use to integrate what they discovered from the activity Task of Interpretation Inventory.

- Write a narration (couples therapy–style) of what you
  believe you hear the writer saying (without your point of

view). Do your best to remove any judgmental language, any time-bound assumptions, any of your own ideas. Stick to what you believe the author is saying, even if you disagree with the writer.

- Next, write about your relationship to the text, looking for places of connection (experience, ideals, compatible images, anecdotes, and analogies).

- Next add any comments that challenge what you read, thoughts that speak to what you found wanting or inconsistent or troubling.

- Review your replies from the Fusion of Horizons. Identify the compelling idea that has emerged. Write about it with support from the original text while addressing the unique context into which the text is being read today.

- The last step is to check your interpretation against those of other interpreters. Sometimes you will find that even a sincere idea you formed is misguided or has overlooked a key piece of context. Take that into account before you finalize your own work.

A spirit of play is essential in the Fusion of Horizons. One of the insightful points Gadamer makes is that each era will alter the meaning of a previous generation's interpretation inescapably. We don't only make meaning for the era in which the original communiqué lived, but we find ourselves reconsidering that meaning at another point in time. All ancient sacred texts are a prime example of this exact scenario.

If we harken back to my Bapa's love letter in the introduction, I might write an interpretation that chooses to focus on the changing meaning of the language "making love" to discuss how our culture's sexual habits have shifted how we use that language over the decades of the twentieth century. My grandfather's writing included the modifier "first" as in "where I *first* made love to you." Part of what jinxes the surface impression of the "made love to you" language is the idea of repeated acts. "Making love" in a sexual sense can be repeated. That means my interpretation would be impacted by that modern awareness. I might choose to think about my grandfather's attempts to bring his wife's mind back to their relationship through both the original declaration and the hint of their intimate shared sex life of their sixty plus years together. The interpretation would not be only about identifying whether or not they had sex before marriage (though if I felt strongly about that, it could be included). Rather, the interpretation would be one that allows a comment on how that letter fit with the time period in which it was written, the lifelong relationship between my grandparents, and the power of sexuality and romance that carries us even when faced with challenges like dementia and end of life.

Ultimately, to think critically is to interpret. The more we help our kids learn to pose questions to themselves that enable them to be conscientious, caring, and clear, the better their interpretations will be. The most challenging part of committing to an interpretation is the recognition that any interpretation a person makes is subject to new scrutiny and revised understanding at a later date. The sooner we can help our young people recognize that they are not trying to secure a once-for-all-time doctrine, but are contributing to a stream of ideas that ebb and flow, the sooner they will enjoy the art of critical thinking and interpretation as an expression of self, their relationship with others, and sublime ideas.

CHAPTER 13

The Courage to Change Your Mind

You have the right to change your mind.

—Oprah Winfrey

One of the most difficult facts to accept about your own perspective is that it doesn't always make sense to the people in your life. You can argue, clarify, empathize, share, reason, explain, provide anecdotes and data, and yet the net effect may still be: they don't see it the way you do. I've found that it takes this inner Herculean resolve in that moment to shift gears and say, "So how is it for you? How do you see things?" Then I try really hard to respect the other person's perspective with as much willingness as I can muster to see how that viewpoint coheres for that person. I notice my reactivity and honor it, noting what's at stake for me—which opinions, which ideas, which communities. And then, I set all of it temporarily aside.

- I try to appreciate the internal logic of the position I don't hold.
- I imagine to myself that this person has perceptions and a community logic story that inform how they think.
- I ask myself if there's anything new for me to consider— any possible contribution to my own ideas that I've overlooked.
- I try to identify what's at stake for this other person if they were to reconsider their view or to even simply hear mine.

I tell my students: none of this is accomplished in a single sitting. Sometimes the engagement with uncomfortable ideas goes on for weeks, months, or years. Staying in the conversation matters. Choosing to see people as individuals and members of communities helps. Remembering what's at risk in my life when I consider viewpoints I don't want to be true lets me find empathy for the similar struggle my "opponent" feels and faces.

Honestly, it's the hardest work I ever do, and I do it pretty darned imperfectly. Yet I've found that it's worth the effort. It's what I hope others do for me. It's how I hope we're raising our children. It takes time to learn how to be in communities where a variety of perspectives co-exist. It's so much fun to be in fan communities of people who agree with me. The craving for common ground is human. We like the illusion of shared certainty. Making space for dissent feels like allowing a pebble to stay in a comfortable shoe. Yet critical thinkers know that it's through dissent that we grow and are provoked to do more research. We can make space in our lives for both, our communities built from shared beliefs and those where we welcome a wider array of ideas.

There's no easy path to mutual understanding. There's no silver bullet of facts that unites and aligns us. Critical thinking requires enormous emotional resources to deal with all that complexity. Your kids need to know that it's important to take breaks, to find their sense of humor, and to hang out with people different from them in their hobbies, not just at protests. You can model for them that not every conversation needs to be a fight for agreement. It's okay to not reach a mutually satisfying conclusion. It's all right to continue the discussion on another day. We can create space to focus on what's pleasurable and relaxing, taking time away from the hard work of evaluation and analysis. As the Caines say, "Sometimes the act of trying to understand actually prevents understanding." I've found that social media conversations about touchy topics go best when I frame the discussion as a search for more information, more insight, more disclosure of why an individual has a stake in the outcome of the arguments, rather than the expectation that we come to a shared perspective. The benefit is mutual air-clearing and a better grasp of what animates a person's dearly held point of view.

Dr. Peter Elbow, my writing mentor, puts it this way: "Most accounts of good thinking are versions of what I call the doubting game: the ability to see flaws in someone's thinking—which is especially valuable when those flaws are hard for most people to see. This ability usually calls on logic." Elbow questions this habit of practice. When faced with ideas that seem *wrong* at first glance, he suggests a better way to generate insight. Can we push the pause button on our knee-jerk reaction to combat the errors in the thinking? Instead, he suggests we enter what he calls the *believing game*. "The believing game teaches us to understand points of view from the inside. Instead of propositional language, it asks for words that help us experience an idea: imaginative, metaphorical, narrative, personal, and even poetic language. And not just words. Images and sounds and body movements are particularly helpful for entering into alien ideas. Role playing—and yes, silence. When someone says something that everyone else thinks is wrong, often the most productive response is merely to listen: force yourself not to reply at all." The affective side of us controls how we make meaning for ourselves, yet we wind up relying on logic and argument to persuade others. It's uncanny!

Yet it turns out that we can advance a conversation more effectively when we withhold a reply and attempt to experience the meaning someone else is generating for themselves. As we've discovered in this conversation about critical thinking, our stories deeply inform how we think. The more we exchange those stories, the more we can appreciate the complexity of the ideas in conflict rather than reducing one another to representations of "evil." By complexifying the topics, we discover that meaningful solutions must take everyone into account, too.

Sometimes the best we can do is admit that the topic is prickly and multifaceted and deserves more research and thought. As Supreme Court Justice Harry Blackmun wrote eloquently in his opinion after the polarizing 1973 decision in *Roe* v. *Wade*, how we understand any controversial topic hinges on "[o]ne's philosophy, one's experiences, one's exposure to the raw edges of human existence, one's religious training, one's attitude toward life and family and their values, and the moral standards one establishes and seeks to observe. . . ." No wonder we struggle to think well together!

Our biggest challenge in raising critical thinkers, then, is making room in the adult-child relationship for dissent. We may find it difficult when kids think their way away from our more reasonable worldview. Yet if you choose to raise children who bravely face new evidence, who feel comfortable asking questions, who challenge the status quo, and who know that a pivot to where the information takes them is welcome, you can be sure they will test beliefs you hold. How you handle that moment has a lot to do with the eventual closeness you can find with adult children. In fact, what our kids need to know is that there is one community that will not reject them for being critical, nuanced, flexible thinkers: their family. And if they can't find that supportive community at home, they most certainly should be able to find it in school.

We can ask good questions that allow our kids to shake their own thinking out in the sunlight, to see if it makes sense when they explain it to us. We can urge them on with heart rather than suspicion. We can trust that better data and more insight will follow an honest exchange of ideas. These are the conditions that lead to closeness and intimacy. Social media, affinity groups, faith communities, friends—there's no guarantee that our children will be supported and understood when they veer away from whatever the accepted logic story is for that group. But if they can know that there is one place where their ranging minds are always welcome, and that place is with you, you will have given them the most robust intellectual and emotional gift they can ever receive— the freedom and right to change their minds, while still being loved and known. We all crave relationships that offer us these gifts.

To help our kids trust their own resilience, we can show them that they will survive a change in thinking because we have. They can know it's possible to thrive because they will have seen you navigate your own evolving beliefs. One way to think about raising critical thinkers, then, is to imagine that you are preparing your children and students to navigate change *with courage*. Fear thwarts good thinking. To be nimble-minded means that a student is willing to discover a flaw in an argument. Adept critical thinkers seek new information and are brave enough to consider it.

Think through a changed way of thinking you've chosen for yourself.

- Can you identify the cost?
- Can you identify the gain?
- What did it take to align with that shift?
- How did you overcome the costs?
- What about the gains led you to believe it would be worth the costs?

The evidence that anyone is, in fact, a critical thinker is that they've changed their mind about a viewpoint they used to hold. Frequently that change costs something—standing in a group, reassurance about the afterlife, how a person votes, the way a person raises children, a marriage, favorite foods, how the person spends money, choice of medical treatment, the feeling of being right, altered habits. What is given up is not necessarily painful—perhaps the thinker gives up a doom-and-gloom outlook in favor of optimism! What was feared is overcome, no longer worthy of obsessed anxiety. No matter how any of us changes our thinking, consequences follow. We only change when we can't unsee what we now see.

Our kids need to know that if they do overturn beliefs or opinions, they can survive attacks or challenges from followers on social media. You can let them know they will not lose ground in building a meaningful life, even if they experience rejection by extended family members. You can help your young people learn how to set boundaries and find community support. You can show them that they are leading lives of integrity, not pretense, and are worthy of respect and kindness. Remind them that their value is not contingent on agreement from others.

Our students need to believe that they can rely on parents and teachers who will stand by them, not abandon them—even when we find their reasoning limited or incomplete. Let me be blunt: you can't be the community that ejects your child from membership. Your child's pursuit of intellectual honesty deserves to be honored by you, or they will learn to be propagandists for a position, or worse, they will secretly hold their subversive beliefs until they're out from under your control.

The ideal context for critical thinking is humility. Our kids know the difference between an adult who says, "That's interesting. Why do you think that?" and one who implies, "How on earth did you come up with that idea?" It takes trust to believe that a child can adopt and shed ideas. Too often, we project onto our children the worst possible set of beliefs and outcomes. Sometimes kids have to try *living with* a belief before they can tell if it's right for them. When you were fifteen, twenty-two, and maybe even thirty-five . . . was that the end of your thinking? Did you arrive at a conclusive, for-all-time understanding of life and all that's in it? Do you agree today with every viewpoint your parents held about money, sex, religion, and politics? Your kids will develop views of their own, too, just like you did. The goal of critical thinking is not certitude. It's intimacy, remember? The best way to help our children use their powerful minds for good is to teach them the flexibility of thought and heart that enables to them to think, to think again, to rethink, and to think some more. We need more people with a spirit of inquiry. We need communities of people brave enough to put cultivating insight ahead of being right. We can begin with our people.

ACKNOWLEDGMENTS

My interest in thinking well has been nourished over a lifetime by my smart, loquacious, opinionated family. Thanks to my father, John E. Sweeney (a lawyer for sixty years), who taught me early to support my assertions. I love you. A special thank-you to my son, Jacob, another lawyer, who stepped in to verify my research and conduct the first edit of the book all the way from Bangkok. What fun we had together!

A particular thanks to my late aunt, Dr. June O'Connor, who was once a nun and then a PhD in the field of ethics and religion at the University of California, Riverside. She modeled to me how to hold strong ethical positions while making space for conversation and divergent points of view. I have missed her every day, particularly as I wrote this book. I carry her memory in my heart, but also in my mind.

The following Brave Writer colleagues have been especially valuable in offering a wide array of resources and in-depth conversations that contributed to my research: Dawn Smith, Kirsten Merryman, Jeanne Faulconer, Jen Holman, Cindy Clark, and Stephanie Elms. Our "think tank" makes me a better thinker and writer. I appreciate each of you.

Special thanks to: friend and colleague Dr. Adam Clark (Xavier University), for his contribution to my chapter about "encounter"; blogging buddy from the early days, Dr. Andrew Tatusko (Penn State), for his insights into asymmetrical reciprocity; Dr. Gholdy Muhammad, for her generous help in thinking more deeply about identity; friend and colleague Rita Cevasco SLP, for her expertise in the field of literacy; my writing mentor and friend Dr. Peter Elbow, for his valuable insights into the "believing game"; my local and wise friend Leslie Hershberger (Enneagram specialist and business consultant), for helping me grasp the power of individual temperaments in worldview formation; and school teacher and conference speaker Ash Brandin, for their expertise into the value of video games.

A particular thanks to Dr. Barbara Oakley. Our lengthy conversations made this a far better book. Thank you for your careful reading of my work, your faith in my writing, your enthusiasm for my ideas, and your beautiful foreword.

Early discussion with my agent, Rita Rosenkranz, gave me clarity of direction, insights that helped me hone the structure of the book, and validation in this effort. Joanna Ng, my editor at TarcherPerigee, is a dream! She offered precise, perceptive edits, encouragement when I most needed it, and thoughtful challenges that enabled me to do my best work. Thank you, Rita and Joanna, for choosing to partner with me. I consider myself the luckiest writer to get to benefit from your talents. Let's keep doing it!

Of note: many of the resources included in this book were first tried and tested in the Brave Writer environment in our online classes and by our families who use our curricula. I appreciate each of you! Brave Writer, my company, was founded in January 2000 and serves a global community in the field of education and writing.

After all the research, all the thinking, all the writing was over—it amused me to discover that even before the copy had been typeset, some of the ideas I expressed in this book were challenged and recast by thought leaders in our society. Where Joanna and I could, we made last-minute adjustments. But it goes to show that when you embark on a study of thinking, even the thoughts about how we think are up for endless review. I'm deeply grateful to the world of people who carefully consider the impact of language and how it shapes our imaginations. The work is never done, and we never arrive. But each vista helps us see something new—something we might have missed. And isn't that the work of critical thinking in the end? It's the art of navigating a highway as it is being built. I'm grateful to all my fellow thinkers who are willing to shift gears and change directions as needed, to bring more light and optimism to living among one another. If that's you, I thank you, too, for what you bring to the feast at our shared table. "We're one, but we're not the same." Bono got it right.

NOTES

INTRODUCTION

xv   **"He's making violent love to me, Mother!":** *It's a Wonderful Life*,
      directed by Frank Capra, written by Frances Goodrich, Albert
      Hackett, and Frank Capra (Los Angeles, CA: Liberty Films,
      1946).

PART 1 ✳ WHAT IS A CRITICAL THINKER?

1   **"The pupil is thereby 'schooled'":** Mark K. Smith, "Ivan Illich:
      Deschooling, Conviviality and Lifelong Learning," Infed.org, April 8,
      2021, https://infed.org/mobi/ivan-illich-deschooling-conviviality
      -and-lifelong-learning/.

1   **"Sadly, children's passion for thinking often ends":** bell hooks,
      Teaching Critical Thinking (New York and London: Routledge, 2010), 8.

2   **Educational expert Arthur Costa explains that critical thinking is
      active:** Arthur Costa, "Habits of Mind," in Arthur Costa, ed.,
      Developing Minds (Alexandria, VA: ASCD, 2001), 80. Costa identifies
      sixteen habits of mind: persisting; managing impulsivity; listening to
      others—with understanding and empathy; thinking flexibly; thinking

about thinking (metacognition); striving for accuracy and precision; questioning and posing problems; applying past knowledge to new situations; thinking and communicating with clarity and precision; gathering data from all the senses; creating, imagining, and innovating; responding with wonderment and awe; taking responsible risks; finding humor; thinking interdependently; and learning continuously.

CHAPTER 1 ✳ SAYS WHO?

5   **"That's it. That's the real story. I was framed":** Jon Scieszka, *The True Story of the 3 Little Pigs* (New York: Puffin, 1989), 31.

13   **"resisters had higher measures of executive control in cognitive tasks":** Daniel Kahneman, *Thinking Fast and Slow* (New York: Farrar, Straus and Giroux, 2011), 47. I found this book riveting. The studies combined with Kahneman's expert analysis provide countless tools for how to take that "academic selfie" so that we can detect the flaws in our own thinking.

13   **"children who had shown more self-control as four-year-olds":** Kahneman, *Thinking Fast and Slow*, 47.

13   **"are prone to answer questions with the first idea that comes to their mind":** Kahneman, *Thinking Fast and Slow*, 48.

16   **"The results were spectacular: the words that were presented":** Kahneman, *Thinking Fast and Slow*, 66.

CHAPTER 2 ✳ SEPARATING THE FACTS FROM THEIR FICTIONS

24   **"The function of education is to teach one to think intensively":** Dr. Martin Luther King Jr., "The Purpose of Education," *Maroon*

Tiger (January–February 1947), 10, https://kinginstitute.stanford.edu /king-papers/documents/purpose-education.

28   **"Facts are stubborn things":** https://quoteinvestigator.com/2010 /06/18/facts-stubborn/.

31   **"Perspective, as any art student knows, is the technique":** Glenn Aparicio Parry, *Original Thinking* (Berkeley, CA: North Atlantic, 2015), 18.

32   **"After perspective, the human eye and consciousness came to be thought":** Parry, *Original Thinking*, 20.

32   **"The thing that really surprised me was that it":** Kenneth Chang, "For Apollo 11 He Wasn't on the Moon. But His Coffee Was Warm," *New York Times*, July 16, 2019, https://www.nytimes.com/2019/07/16 /science/michael-collins-apollo-11.html.

CHAPTER 3 ✳ CURIOUSER AND CURIOUSER: A PROBLEM-POSING EDUCATION

41   **"I think what I learned from Trix":** Mo Willems, interview by David Marchese, "Mo Willems Has a Message for Parents: He's Not on Your Side," *New York Times*, November 16, 2020, https://www.nytimes .com/interactive/2020/11/16/magazine/mo-willems-interview.html.

42   **"Frequently, by the time children reach 3rd grade":** Thomas Jackson, "The Art and Craft of 'Gently Socratic' Inquiry," in Arthur Costa, ed., *Developing Minds* (Alexandria, VA: ASCD, 2001), 459.

42   **"banking concept":** Paulo Freire, *Pedagogy of the Oppressed* (New York: Bloomsbury, 2017). Freire's description of the banking concept of education is found in chapter 2.

43   **"Students are generally used to working with a textbook":** Chauncey Monte-Sano, Susan De La Paz, and Mark Felton, *Reading, Thinking, and Writing About History* (New York: Teachers College, 2014), 2.

43   **"Education is suffering from narration sickness" and "The teacher talks about reality":** Freire, *Pedagogy,* 71.

43   **"sonority":** Freire, *Pedagogy,* 71.

43   **"If students are only to memorize facts":** Marcy Cook, "Mathematics: The Teaching Arena for Problem Solving," in Arthur Costa, ed., *Developing Minds* (Alexandria, VA: ASCD, 2001), 288.

47   **"Such rigidity is maddening, and I believe" and "Two plus two is four":** Betty Edwards, *Drawing on the Artist Within* (New York: Fireside, Simon & Schuster, 1986), 35. Edwards offers her own example of the "hot iron" conundrum in her book, but I've recast it here to match the aim of this section. One important caveat to my comments on multiple choice tests came from a dialogue I had with Dr. Barbara Oakley (author of the foreword). According to Oakley, when patiently and thoughtfully crafted, good multiple choice questions (particularly at the undergraduate and postgraduate levels) both can lead to a robust measure of what a student has learned as well as offering a student a chance to exercise critical thinking. The caution still stands, however. Multiple choice tests must consider the aim of the question, not merely require the student to guess what the creator had in mind.

49   **"as teachers, our role is to take our students":** hooks, *Teaching Critical Thinking,* 43.

49   **"The art of questioning becomes the key":** Cook, "Mathematics," 288.

49   **"asking good questions, providing good problems":** Cook, "Mathematics," 291.

50   **"We do not want the intellectual life of a classroom":** Cook, "Mathematics," 287.

50   **"Conversations are not one-dimensional":** hooks, *Teaching Critical Thinking*, 46. See also my earlier book, *The Brave Learner*, pages 76–77, for a more complete treatment of the idea of Big Juicy Conversations.

51   **"We're most curious when we know a little" and "emotional consequences":** Jonah Lehrer, "The Itch of Curiosity," *Wired*, August 3, 2010, https://www.wired.com/2010/08/the-itch-of-curiosity.

52   **"Learning is timely, not timeless":** Michael Luntley, "What's the Problem with Dewey?" *European Journal of Pragmatism and American Philosophy* VIII-1 (2016): para 28, https://journals .openedition.org/ejpap/444.

CHAPTER 4 ✳ KEEN OBSERVATION: THROUGH THE LOOKING GLASS

67   **"We mostly see what we have learned to expect to see":** Betty Edwards, *Color* (New York: TarcherPerigee, 2004), 10.

71   **"Psychologist Lev Vygotsky . . . contended that linguistic":** Alice G. Brand, "The Why of Cognition: Emotion and the Writing Process," *College Composition and Communication* 38, no. 4 (1987): 437, accessed February 3, 2021, www.jstor.org/stable/357637.

71   **"The construct of memory is central to cognition":** Brand, "The Why of Cognition," 437.

77   **"The brain is the ultimate reductionist":** Costa, "Habits of Mind," 83.

CHAPTER 5 ✳ CRITICAL THINKING STARTS WITH CARING

89   **"In brief, the ideal critical thinker is disposed to care":** Robert Ennis, "Goals for a Critical Thinking Curriculum and

Its Assessment," in Arthur Costa, ed., *Developing Minds* (Alexandria, VA: ASCD, 2001), 44.

92   **scaled model reduced by a factor:** Lunar and Planetary Institute, https://www.lpi.usra.edu/education/explore/solar_system/activities /3_PlanetScale_1Billion.pdf.

92   **"Playing a game is the voluntary attempt to overcome unnecessary obstacles":** Bernard Suits, *The Grasshopper: Games, Life, and Utopia* (Toronto: University of Toronto Press, 1978); Bradley J. Morris, Steve Croker, Corinne Zimmerman, Devin Gill, and Connie Romig, "Gaming Science: The 'Gamification' of Scientific Thinking," *Frontiers in Psychology* 4 (2013), https://www.frontiersin.org /articles/10.3389/fpsyg.2013.00607/full#h8.

93   **"thematic attractors" and "around which we organize our thoughts and ideas":** Renate Caine and Geoffrey Caine, *Making Connections* (Menlo Park, CA: Addison-Wesley, 1994), 142. Highly recommend this book for a carefully researched and highly readable description of how our brains generate meaning while learning.

93   **"They provide a personalized focal point":** Caine and Caine, *Making Connections*, 142.

93   **"think creatively, tolerate ambiguity, and delay gratification":** Caine and Caine, *Making Connections*, 143.

95   **"The discussion about video games has focused on fears":** Niklas Johannes, Matti Vuorre, and Andrew K. Przybylski, "Video Game Play Is Positively Correlated with Well-Being," *PsyArXiv*, November 13, 2020, https://doi:10.1098/rsos.202049.

95   **"Non-gaming has been found to put boys, in particular, at greater risk for problems":** Morris et al., "Gaming Science: The 'Gamification'

of Scientific Thinking," *Frontiers in Psychology* 4 (2013), https://www
.frontiersin.org/article/10.3389/fpsyg.2013.00607.

95   **"There are now studies that show equally positive results":** Morris
et al., "Gaming Science."

96   **"Positive stress helps players achieve 'flow'":** Morris et al.,
"Gaming Science."

97   **"Kids can't self-regulate almost anything when young":** Ash
Brandin, educator and conference speaker. See https://www
.ashbrandin.com for more information on how video gaming
provides educational benefits to kids. See also my interview with Ash
on the *Brave Writer* podcast: https://blog.bravewriter.com/2021/05
/12/podcast-educational-value-video-games-ash-brandin/.

98   **In fact, research shows that students *enjoy* the experience of
exercising control (autonomy):** Caine and Caine, *Making
Connections*, 143.

99   **"bad stat is harder to kill than a vampire":** Joel Best, *Stat-Spotting*
(Berkeley: University of California Press, 2013), 10. All of Best's books
on statistics are filled with powerful explanations of how stats can be
used to manipulate readers. This particular volume is slim and offers
an easy-to-use reference. It makes an excellent tool for working with
teens in particular.

101   **"Exploring an unfamiliar forest, experienced hikers know":**
Sam Wineburg and Sarah McGrew, *Lateral Reading: Reading Less and
Learning More When Evaluating Digital Information* (October 6,
2017), Stanford History Education Group Working Paper No.
2017-A1, available at SSRN: https://ssrn.com/abstract=3048994 or
http://dx.doi.org/10.2139/ssrn.3048994.

102   **Fairly quickly, the fact-checkers were able to determine:**
Wineburg and McGrew, *Lateral Reading*.

CHAPTER 6 ✳ IDENTITY: THE FORCE TO RECKON WITH

113 **"And all the worlds you are":** Jacqueline Woodson, *Brown Girl Dreaming* (New York: Penguin, 2014), 319–20.

114 **"Imitation is part of the learned pattern of dispositions and actions":** Marcus Mescher, *The Ethics of Encounter* (New York: Orbis Maryknoll, 2020), 131.

114 **"Children imitate parents, adults emulate those they admire":** Mescher, *Ethics*, 131.

114 **"We will never know how fully we've":** Ezra Klein, *Why We're Polarized* (New York: Avid Reader, 2020), 261. A particularly good look at our community identities and how those inform our beliefs.

115 **"Sociologist C. Wright Mills . . . described using a 'sociological imagination'":** Anne Helen Peterson, "Other Countries Have Social Safety Nets: The U.S. Has Women," interview with sociologist Jessica Calarco, November 11, 2020, https://annehelen.substack.com /p/other-countries-have-social-safety.

115 **"I have come to see white privilege as an invisible package":** Peggy McIntosh, "Unpacking the Knapsack of White Privilege," excerpted from her working paper, "White Privilege and Male Privilege: A Personal Account of Coming to See Correspondences Through Work in Women's Studies," 1988, https://psychology.umbc .edu/files/2016/10/White-Privilege_McIntosh-1989.pdf.

122 **"The most fundamental idea in this conception of justice is the idea":** John Rawls, *Justice as Fairness* (Cambridge, MA: Belknap, 2001), 5. This book is a powerful distillation of the values and aims of a liberal democracy—that is, a democracy guided by a constitution. A must-read for anyone invested in how our society forms its laws and fights its battles in the courts.

122   "for the purpose of promoting the health, safety, morals, or general welfare of the community": David J. Christiansen, "Zoning and the First Amendment Rights of Adult Entertainment," 22 Val. U. L. Rev. 695 (1988). Available at: https://scholar.valpo.edu/vulr /vol22/iss3/12.

122   "The central concern in Euclid was whether the creation": Christiansen, "Zoning."

124   "who we are, who others say we are (both positive and negative features), and whom we desire to be": Gholdy Muhammad, *Cultivating Genius* (New York: Scholastic, 2020), 67.

126   "Our students, and arguably adults, are always looking for themselves in spaces and places": Muhammad, *Genius*, 69.

126   "My parents were my first teachers, and my first librarians": *Here Wee Read* podcast hosted by Charnaie Gordon, guest Kwame Alexander, season 1 episode 1, http://hereweeread.com/podcast (minutes 26:12–28:07).

131   "[I]dentity doesn't just shape how we treat each other. It shapes how we understand the world:" Klein, *Polarized*, 79.

CHAPTER 7 ✳ READING: UP CLOSE AND PERSONAL

139   "Close reading, then, should not imply that we ignore": Kylene Beers and Robert E. Probst, *Notice and Note* (Portsmouth, NH: Heinemann, 2013), 36.

143   "A reader must call upon both word knowledge": Neil Anderson, 2014; J. P. Gee, 2003; Stephen Kucer, 2005; Margaret Moustafa, 1997; and Michael Pressley, 2001, "To Understand, You Need to Be a Part of the Conversation," *The Literacy Bug*, 2014, https://www .theliteracybug.com/conversation. The blog and podcast put out by

The Literacy Bug provide helpful analysis of how to go from basic decoding skills to the richer, more meaningful tasks of becoming— becoming readers, writers, speakers, knowers, and connectors.

143 **"Visual literacy is the ability to construct meaning from images":** Shane MacDonnchaidh, "Teaching Visual Literacy in the Classroom," accessed May 16, 2021, https://www.literacyideas.com/teaching -visual-texts-in-the-classroom.

148 **"Deeper literacy is metacognitive":** Rita Cevasco, SLP and founder of Rooted in Language, private email correspondence. Rita's company, Rooted in Language, provides the kind of integrated approach to literacy that I talk about here. Her tools are widely loved in home education circles and are particularly valuable for kids who struggle with learning disabilities.

149 **Ultimately, comprehension is tied to background knowledge, linguistic concepts, and underlying oral language skills:** Cevasco, email.

162 **In 2015, Young Adult author Corinne Duyvis:** As of this printing, there are some new concerns about the #OwnVoices movement. In some cases, authors prefer to conceal their identities for the sake of personal privacy and safety. See also: https://diversebooks.org/why -we-need-diverse-books-is-no-longer-using-the-term-ownvoices/.

CHAPTER 8 ✳ READING: GO SLOW TO GO DEEP

165 **"As we go ever deeper into our own insights":** Maryanne Wolf and Joan Richardson, "Maryanne Wolf: Balance Technology and Deep Reading to Create Biliterate Children," *Phi Delta Kappan* 96, no. 3 (2014): 14–19, accessed May 17, 2021, http://www.jstor.org/stable/24375937.

166 **"[T]his discovery of yours [writing] will create forgetfulness in the learners'":** Plato, *The Phaedrus,* http://classics.mit.edu/Plato /phaedrus.html.

167   **St. Augustine in CE 380 showed genuine surprise:** Nicholas Carr, *The Shallows* (New York: Norton, 2020), 60. The entire book provides a superb, in-depth examination of the impact of online reading and how it has shifted the way we pay attention and make meaning from what we read.

168   **"Deep attention is superb for solving complex problems represented by a single medium":** N. Katherine Hayles, "Hyper and Deep Attention: The Generational Divide in Cognitive Modes," *Profession,* (2007): 187–99. JSTOR, accessed February 11, 2021, www.jstor.org/stable/25595866.

168   **"The development of knowledge became an increasingly private act":** Carr, *Shallows*, 67.

168   **"In an evolutionary context, no doubt hyper focus":** Hayles, "Hyper," 188.

169   **"The seemingly innocuous features . . . —the 'like' and 'heart' buttons":** Carr, *Shallows*, 233.

169   **"As a society, we devote ever less time to reading printed words":** Carr, *Shallows*, 110.

170   **"One thing is very clear: if, knowing what we know":** Carr, *Shallows*, 115–16.

170   **"Until I am convinced by research to the contrary":** Wolf and Richardson, "Maryanne Wolf," accessed February 11, 2021.

173   **(1) it slows down the reader, (2) it gives auditory feedback, and (3) it recruits attention:** Cevasco, private correspondence.

176   **"There's research that shows that having a phone or computer device in the room":** Carr, *Shallows*, 230.

176   **Political commentator Ezra Klein shared on his podcast that:** Ezra Klein, *The Ezra Klein Show*, https://www.vox.com/podcasts/2020

/7/1/21308153/the-ezra-klein-show-the-shallows-twitter-facebook
-attention-deep-reading-thinking. This episode features an interview
with Nicholas Carr, cited page 305, for his book *The Shallows*.

179   **Copy work (transcription) is gaining popularity in literacy research
as well:** Jeanne Wanzek, Brandy Gatlin, Stephanie Al Otaiba, and
Young-Suk Grace Kim, "The Impact of Transcription Writing
Interventions for First-Grade Students," *Reading & Writing Quarterly*
33, no. 5 (2017): 484–99, https://www.tandfonline.com/doi/full
/10.1080/10573569.2016.1250142.

CHAPTER 9 ✳ EXPERIENCE: ENTERING MORE INTIMATE TERRITORY

183   **"It's easier to act your way":** Richard Pascale, Jerry Sternin, and
Monique Sternin, *The Power of Positive Deviance: How Unlikely
Innovators Solve the World's Toughest Problems* (Cambridge, MA:
Harvard Business Review, 2010).

184–85   **"In daily life we never understand each other":** E. M. Forster, *Aspects
of a Novel* (San Diego: Harcourt Brace Jovanovich, 1927), 67. Forster
does address the characteristics of a novel's characters as either flat
or round and concedes that a flat character is a two-dimensional
caricature—which gives the reader less access to the true thoughts
and feelings of a person. Round characters are more likely to deliver
the complexity that Forster is getting at here.

186   **"If working memory is the mind's scratch pad, then long-term
memory is its filing system":** Carr, *Shallows*, 123.

186   **"One of the most effective ways to encourage information to make
that important jump":** MacDonnchaidh, "Visual Literacy." The
website literacyideas.com includes excellent activities to try with your
kids to explore how visual literacy works.

188   **"The challenge is, some students do indeed have something akin to race-car brains":** Barbara Oakley, *Uncommon Sense Teaching* (New York: TarcherPerigee, 2021), 16.

189   **"The terms *working memory* and *intelligence*":** Oakley, *Uncommon*, 14.

190   **"controlled release of energy that's self-sustaining":** David C. Roy, *Wired*, https://www.youtube.com/watch?v=ROP45rjvOHg&feature=youtu.be. I recommend viewing his sculptures to get a firsthand grasp of how Roy puts his knowledge to practice and iterates accordingly.

196   **"Emotions, perceptions, and reminders all stir the imagination":** Edmund Blair Bolles, *Remembering and Forgetting: An Inquiry into the Nature of Memory* (New York: Walker, 1988), 181.

197   **"It takes the traditions of a people not celebrated in the global":** Christopher Byrd, "Video Game Review: In 'Never Alone' Native Alaskans Explore the Future of Oral Tradition," https://www.washingtonpost.com/news/comic-riffs/wp/2014/12/29/never-alone-review-native-alaskans-explore-the-future-of-oral-tradition/.

200   **"I was on the antislavery side, so I got up and talked to the class":** Nicole Philip, "'It Was Very Humiliating': Readers Share How They Were Taught About Slavery," *New York Times Magazine*, September 27, 2019, https://www.nytimes.com/interactive/2019/09/27/magazine/slavery-education-school-1619-project.html.

200   **"crashing waves and spooky thunderbolts":** Philip, "'It Was Very Humiliating.'"

201   **In the winter of 2021, a middle school teacher in Mississippi:** Larrison Campbell, "Rage Erupts After Mississippi School Asks Kids to Pretend to Be Slaves," March 3, 2021, https://www.thedailybeast.com/purvis-middle-school-and-mississippi-erupt-over-schools-slave-letter-writing-activity.

201   **The teacher described a student creating an experience:** Mark L. Daniels, "A Living History Classroom: Using Re-Enactment to Enhance Learning," June 2010, https://www.socialstudies.org/social -education/74/3/living-history-classroom-using-re-enactment -enhance-learning.

CHAPTER 10 ❋ ENCOUNTER: OVERWHELM THAT OVERTURNS

205   **"Love and compassion have to be stretched wide enough":** Mescher, *Ethics*, 141.

208   **"[T]he woods are just about the safest place in the world":** Robin Wall Kimmerer, *Braiding Sweetgrass* (Minneapolis, MN: Milkweed, 2013), 223. Kimmerer's book is a fabulous example of bringing multiple skill sets together to create a far richer understanding of a subject of study. Her work in the field of botany is a multilayered approach to critical thinking, which takes advantage of both scientific research and Potawatomi community narrative in particular.

211   **"Encounters offer a glimpse that there is always more to learn about ourselves, others, and the world":** Mescher, *Ethics*, xi.

211   **"Every encounter involves a choice: to engage or ignore, to accept or reject":** Mescher, *Ethics*, xii.

212   **"responsible risks":** Costa, "Habits of Mind," 84.

215   **"He stood and made the motions of catching the ball, cradling it, and then throwing":** Joseph Bruchac, *The Children of the Longhouse* (New York: Puffin, 1998), 109.

221   **Even so, when Americans are polled, they long for a little generosity:** Gallup Poll, May 18, 2012, https://news.gallup.com/poll/154715

/americans-negativity-moral-values-inches-back.aspx. Thanks to Marcus Mescher for introducing this poll in his discussion of tolerance in *The Ethics of Encounter*.

224   **"If I do not stop, if I do not look, if I do not touch, if I do not speak"**: Pope Francis, TED Talk, "Revolution of Tenderness," https://qz.com /968060/pope-franciss-ted-talk-the-full-transcript-and-video/.

PART 3   ※   THE RHETORICAL IMAGINATION

229   **"Much intellectual work embraces the art of the possible"**: hooks, *Teaching Critical Thinking*, 139.

229   **"We live in a world where small children"**: hooks, *Teaching Critical Thinking*, 60.

230   **"Creativity and critical thinking are of particular importance in scientific research"**: Pitchai Balakumar, Mohammed Naseeruddin Inamdar, and Gowraganahalli Jagadeesh, "The Critical Steps for Successful Research: The Research Proposal and Scientific Writing: A Report on the Pre-Conference Workshop Held in Conjunction with the 64th Annual Conference of the Indian Pharmaceutical Congress—2012," *Journal of Pharmacology and Pharmacotherapeutics* 4, no. 2 (2013): 130–38, https://www.ncbi.nlm.nih.gov/pmc/articles /PMC3669572/.

234   **"When a teacher lets loose an unfettered imagination in the classroom"**: hooks, *Teaching Critical Thinking*, 62.

CHAPTER 11   ※   THE SURPRISING ROLE OF SELF- AWARENESS IN CRITICAL THINKING

235   **"The body knows things"**: Sue Monk Kidd, *The Secret Life of Bees* (New York: Penguin, 2002), 69.

238   **our in-group attachments release oxytocin:** Carsten K. W. De Dreu, Lindred L. Greer, Gerben A. Van Kleef, Shaul Shalvi, Michel J. J. Handgraaf, and Douglas S. Massey, "Oxytocin Promotes Human Ethnocentrism," *Proceedings of the National Academy of Sciences of the United States of America* 108, no. 4 (2011): 1262–66, accessed May 23, 2021, http://www.jstor.org/stable/41001849.

238   **"escalation of commitment" (commitment bias):** "Why do people support their past ideas, even when presented with evidence that they're wrong?" Decision Lab, accessed May 23, 2021. https://thedecisionlab.com/biases/commitment-bias/.

239   **"Insight is much more important in education":** Caine and Caine, *Making Connections*, 103.

250   **The *Guinness World Records* book claims that more than five billion copies:** Accessed May 24, 2021, https://www.guinness worldrecords.com/world-records/best-selling-book-of-non-fiction.

250   **The entire Bible has been translated into over seven hundred languages worldwide:** Accessed May 24, 2021, https://www.wycliffe .org.uk/about/our-impact/. Wycliffe is a mission organization dedicated to translating the Bible into every spoken language on the planet.

250   **"[t]he scrolls have shown how biblical texts are actually fungible":** Matthew Rozsa, "What the Newly-Discovered Dead Sea Scrolls Tell Us About History," March 18, 2021, https://www.salon.com/2021/03 /18/what-the-newly-discovered-dead-sea-scrolls-tell-us-about -history/.

251   **"[we] project onto them a perspective that complements [our] own":** Iris Marion Young, *Intersecting Voices* (Princeton, NJ: Princeton University Press, 1997), 45.

251 "Officials thought they had objective grounds for this judgment": Young, *Intersecting*, 42.

252 "The majority of the respondents said that they would rather be": Young, *Intersecting*, 42.

252 "When asked to put themselves in the position": Young, *Intersecting*, 42.

253 "This implies that we have the moral humility to acknowledge that even though there": Young, *Intersecting*, 53.

254 "Questions can express a distinctive form of respect for the other": Young, *Intersecting*, 55.

254 "Respectful listening thus involves attentive": Young, *Intersecting*, 55.

254 "A moral point of view requires a person to think about a question": Young, *Intersecting*, 59.

257 "patterns of thought that are destined to be compared with each other": Parry, *Original Thinking*, 143.

262 "The hallmark of a productive debate": Instagram @adamgrant, July 15, 2021, https://www.instagram.com/p/CRWUyKJpOV0/.

CHAPTER 12 ❄ THE ART OF INTERPRETATION

263 "The issue therefore is not about finding the truth the author wrote": Paul Regan, "Research in Hermeneutics, Phenomenology, and Practical Philosophy," *Meta* IV, no. 2 (December 2012): 286–303, ISSN 2067–3655, www.metajournal.org (PDF, page 292).

264 "To understand [a text] does not mean primarily to reason one's way back into the past": Hans-Georg Gadamer, *Truth and Method* (London: Continuum, 1960), 398.

266   **"We talk about how many women were raped last year":** Jackson Katz, last visited on May 27, 2021, https://www.jacksonkatz.com /news/man-behind-viral-quote/.

268   **"Her works reflect dated cultural attitudes toward":** Niraj Chokshi, "Prestigious Laura Ingalls Wilder Award Renamed Over Racial Insensitivity," *New York Times*, June 26, 2018, https://www .nytimes.com/2018/06/26/books/laura-ingalls-wilder-book-award .html.

CHAPTER 13 ✳ THE COURAGE TO CHANGE YOUR MIND

285   **"Sometimes the act of trying to understand actually prevents understanding":** Caine and Caine, *Making Connections*, 161.

285   **"Most accounts of good thinking are versions of what I call the doubting game":** Peter Elbow, "The Believing Game or Methodological Believing," *Journal for the Assembly for Expanded Perspectives on Learning* 14 (2009), http://works.bepress.com /peter_elbow/41/.

285   **"The believing game teaches us to understand points of view from the inside":** Elbow, "Believing," 14.

286   **"[o]ne's philosophy, one's experiences, one's exposure":** Justice Harry A. Blackmun, Roe et al. v. Wade, District Attorney of Dallas County no. 70–18, Supreme Court of the United States, 410 US 113, January 22, 1973, http://law2.umkc.edu/faculty/projects/ftrials /conlaw/roe.html.

INDEX

ABOUT THE AUTHOR

Julie Bogart is the creator of the award-winning, innovative Brave Writer program, teaching writing and language arts to tens of thousands of families every year. She homeschooled her five now grown children for seventeen years and is the founder of Brave Learner Home, which supports thousands of parents through coaching and teaching. She has also taught as an adjunct professor of theology at Xavier University. Bogart is the author of *The Brave Learner*.